HOLY SPIRIT
THE BONDAGE
BREAKER

DESTINY IMAGE BOOKS BY DAVID DIGA HERNANDEZ

Holy Spirit: The Bondage Breaker

Praying in the Holy Spirit: Secrets to Igniting and Sustaining a Lifestyle of Effective Prayer

Encountering the Holy Spirit in Every Book of the Bible

Carriers of the Glory: Becoming a Friend of the Holy Spirit

HOLY SPIRIT
THE BONDAGE
BREAKER

EXPERIENCE
PERMANENT DELIVERANCE
FROM MENTAL, EMOTIONAL,
& DEMONIC STRONGHOLDS

DAVID DIGA HERNANDEZ

DESTINY IMAGE® PUBLISHERS, INC.
P.O. Box 310, Shippensburg, PA 17257-0310
"Publishing cutting-edge prophetic resources to supernaturally empower the body of Christ"

This book and all other Destiny Image and Destiny Image Fiction books are available at Christian bookstores and distributors worldwide.

For more information on foreign distributors, call 717-532-3040.

Reach us on the Internet: www.destinyimage.com.

ISBN 13 TP: 978-0-7684-7240-0

ISBN 13 eBook: 978-0-7684-7241-7

ISBN 13 HC: 978-0-7684-7243-1

ISBN 13 LP: 978-0-7684-7242-4

For Worldwide Distribution, Printed in the U.S.A.

1 2 3 4 5 6 7 8 / 27 26 25 24 23

DEDICATION

I dedicate this book to those wearied by spiritual struggle and who desire to finally be free.

ACKNOWLEDGMENTS

I want to acknowledge and honor the precious Holy Spirit who has revealed these truths by His Word.

I also wish to acknowledge my wife, Jessica, and my daughter, Aria, as they have lovingly released me to perform the work of writing this book. As I wrote over the course of several months, they shared in the sacrifice of time.

Finally, I wish to acknowledge the entire DHM team and our wonderful DHM partners. Together, we are spreading the gospel of Jesus Christ all around the world through events and media.

CONTENTS

Introduction 11

1   Enough Is Enough 15

2   What Is a Stronghold? 19

3   Darkness Returns 29

4   The Spirit of Truth 35

5   Open Doors 43

6   Identifying Strongholds 61

7   Commanding the Forces of Darkness 71

8   Strongholds, Thoughts, and Emotions 103

9   Help Me, Holy Spirit 131

10   The Stronghold of Temptation 141

11   The Stronghold of Addiction 159

12   The Attack of Sickness 175

13   Christians and Demon Possession 189

14   The Stronghold of Fear and Torment 241

15   The Stronghold of Accusation 267

16   The Stronghold of Depression 275

17   Other Strongholds 285

     Staying Free 295

     About the Author 299

INTRODUCTION

There is no spirit more powerful than the Holy Spirit. No lie can linger in the light of the Spirit of Truth. No addiction, torment, fear, or confusion can fight against the power of the Holy Spirit.

For the Lord is the Spirit, and wherever the Spirit of the Lord is, there is freedom (2 Corinthians 3:17 NLT).

God's will for you is total victory. The life of the believer is meant to be one of spiritual vitality, strength, and freedom. Though you will face hardships, even in life's most difficult circumstances you can and should be spiritually victorious. Sadly, many believers go years under the heavy weight of demonic deception, and that deception wreaks havoc in their lives through the bondage it creates. Worse still, many of God's children knowingly or unknowingly accept at least some form of spiritual defeat as a given. They think spiritual struggle is a normal part of the Christian life. Indeed, trials are part of the Christian life, but never spiritual weakness or bondage. Even with outer trouble, we should live with inner peace and joy—totally stabilized within.

Perhaps you may be in a spiritual bondage. That bondage is not your cross to carry. Spiritual defeat isn't a sacrifice made unto God. There's no doubt in my mind that you can and should be set free and then permanently remain free from all forms of demonic influence.

Whether you're in spiritual bondage or you simply want to better minister freedom to others, the truths within this book will challenge, encourage, and transform you.

The Holy Spirit is your partner in living in the truth that will set you free. Whatever the bondage and no matter how many times you have tried to be free, I can assure you of this: the Holy Spirit's presence in your life will be the key to permanently breaking every chain of bondage. This book presents the truth about deliverance, spiritual warfare, and hell's strategies, while emphasizing the power of the Holy Spirit over demonic power. The principles I share are derived from and directly backed by Scripture, so that the solutions presented are God's solutions—not human religious directives. You'll be given truth, not tradition.

To get the most out of this book, I recommend reading it from start to finish without skipping around.

> For precept must be upon precept, precept upon precept; line upon line, line upon line; here a little, and there a little (Isaiah 28:10 KJV).

We must be grounded in basic biblical principles before we can deal with the specifics of each individual kind of stronghold. I address:

+ Identifying strongholds
+ Tearing down strongholds
+ Demonic power
+ Open doors
+ Truth
+ Deception

- Spiritual warfare
- Other key truths

This book also presents revelatory strategies you can use against these specific strongholds:

- Temptation
- Addiction
- Fear and torment
- Accusation
- Depression
- Distraction
- Offense
- Confusion

I've included a chapter on how the enemy can use sickness against the believer, though sickness is categorized as an "attack" instead of a "stronghold." Also, I share my personal testimony of how the Lord broke the power of anxiety in my life. As we take this deep dive into God's Word, layers of deception will be exposed and removed.

Rest assured, God did not create you to live in any form of spiritual defeat. You don't have to settle for anything less than absolute spiritual victory for all the days of your life here on earth. It's time to finally break the cycle of torment, fear, habitual sin, heaviness, and confusion. You can be free, once and for all, and God's Word has the answers. You're going to overcome. You're going to have peace and joy. A life of spiritual victory is waiting for you on the other side of truth. Get your hopes up. Let your faith rise. The Holy Spirit is your Bondage Breaker.

So if the Son sets you free, you are truly free (John 8:36 NLT).

1

ENOUGH IS ENOUGH

My wife, Jess, and I sat down for a Sunday brunch. We were celebrating our anniversary, and our plan was to go on a hike after we finished our meal. Jess and I had been looking forward to that day. We were in a busy season of life, so it had been weeks since we had the opportunity to do something like that. Were it not for our anniversary, I'm not so sure we would have been so intentional about our day trip. I remember the look on Jessica's face. She sat across the table from me and smiled with contentment. Finally getting some time for "just us," we were in great moods.

Only minutes after we received our food, I sensed a familiar yet unwelcome feeling. In my mind, I pleaded with myself, "Please, not now, not now, not now." There's never a good time for what was happening to me, but I also can't think of a worse time than an anniversary date. I did my best to ignore it, to suppress it, but I knew that I would eventually lose control...again.

Trying to distract myself from the internal battle, I stared at Jess as she spoke about something. I wasn't able to focus enough to make out what she was saying.

Then it got worse. There was a ringing in my ears. I felt blood rush to my face. My heart began to beat so heavily that I could feel my pulse in my neck. My vision became blurry, and my face went numb. I was having a full-blown panic attack—there in public, in front of my wife, in the middle of our anniversary brunch.

In moments of panic, reason rarely prevails. I knew it was "just another panic attack." However, anxiety always insists on asking, "But what if it's more?" I couldn't bring myself to be logical. As I did during almost every other panic episode, I imagined the worst-case scenario, that I was dying. Logic told me, "It's just anxiety. Calm down. It'll pass." Fear shouted, "You're dying! Get to a hospital now!"

With no regard for anyone but myself, I grabbed my wallet, ran up to our waitress, and paid the bill. I fumbled for words as I fretted, "I need to get out of here now. I have to pay this bill. Take the money. Keep the change." In an almost motherly way, the waitress looked at me and assured, "Your color looks fine. You're talking normal. Sweetie, you're just having a panic attack." I had never before met that woman. I can only assume that her boldness was prompted by the Holy Spirit. That moment, I was much too fearful to listen for His voice myself. Looking back, I can see He was trying to speak to me through her. I know He was saying, "Don't let fear win. Don't allow fear to steal this moment from you. Don't allow fear to steal this moment from Jess."

Had I been at all reasonable, I would have paused and realized what was happening. I would have remembered the countless times when I had survived a panic attack in the past. I would have breathed slowly for a few minutes, prayed, and then moved on with my day. Unfortunately, on that day, I chose fear.

Like so many times before, I found myself waiting to be seen at Urgent Care. Jess had driven me there in our car, and she sat next to me in the waiting room, comforting me. I remember sitting on a waiting-room chair, slumped over with my hands in my face. I was covering my face to help myself calm down, but I was also embarrassed by the scene I had caused. My body was shaking. Jess placed her hand on my back and sat with me. There was really nothing to be said.

As we waited for the urgent-care staff to call my name, the panic began to subside. After about forty-five minutes of waiting, I became level again. I felt the panic release my body. Jess and I left the hospital without me being examined by a doctor. I didn't need to be examined. I knew exactly what had happened to me, because it had happened to me so many times before.

As Jess and I drove home, all I could do was apologize to her again and again. She was so sweet and understanding about it, insisting that there was no need to apologize. Yet I felt so angry with myself for allowing yet another panic attack to ruin yet another beautiful moment. I kept thinking about how Jess was smiling just before I allowed my anxiety to get the better of me.

Then, of course, the enemy began to relentlessly taunt, "Aren't you a man of God? You're so weak. You're a fake." I felt so helpless and ashamed. I was also confused. I asked myself serious questions: *Haven't I already been set free from this? How many more times am I going to have to defeat this darkness? How can this continue to happen when I'm walking with the Holy Spirit? How is this possible in the life of a faith-filled believer?* "Lord," I prayed, "I've seen You do miracles for so many others. Why won't You do this miracle for me?"

Absolutely exhausted, I was tired of my battle with anxiety. Actually, it wasn't just anxiety I battled. I battled the devastating duo that is anxiety and depression. Truly, I was tired of it. I was tired of the heaviness that weighed upon me. I was embarrassed by my struggle. I felt faithless and fake.

I had read of the great revivalists and evangelists of times past. Some of them had lost their minds due to the pressures of ministry and the heaviness of mental and emotional battles. I wondered, *Am I going to repeat their mistakes? Will I be remembered as an evangelist who lost his mind?*

How could a minister of the gospel suffer with anxiety and depression? How was it possible for such bondage to find a place in my life?

Was I being attacked? Was I under witchcraft? A curse? Was it demon possession, oppression, or just an emotional problem? Was it an "open door"? What exactly was happening?

"Whatever this is", I decided, "Enough is enough."

2

WHAT IS A STRONGHOLD?

(For the weapons of our warfare are not carnal, but mighty through God to the pulling down of strong holds;) Casting down imaginations, and every high thing that exalteth itself against the knowledge of God, and bringing into captivity every thought to the obedience of Christ (2 Corinthians 10:4-5 KJV).

The context of that portion of Scripture is Paul's defense of his apostolic authority. Some divisive people had begun to challenge Paul's divine calling by undermining him before the members of the Corinthian church. Those wannabe apostles were jealous of Paul's God-given influence. Paul referred to his takedown of the slanderous deceptions as the *"pulling down of strong holds."* Context considered, here's a takeaway principle: deception is like a stronghold.

In the natural, a stronghold is a fortress or a fortified place. This could be like a castle, tower, or a well-defended hold of any sort. In the spiritual realm, a stronghold is a mindset based on deception. A stronghold is an ungodly imagination, an argument against the truth, or a deceptive way of reasoning. Strongholds are deceptive thought patterns. These deceptive thought patterns can become safe havens for works of the flesh, as well as demonic influence. Once established, these ungodly thought patterns become ungodly behavior patterns, and those ungodly behavior patterns are what we refer to as "spiritual bondage."

If you want to be permanently freed from spiritual bondage, you have to get to the root of the issue. You have to address the problem beyond just the symptoms of your actions and feelings; you have to get to the source of the deception. For the believer, the root of every kind of spiritual bondage is a stronghold of deception. Deception is the root of all defeat. The devil is the father of all deception. Spiritual warfare is the fight to believe God's truth over the enemy's lies. What we believe can give power to or take power from the devil and the sin nature. Thankfully, we're told how to deal with strongholds of deception.

Paul writes, *"For the weapons of our warfare are not carnal."* This, of course, speaks to the spiritual nature of how the believer engages in battle. Though the spiritual can often affect the material and vice versa, you and I don't fight our enemy through carnal means. Demons and deceptions don't respond to shows of physical strength. They're not impressed by intellect, by what we think we know about them or the spiritual realm. Nor does emotion work against the enemy. Neither deceptions nor demons have any compassion toward us, so our frustrations or sorrows cannot persuade them to show mercy. Screaming and yelling don't intimidate them. Human effort cannot remove or silence them. Moreover, we can't outthink them. So we use God's weapons, which are the powerful effects of truth and divine authority.

The phrase *"mighty through God,"* tells of the effectiveness of our weapons and how our spiritual weapons accomplish for the sake of God's cause.

"To the pulling down of strongholds" is especially powerful. What's being described is the absolute destruction and the complete removal of the spiritual obstacle. To visualize this insight, picture a brick wall. If the wall were to be pulled down in the way described in this verse, not

one brick would be left upon another. This is more than the toppling of a structure—it's the vanishing of it. The Scripture isn't describing a damaged stronghold or a partially removed barrier. It's not even describing a pile of rubble. The Bible tells us of a path completely cleared. Not even a hint of the stronghold can remain. Stepping into victory, you wouldn't even have to worry about getting a pebble in your shoe. That's what God promises—total victory.

> *So if the Son sets you free, you are truly free* (John 8:36 NLT).

When Paul writes, "*Casting down imaginations,*" he is speaking of reasonings, mindsets, or deception. These "*imaginations*" are the things we tell ourselves that don't align with divine truth. They are also the lies that demons tell us repeatedly. So "*casting down imaginations*" is a reference to the dispelling of deception.

We are told that "*Every high thing that exalts itself against the knowledge of God*" will be torn down. This can be both every mindset or deception that prevents us from knowing God and every mindset or deception that prevents us from knowing truth *about* God. The former has to do with our personal relationship with God; the latter has to do with our personal revelation about God.

Finally, the Scripture tells us of "*Bringing into captivity every thought to the obedience of Christ.*" I love that the Scripture describes the act of combatting deception as taking captives. Just as the spoils of war are taken only after a city falls, so you cannot take your thoughts captive until you have dismantled the stronghold, the pattern of thinking, in which they find refuge. Demonic and fleshly influence hide in the strongholds that are built upon the lies we believe. When a stronghold is torn down, only then are we able to take our thoughts as captives and bring them under subjection.

So how do you destroy strongholds? To destroy strongholds and take your thoughts captive, you must understand the nature of deception.

THE NATURE OF DECEPTION

Deception isn't exactly the same thing as a lie. A lie is a contradiction of the truth, but deception is what occurs when someone believes the lie. If someone tells you something that contradicts the truth, you've been lied to. If you believe what they tell you, you've been deceived. A lie doesn't become deception until it's believed. This is why the enemy works at making his lies believable, subtle, and even mixed with truth. If a lie is crafty, it's more likely to be embraced.

This is how strongholds work: The enemy lies to you through his demons, secular culture, other people, media, and even you. Every day, you are bombarded by lies. Every so often, a lie will slip past your guard. The lie, once believed, becomes deception. That deception becomes a thought pattern. That thought pattern becomes a behavior. That behavior becomes a habit. That habit becomes a long-term cycle. That cycle is what we call spiritual bondage.

Most believers spend years trying to address the surface of a stronghold, which would be the bad habits or the negative feelings. They go after the symptoms instead of the sickness, the fruit instead of the root, the consequence instead of the cause. They go after the bondage instead of the stronghold that is causing the bondage. This would be like trimming a tree instead of uprooting it. You can trim a tree to look tame for a season, but its leaves will grow again if it isn't cut down at the root. This explains why some can experience a form of freedom or deliverance for days, weeks, or even months, only to find themselves back where they started. They keep addressing the outcome while ignoring the origin.

Even if you can elevate your mood and temporarily quit bad habits through a positive experience or even a spiritual encounter, if you don't address the root lie, you'll eventually just fall back into your old patterns. Even if you use discipline and willpower to resist a habit for an extended period of time, if you don't address the root deception, you'll eventually just go back to the habit again. And when you do fall back into your old ways, the discouragement from having tried and failed will just compound the problem.

Lies become deception. Deception becomes a thought pattern or a way of feeling. Those thoughts and feelings become actions. Those actions become habits. Those habits become cycles. That's bondage.

Lies = Deception = Thought/Feeling Patterns = Actions = Habits = Cycles = Bondage

The bondage that results from a stronghold can be terribly destructive. It can produce torment, depression, anxiety, addiction, paranoia, sinful cravings, confusion, and even issues as severe as mental instability, night terrors, suicidal ideation, hallucinations, and the hearing of voices. Strongholds are that destructive. That's how effective deception can be. No matter the symptom, the source is a stronghold of deception, and, therefore, the solution is truth. To live in that truth is the essence of spiritual battle. Thankfully, God has equipped us to have victory.

THE ARMOR OF GOD

Your mind is the battlefield. Whenever you choose to believe the truth, peace advances. Whenever you choose to believe the lies of the enemy, darkness advances. Strongholds are built, brick by brick, by lies.

Strongholds are dismantled, brick by brick, by truths. This is why we must make a practice of *"Bringing into captivity every thought to the obedience of Christ."* We do this by making use of the spiritual gear God has provided.

> *A final word: Be strong in the Lord and in his mighty power. Put on all of God's armor so that you will be able to stand firm against all strategies of the devil. For we are not fighting against flesh-and-blood enemies, but against evil rulers and authorities of the unseen world, against mighty powers in this dark world, and against evil spirits in the heavenly places. Therefore, put on every piece of God's armor so you will be able to resist the enemy in the time of evil. Then after the battle you will still be standing firm. Stand your ground, putting on the belt of truth and the body armor of God's righteousness. For shoes, put on the peace that comes from the Good News so that you will be fully prepared. In addition to all of these, hold up the shield of faith to stop the fiery arrows of the devil. Put on salvation as your helmet, and take the sword of the Spirit, which is the word of God. Pray in the Spirit at all times and on every occasion. Stay alert and be persistent in your prayers for all believers everywhere* (Ephesians 6:10-18 NLT).

The word *strategies* in verse 11 is translated from the Greek word *methodeia*, which means "deceit, cunning arts, trickery." So the strategies of the enemy have primarily to do with deception. In verse 11, we also see the phrase *"so that you will be able to stand firm against all strategies of the devil."* This is key. Notice that the Bible doesn't say that the armor of God will help you to stand against only *some* of the strategies of the enemy. It says, *"all strategies of the devil."* This means that the armor of God is all that we need in order to stand against all that the enemy can do.

Of course, Scripture certainly gives us many other revelations about spiritual warfare. So I'm not saying that other biblical insights on spiritual warfare aren't needed. I just mean that the armor of God can defeat every single conceivable strategy that the enemy can use against the believer.

Looking at the various pieces of armor, we see a consistent theme: the combatting of deception.

Paul writes that we are to *"put on"* God's armor. This is an instruction. So we carry at least some responsibility in the application of the armor of God.

The first piece of armor listed is the belt of truth. If we are to be successful in the application of the rest of God's armor, we must be committed to the truth.

The second piece of armor listed is the breastplate of righteousness. Paul would be referring to Roman or Israeli armor. So the breastplate, which protected vital organs against enemy attack, would need to be properly fastened by the belt. Thus, we gather that the breastplate of righteousness must be held in place by the belt of truth. Truth holds righteousness to you. You can't live righteously if you don't live in truth.

The breastplate of righteousness represents the righteousness of God given to His children. We are made righteous when we put our faith in the Lord Jesus (Romans 4:3). This is righteousness that could not be earned but only gracefully gifted by God to those who believe. Righteousness comes by faith, but to experience here on earth the full benefits of the righteousness gifted to us, we must know and live by the truth.

The shoes of peace represent our readiness to spread the gospel. The King James Version words it this way: *"And your feet shod with the preparation of the gospel of peace."* Two things to note here: First, in God's Kingdom, we don't take territory in the manner of worldly conquerors.

We take territory with the spreading of the message of the gospel. We step foot on and claim enemy territory by winning souls. Second, the gospel is truth. So again we see a theme—truth versus deception.

Then there is the shield of faith. The shield being described in the text is a large shield, one that would cover the entire body of its holder. When we place our faith in Christ's sacrifice, in the Holy Spirit's power, and in the Father's promises, we are using the shield of faith. It is our faith in God and His Word that acts as a shield to protect us from the fiery darts of the enemy. The fiery darts represent the devil's lies and deceptions. Deception, like fire, spreads if it's not quenched. How do we stop that fire from spreading? How do we shield ourselves from the darts? We use the shield of faith by placing our confidence in what God says. This belief, this deep conviction, quenches the fiery darts, the lies of the enemy. Examining the shield of faith, we again see that spiritual warfare is about truth versus deception.

Next, we have the helmet of salvation. An effective way to discover a Scripture's meaning is to compare that Scripture with other Scripture. Thankfully, we have another mention of the helmet of salvation in First Thessalonians. This sheds light on the helmet's meaning.

> But let us, who are of the day, be sober, putting on the breastplate of faith and love; and for an helmet, the hope of salvation (1 Thessalonians 5:8 KJV).

The helmet of salvation is the hope of salvation. This "knowing" that we have regarding our salvation is ultimately rooted in truth.

Finally, we have the sword of the Spirit. Now the sword, unlike the other pieces of armor, is offensive, as opposed to defensive. Granted, we could say that the shoes of peace are offensive too, in that they are the means by which we take ground from the enemy. However, the sword is our primary weapon of offense. The Sword of the Spirit is the inspired

Word of God. With the other pieces of armor, we defend ourselves against lies and deception. With the sword, we destroy the source of those lies. Yet again, we see the theme—truth versus deception.

So if every piece of the armor of God is purposed against deception and the armor of God is all we need to stand against all the attacks of the enemy, we can conclude that, fundamentally speaking, all of the enemy's methods are based on deception. There you have it—spiritual warfare is the fight to believe God's truth over the enemy's lies.

While the Bible does address other aspects about spiritual warfare and the enemy's nature, we can conclude that deception is at the heart of all enemy strategy and that we can always win against him by knowing and living in the truth.

Thank God that we are given what we need to stand against *"all strategies"* of the devil. God has fully exposed the enemy through the Word. He doesn't leave us second guessing or lacking. God doesn't hide our freedom behind demonic mysteries or ancient secrets. The Bible is clear that truth is the key to victory. Thus, we know that the only power the enemy has over us is what he can deceive us into giving to him. I know it may not always feel or seem that way. Sometimes, it can feel as though the enemy carries more power over us than just deception alone.

However, it's still absolutely true that the enemy's only power over you is deception. Some Christians don't want to accept that simple truth, because they base their identity around their man-made spiritual warfare tactics. Such simplicity would render their "tactics" needless. Other Christians reject that simple truth out of paranoia. They hear so much preaching about how ignorance of the devil's tactics can result in spiritual weakness. Thus, they confuse confidence in truth for "dropping their guard." They think God's solutions are too simple, and they don't trust that simple truth will be effective enough to make them and keep them free.

Granted, it's true that we should be aware of the enemy's tactics. However, what we know of the spiritual realm must be based on the Word, and we have to trust that the Word gives us all we need to be victorious.

To the point, the Word clearly reveals that the enemy is powerless against Spirit-filled believers if he cannot deceive them. Strongholds, spiritual bondage, demonic attack—it's all based on deception. Freedom, the armor of God, spiritual victory—it's all based on truth.

3

DARKNESS RETURNS

My battle with anxiety and depression started when I was a child, and it wasn't just a psychological issue—it was a spiritual one. Even at the age of seven, I was very much aware of the supernatural realm. I could sense the war over my soul, the conflict between light and darkness. Because I don't think it's healthy to emphasize demons or demonic power, I don't often talk about this aspect of my testimony. However, I do think it's important to share with you what I went through, so that you can be encouraged to know that it's possible to overcome even the most severe spiritual battles and strongholds.

The attack on my life proved to be generational. My great-great-grandfather was a powerful warlock who practiced in Zacatecas, Mexico. People from all over the region would come to receive healing and even pay him to place hexes on their enemies. The source of his power was demonic, and there were definitely consequences to my great-great-grandfather's actions. The demonic influence that he established had become familiar to my family. That familiarity lasted generations.

As little girls, my grandmother and her sister would play a game involving demonic power. They would sit down and move objects by simply willing the objects to move. One of their favorite things to do was open and close drawers and cabinets by simply concentrating their "energy" on the objects. My grandmother explained to me, "We thought it was just something normal that all kids were able to do. It was a game to us. We didn't know it was evil at the time." Thankfully, after their parents became born-again believers, those demonic displays of power were just no longer possible. However, that didn't mean that the demonic attacks against my family just ceased. Growing up, my cousins and I would experience strange demonic phenomena. Honestly, we thought it was normal.

In many other instances when I had friends over, my friends would become uneasy and report sensing "something" else in the house with us. As a very young child, I often saw and would hold conversations with demonic entities. I'm not proud of this. It's just important that you know how deep the darkness was. To put it bluntly, it was tormenting. So I'm sure you can understand why I was so embattled. Because my family had eventually become Spirit-filled and born-again, there were limits to what the demonic powers could do to me personally, but the demonic entities certainly did what they could.

I recall seeing faces in the walls of my room, hearing whispering voices, and physically seeing dark beings come near me. It wasn't until I was born again at the age of eleven that I found my first breakthrough. The moment I received Christ, the torment ceased. The depression lifted. The anxiety faded away. The demonic activity just stopped, and I mean within seconds of me being born again. I dedicated the first two years of my salvation to daily praying for four to eight hours and daily reading dozens of chapters of the Bible. I became a committed follower of Christ, and that changed my life.

Two years after I was born again, at the age of thirteen, I began to preach at youth conferences. For years, I walked in total victory over anxiety and depression. At a certain point, those prior struggles weren't even thoughts in my mind anymore. I literally forgot about my previous years of torment. My new life had begun, and I didn't look back.

During those years of total freedom from depression and anxiety, I even began to learn more about the Holy Spirit, prayer, spiritual warfare, and such truths. I was having a real and personal revival. My faith was growing stronger, my joy was increasing, and my peace was consistent. My friendship with the Holy Spirit began to flourish and, along with that friendship, eventually came an evangelistic ministry.

This is where things turned. I became busier and busier with ministry and had less and less time to spend in the secret place of prayer. As the ministry began to grow, so did my reputation as a man of "faith and power." Years into the beginning stages of what some might call success, I became so confident in what I did for the Lord, that, for a season, I became reliant upon my own strength. I still loved the Lord. I still walked with and knew the Holy Spirit. I still lived clean. I prayed for the sick, drove out demons, prophesied, won souls, and preached. My ministry travel schedule began to pick up pace. Everything seemed to be going well, but that hint of self-reliance was more of a problem than I realized.

Gradually, my depression and anxiety began to re-emerge. There was no single instance I can remember that would make me say, "There! That's when it came back." It just crept in slowly. The busier I became, the more known I became, the more pressures began to pile on, it just inched its way back into my life. By the time I turned nineteen, my depression and anxiety had once again become a problem for me. So there I was, a minister who prayed for the sick and who was able to cast out demons, yet in need of a spiritual victory himself.

Dear reader, perhaps you too have found yourself in a similar circumstance. Maybe there's a bondage from which you desire to be finally and permanently free. Maybe there's a stronghold that has re-emerged or often re-emerges. You might be wondering why the cycle keeps repeating.

Every time the cycle repeats, the discouragement gets a little worse. Every time the cycle repeats, hope weakens that much more. Every time the cycle repeats, you're left wondering if freedom is ever going to happen for you, if you'll ever truly be permanently rid of the bondage. I'll admit it. That's what happened to me. I had been free for so long that I became discouraged by the thought that my struggle could return. It was as though its return proved that no matter how long I would be free, the darkness would always return. I doubted, *Will I ever truly be free? Was it all just a matter of time before the problem would return? Will I always be inevitably bound, no matter what?*

Wanting to understand why I was struggling the way I was struggling again, frustrated by my many seemingly fruitless attempts to be free, I determined to find deliverance—once and for all. I tried everything I could. When I say I tried everything, I mean it. I went to conferences, worship nights, revival meetings, and church services. I was prayed over by prophets, evangelists, apostles, and deliverance "specialists." The teachers tried to teach it out of me. The pastors tried to pastor it out of me. The counselors tried to counsel it out of me.

For a time, I even went the route of medication and therapy. I received prophetic words, was prayed over with oil, and even had shofars blown over me. I read the books and watched the seminars. I verbally renounced every possible demonic influence from every possible source from every previous generation. I prayed the curse-breaking prayers and made the faith-filled confessions. Some of those things would work for a season. Still, no matter what I did, anxiety and depression would always seem to find their way back to me.

Certainly, I believe in prayer, deliverance, and God's ability to set people free. Countless times, I've seen Him work through some of these ways I've listed. I'm just being honest with you in telling you that, for a certain period in my life, absolutely nothing seemed to be working for me, and I just didn't know why. Fellow believers accused me of being spiritually weak. As hard as it is to admit, there was some truth in what they told me. Still, it was all very discouraging.

I wanted to be free and without even a hint of depression or anxiety. The struggle wasn't always debilitating. Day-to-day, I just lived knowing that I could at any moment slump into depression or shoot into anxiety. It wasn't always boiling, but every day it was on a slow simmer. There was a subtle sense of heaviness. Some days it was really bad, but most days it was simply inconvenient. I yearned to be free "indeed." So this back-and-forth struggle, this years-long search for permanent victory, lasted through many phases of my life, and even all the way up until that day when I allowed a panic attack to ruin an anniversary date with my wife, Jessica.

I was ready for the solution. I had been in deep darkness, and I was looking for that marvelous light of freedom. I turned to my dear friend, the precious Holy Spirit. I asked Him to teach me. I told Him, "I don't care what the answer is. Even if it means I have to correct my theology and deeply held beliefs, I just want to know the truth that will set me free. Help me, Holy Spirit!"

4

THE SPIRIT OF TRUTH

And you will know the truth, and the truth
will set you free (John 8:32 NLT).

DECEPTION BRINGS DEFEAT

If you are still bound, there's a lie you still believe. If you're living in bondage, you're living in a lie. If you're spiritually defeated, you're deceived. Where there is spiritual defeat, there is always spiritual deception. If you are not walking in spiritual victory, then somewhere, hidden among your many thoughts and beliefs, is a lie that you unknowingly or unwillingly embrace. No demonic power can match the Holy Spirit's power in you. So the enemy's only hope at victory is to deceive you into defeat. Deception is the only power the enemy has over the believer.

There's an old analogy that's often used to demonstrate the negative effect of limiting beliefs. It goes something like this: A man once observed a group of fully grown elephants being held captive by thin ropes wrapped around their legs and tied to relatively small wooden stakes in the ground. Realizing that the elephants could snap the ropes by even a fractional use of their strength, he wondered why the elephants remained bound when they could at any moment break free. The man sought an explanation from an animal trainer who was working nearby. The trainer explained, "Since these elephants were young, we've used ropes of this size to bind them. When they were younger, smaller, and weaker, these ropes were enough to keep them bound. They've been conditioned to believe that they cannot break free from these ropes. So, even though they're strong enough to break free, they simply choose not to try, because of the simple belief that they can't."

The same is true for the believer. I don't mean that positive thinking alone can bring about freedom, and I would never be dismissive of anyone's struggle. I understand that spiritual bondage isn't something you can just "snap out of." Well-meaning people will tell you to "just believe," as if that suggestion alone holds breakthrough power. So I'm certainly not trying to communicate that overcoming strongholds is as simple as a happy thought. However, it is true that if you're in spiritual bondage, you're not making full use of the power God placed within you. So how can we make use of this power?

THE SPIRIT OF TRUTH

Knowing the truth is much deeper than simply thinking a happy or positive thought. This knowing is a spiritual knowing. Thus, as with all things spiritual, we need the help of the precious Holy Spirit. His role in your freedom is crucial. He is the One who guides us in the truth.

> *When the Spirit of truth comes, he will guide you into all truth. He will not speak on his own but will tell you what he has heard. He will tell you about the future* (John 16:13 NLT).

If it's the truth that sets us free and it's the Holy Spirit who guides us in truth, then the Holy Spirit is truly the Bondage Breaker. Without the guidance of the Holy Spirit, we cannot know truth. Without the truth, we cannot be free.

All of us have blind spots. All of us get something wrong at some point. All of us need to be reminded of the truths we forget. Lies come against us in all forms. Demons deceive. Your own thoughts can be deceiving. Even your emotions can play a part in convincing you to believe something that contradicts Scripture. We have preferences and leanings. We see through foggy lenses. We assess through faulty perceptions. We are influenced by upbringing, culture, opinions, and even by what we hope is true. This is precisely why we need the Holy Spirit. He has no blind spots, and He can help you see yours.

You can come to know a fact by receiving information, but you can only know the truth by receiving revelation. Only revelation brings true and lasting transformation. Revelation comes only by the Holy Spirit. He is the Teacher.

So how do you create a connection with the Holy Spirit? That's the amazing part. If you're a born-again believer, you're already connected to Him.

ALREADY ONE

Your body is a shell. Your soul is your mind, will, and emotions. Your spirit is your deep and direct connection with God. Your spirit is what was brought to life when you were born again (John 3:3-8). The innermost part of you, who you really are, is your spirit. Your spirit is now and forever directly connected with the Holy Spirit. As a born-again believer, you don't have to work to connect with the Holy Spirit. That's already done. Sure, your body is perishing. Yes, your soul is being sanctified. But your spirit is already complete. Your spirit is one with the Holy Spirit, right at this very moment.

But the person who is joined to the Lord is one spirit with him (1 Corinthians 6:17 NLT).

Oneness with the Holy Spirit is not something to be experienced then and there, but here and now. Oneness isn't just for Heaven later. You are living in that oneness even as you exist here on earth. As born-again believers, we are not striving for connection with God. We're already connected. This may be difficult to believe, especially if you're struggling to be free from a stronghold. You may feel the struggle in your emotions and battle the negative thoughts in your mind. You may even feel heaviness in your body as a result of your inner struggle. Yet despite what you sense in the outer shells of your being, you must be aware of the reality that your spirit is free and connected with God. Spiritual bondage can only go so deep, because spiritual connection with God is at the core of who you truly are.

Many believers go their entire lives without realizing this connection. You may even view your walk with God like climbing a ladder. On days you do well, you go up the ladder. On days you fail or make a mistake, you take a few steps down. Such a view of your walk with God is what contributes to defeat. Our relationship with God isn't a rigid, points-based system. Here's how the Bible describes your relationship with the Lord:

But it was to us that God revealed these things by his Spirit. For his Spirit searches out everything and shows us God's deep secrets. No one can know a person's thoughts except that person's own spirit, and no one can know God's thoughts except God's own Spirit. And we have received God's Spirit (not the world's spirit), so we can know the wonderful things God has freely given us. When we tell you these things, we do not use words that come from human wisdom. Instead, we speak words given to us by the Spirit, using the Spirit's words to explain spiritual truths. But people who aren't spiritual can't receive these truths from God's Spirit. It all sounds foolish to them and they can't understand it, for only those who are spiritual can understand what the Spirit means (1 Corinthians 2:10-14 NLT).

God's Holy Spirit communes with your spirit. The deepest depths of God know the deepest depths of you. This reality is now. All day, every day you are fellowshipping with God by the Holy Spirit. Deep is calling unto deep.

Deep calleth unto deep at the noise of thy waterspouts: all thy waves and thy billows are gone over me (Psalm 42:7 KJV).

It's the outer shells of you that are being worked on—your body and soul. Your spirit already experiences God's joy, love, peace, power, and holiness. In the Spirit, you know God. In the Spirit, you are complete, always connected with God. In the spirit, you are free.

This is why I have a small issue with the phrase "spiritual growth." Of course, like anyone else, I use that phrase, but in reality, your spirit doesn't grow. Your spirit is already fully mature, because your spirit is already one with God. Spiritual growth isn't your spirit growing at all—it is the rest of you catching up with who you already are in the spirit. Spiritual growth isn't the actual strengthening of your spirit, for your spirit is already as strong as it can be. Spiritual growth is when your spirit begins to influence and affect your outer shells, your body and soul.

So then if we're already connected with the Holy Spirit, why do we sometimes experience spiritual bondage?

REVELATION BY THE SPIRIT

Most Christians just never come to realize the fullness of their connection with God. Because they lack revelation of who they are in Christ, they simply leave God-given power unused. They live under deception, thinking of themselves as satan's victims, rather than as God's children. They live as though they are merely physical beings who struggle against the powers of darkness. Because of this, they accept their spiritual bondage as a normal part of the Christian life. Because of this, they never realize that they are spiritual beings who have the power to be victorious. All who are under spiritual bondage need a major revelation of who they are in Christ.

Revelation is when what you already know in your spirit is revealed to your natural mind by the Holy Spirit. The source of revelation is always Spirit. That's the difference between just acknowledging a truth and coming to really know the truth. Revelation takes the inner realities of who you already are in the spirit and causes them to affect the outer aspects of your being.

This deeper, inner knowing is the witness of the Holy Spirit. The witness of the Holy Spirit is the starting point of perfect liberty. Some believers seek their freedom through other means. They look for an encounter or experience to convince them of what they should already know by faith. They wait until their emotions confirm their freedom. They wait until their thoughts stop racing. They wait until their body no longer feels the angst of spiritual attack. They wait for exterior realities to confirm what the Holy Spirit has been saying all along, within.

The precious Holy Spirit faithfully reminds us.

> But when the Father sends the Advocate as my representative—that is, the Holy Spirit—he will teach you everything

and will remind you of everything I have told you (John 14:26 NLT).

The breaking of strongholds begins here: the truth being spoken by the Holy Spirit. The Holy Spirit speaks the truth about your identity, about your divine inheritance of freedom, about the authority and power you carry, about the purpose you have, and other grounding truths.

Additionally, the Holy Spirit contradicts every lie that could potentially become a stronghold.

Bondage looks like this:

Lie = Deception = Thought/Feeling Pattern = Behavior = Habit = Bondage

Freedom looks like this:

Truth = Revelation = Thought/Feeling Pattern = Behavior = Faithfulness = Freedom

So the Holy Spirit speaks the core and grounding truths. He also speaks specific truths that keep us from falling for the daily lies of the enemy. When the demons of hell shout lies, the Holy Spirit speaks truth. When the enemy tempts you to focus on deception, the Holy Spirit draws your attention to Jesus.

He [Holy Spirit] will bring me glory by telling you whatever he receives from me (John 16:14 NLT).

The first step to receiving freedom is to know the truth, and the Holy Spirit will teach you truth and then continue to remind you of whatever truth you might need to remember. The truth sets you free, exposes the strategies of the enemy, grounds you in your identity, and contradicts the lies from satan. This is the starting point. To stay free from lies, all of us need the Holy Spirit's help.

So if the Holy Spirit is the One who helps you to expose and eliminate deception, what can cause you to fall under the power of deception?

5

OPEN DOORS

WHAT I MEAN

As you study the subjects of spiritual warfare, deliverance, and strongholds, you'll often hear the term "open doors." This term is used in a variety of ways: "Don't watch that movie! It's an open door for the devil." "Don't listen to that song! It's an open door for the enemy." "Don't play around with the occult; that's a major open door for demonic influence."

So what do we mean when we say, "open door"? Even though the term itself isn't found in Scripture, the biblical principle most certainly is. Simply put, an open door is anything that would give the enemy the upper hand in your life or that would cause you to lower your guard against the lies of satan. An open door is anything in your life that makes you more susceptible to deception. Another way to word it: an open door is anything you do, say, feel, or think that makes you more receptive to demonic lies. Open doors are spiritual weak points that the enemy can exploit to bring you under the power of deception. Even after you're born again and even if you've already been delivered from a certain bondage, you must maintain a healthy vigilance, for demonic beings are quite persistent.

DEMONS RETURN

Something quite startling is revealed in the following portion of Scripture:

> When an evil spirit leaves a person, it goes into the desert, seeking rest but finding none. Then it says, "I will return to the person I came from." So it returns and finds its former home empty, swept, and in order. Then the spirit finds seven other spirits more evil than itself, and they all enter the person and live there. And so that person is worse off than before. That will be the experience of this evil generation (Matthew 12:43-45 NLT).

Beware, demons return to check for weak points. They come back to check on you. When an evil spirit loses a place of influence, it comes back in an attempt to reclaim what it can. In the case of the unbeliever, a demonic being can return to gain full influence, including actual possession. In the case of the born-again believer, who is not "empty" as mentioned in the passage from Matthew 12, the demon can still return but is limited on what it can do. When a demonic being returns to find influence in the life of the believer, it can come back to attack and deceive—but never again to fully possess, enter, or attach itself to the believer's being in any way whatsoever. The demon has to settle for attacking the believer from the outside.

Still, it'll take what it can get, so that doesn't mean you can just drop your spiritual guard or live in compromise. Demons don't need to be able to fully possess Christians in order to deceive them. For the sake of spiritual vigilance, we ought to consider this important question: why would a demon even need to possess a believer who chooses to live according to its lies? A demon doesn't need to be able to control your body if it can influence your thoughts through deception. So even though the demon cannot literally re-enter the believer's being, it will still return to deceive. For the believer, open doors can never lead to possession, but they can lead to deep deception. That's reason enough to live with spiritual vigilance and to watch for these "open doors."

So what exactly are the "open doors" that can make us more susceptible to deception? More importantly, how does the Holy Spirit help us to keep these doors closed?

Open Door #1: Connections

Your relationships and connections with ungodly people can be open doors for deception.

> Don't be fooled by those who say such things, for "bad company corrupts good character" (1 Corinthians 15:33 NLT).

It's not my intention to make you suspicious of everyone. Even Jesus spent time with those considered wicked (Mark 2:17). You shouldn't isolate yourself and sever all connections with unbelievers. How then would they receive the gospel? How then could they witness your testimony? Superstitious thinking might lead you to believe that someone's demonic spirit might attach itself to you simply because you shook their hand or allowed them to sit next to you. If you are ever greeted by someone who has a demon attached to them, who do you think will have the greater influence—the demon in them or the Holy Spirit in you?

> But you belong to God, my dear children. You have already won a victory over those people, because the Spirit who lives in you is greater than the spirit who lives in the world (1 John 4:4 NLT).

Guard your connections, but don't live in paranoid isolation. There's a balance to be had.

We don't have to live in isolation for fear of being spiritually infected by ungodly people. On the other hand, we shouldn't go partaking in the sinful habits or compromise of unbelievers either. That sort of compromise makes you vulnerable to the deception of their demons. While the demonic spirit in an unbeliever might not be able to possess or own you, it can imprint a whole new deceptive thought pattern onto your mind if you give that individual too much influence in your life. Let a thief have influence over you, and you'll begin to think like a thief. If you follow the ways of someone addicted to pornography, if you listen to their perverse talk, you'll find it much more difficult to resist sexual temptation. Allow a religious person to use convincing words to dishonor the Holy Spirit's power, and watch how doubt begins to form a stronghold in your mind. When you give people influence over you, when they have the power to cause you to compromise, that's when the strongholds that govern their thoughts start to gain power in yours.

The Holy Spirit helps us to keep this door closed by giving us proper discernment. Proper discernment isn't paranoia, criticism, or suspicion. Especially if we've been hurt or betrayed in the past, we may have the tendency to be generally untrusting toward people. So by relying upon the Holy Spirit, we can avoid the unhealthy extremes of both anti-social suspicion that keeps us closed off to connection and foolish apathy that allows ungodly or ill-intentioned people to gain access to our lives.

For some, the concern is that they might be wronged or taken advantage of. For others, the concern is that they might be lonely or isolated. We all want true connection, and none of us want to be betrayed or hurt. So the Holy Spirit gives clear, sensible, and protective guidance for our lives.

While being hunted by King Saul, David, who was set by God's hand to replace Saul, went into hiding. Out of honor for Saul, David refused to retaliate. So David simply waited in hiding, hoping to not be discovered by King Saul, who was angry, jealous, and driven to madness by a demonic being. Several of the men who had gone into hiding with David were defectors from Saul's ranks. Among the men loyal to David were skillful archers.

> All of them were expert archers, and they could shoot arrows or sling stones with their left hand as well as their right. They were all relatives of Saul from the tribe of Benjamin (1 Chronicles 12:2 NLT).

David was also protected by men with swords and shields.

> Some brave and experienced warriors from the tribe of Gad also defected to David while he was at the stronghold in the wilderness. They were expert with both shield and spear, as fierce as lions and as swift as deer on the mountains (1 Chronicles 12:8 NLT).

Those loyal to David had created a wall of protection around him. The archers would handle enemies coming from a distance, and the swordsmen would handle any enemies who might break through that first line of defense. No enemies could get close to or even begin to approach David without being intercepted.

Suddenly, men from the tribes of Benjamin and Judah approached David's encampment. How was David supposed to know whether or not the approaching men were spies sent from Saul? How was he to know their intentions? It was by the Holy Spirit.

> David went out to meet them and said, "If you have come in peace to help me, we are friends. But if you have come to

betray me to my enemies when I am innocent, then may the God of our ancestors see it and punish you." Then the Spirit came upon Amasai, the leader of the Thirty, and he said, "We are yours, David! We are on your side, son of Jesse. Peace and prosperity be with you, and success to all who help you, for your God is the one who helps you." So David let them join him, and he made them officers over his troops (1 Chronicles 12:17-18 NLT).

It was the presence of the Holy Spirit upon the approaching men that caused David to know that they should be allowed to come close.

In the same way, the Holy Spirit guards the door of your relationships, carefully watching over you. You can't see the motives of others, but the Holy Spirit can. You can't always see the spirit in which others are coming, but the Holy Spirit can.

Perhaps you've already sensed His guidance in closing certain doors. Maybe He's already urged you to pull back from, tone down, or even completely sever certain connections. He sees the damage some relationships are doing to you. He hears the conversations that take place behind your back, and even better, He sees into hearts. He carefully watches over you, steering you away from whoever might cause you to distance from Him.

This is why you're sometimes just not comfortable going certain places, doing certain things, or being around certain people. Something in you is irritated, discomforted by something in them. This is why you choose to keep your kids away from certain people, why you hesitate to confide in certain individuals, and even why things just don't "click" with certain connections.

We're not to become paranoid hermits who isolate and suspect everyone of bringing negative influence. I don't mean paranoia and suspicion. I do mean that the precious Holy Spirit helps to guard us against the spiritual setbacks that happen when we closely connect with those whose conversations, influence, and friendships make us more susceptible to deception. I'm a big believer in divine connections; but divine disconnections are just as important.

Open Door #2: Eyes and Ears

What you see and hear can make you more susceptible to deception.

Few things can affect the mind as powerfully as visuals. Visuals have tremendous staying power. The visual experiences that we store in the mind can contribute to the power of issues like trauma, lust, and mental torment (among other issues). This is why the psalmist refused to look at anything vulgar or vile.

> I will refuse to look at anything vile and vulgar. I hate all who deal crookedly; I will have nothing to do with them (Psalm 101:3 NLT).

This is also why Job made a covenant (agreement, promise) with his own eyes. He made a commitment to himself to not look upon a woman with lust in his heart.

> I made a covenant with my eyes not to look with lust at a young woman (Job 31:1 NLT).

The images you allow before your eyes can become imprinted on your mind. Visualization is one of the most powerful forms of thought. The enemy seeks to use these powerful thoughts against us. He uses them to aid in his effort to cloak our minds under the darkness of his deceptive lies.

The enemy takes disturbing, sinful, or distracting visuals and brings them to memory when you're at a weak point. He may bring a tormenting memory to you while you're half-asleep or even remind you of a sexual image when you're trying to pray or read the Word. This is why it's so crucial that we be aware of what we allow to pass into the mind through the eyes. The images and visual experiences we collect can later be used as ammo in the enemy's weapons. He can bring to remembrance a visual or even create a new visual, a composite of all the ungodly things we've witnessed, to produce negative effects.

Spiritually speaking, the ears work in a similar manner to the eyes. The ideas and words we listen to can cause us to become weaker in our fight against deception.

For example, the music you listen to can be leveraged by the enemy to gain a tactical advantage. No doubt, the Bible makes it clear that there's a spiritual element to music. David's harp playing caused demons to flee.

> And whenever the tormenting spirit from God troubled Saul, David would play the harp. Then Saul would feel better, and the tormenting spirit would go away (1 Samuel 16:23 NLT).

The prophet Elisha requested music to accompany him while he prophesied. Something about the music helped to stir the spiritual power in which he was operating.

> "Now bring me someone who can play the harp." While the harp was being played, the power of the LORD came upon Elisha (2 Kings 3:15 NLT).

The anointed music of David expelled demonic influence, and the harp helped to stir the prophetic power on Elisha. Music is spiritual. The enemy can likewise use music. The devil perverts the power and the effect of music to increase the effectiveness of his deception against us.

Something about music has the power to make the soul more receptive to ideas. This is why it's especially important that we monitor the lyrics that come with the music we enjoy. Because music makes us more mentally and emotionally receptive, the words that come upon the music are able to be planted with more depth. So when you listen to music that makes you angry, depressed, doubtful, cynical, prideful, or disconnected from reality, you're making yourself more vulnerable to believing the ideas that the enemy wants to plant in your mind. This is why I'm astonished by believers claiming to be desperate for freedom while also praying inconsistently, reading God's Word rarely, and listening to ungodly music daily. The life of the believer is supposed to be one of victory, but you can't constantly fill your mind with worldly music and then expect to lay hold of that victory. The reception of ungodly music is just one example of how the ears can serve as open doors to deception.

In general, you should be careful about what you listen to, because words are programmers of the mind. Beware of ungodly advice, unholy conversations, dishonoring gossip, and selfish complaining. Over time, these communications can begin to train your mind to follow the patterns of deception rather than the patterns of truth.

> *Death and life are in the power of the tongue: and they that love it shall eat the fruit thereof* (Proverbs 18:21 KJV).

You can hear truth or deception, encouragement or doubt. The words we hear can produce life-giving thought patterns or spiritually unhealthy thought patterns.

Now, I'm not telling you to live in fear, hide in your home, or walk around with earplugs and blinders. We exist and live in this world.

You're going to unintentionally hear things in passing, see images you'd rather avoid, and talk to people who don't watch carefully what they say. Your whole spiritual life isn't going to fall apart because something flashed on your screen or was played in a public place. Furthermore, when you hear an unwelcome sound or unexpectedly see an unwelcome sight, this doesn't mean that demons are able to seize upon the moment and attach themselves to you.

I know of some Christians who are so bound in legalism that they stop to have a renouncing ritual every time they visit a public place. I have even heard teachings that tell people they need an exorcism if they accidentally see an ungodly image flash across their phone screen or unwillingly hear a secular song on the radio at the market. Taking it even further, some will tell you that a single conversation with an unsaved person or even seeing a secular company logo on a product at the store is cause for major concern. That's not how it works at all. That's not how any of this works. I'm not being facetious, nor am I trying to mock anyone. However, this is just powerless, legalistic, virtue-signaling bondage posing as spirituality. It actually causes misery and spiritual heaviness. Sadly, people who believe such defeated, religious myths live in their own very complicated form of bondage. Those who think like that have not placed their faith in the Holy Spirit's ability to guide and protect.

On the other hand, some believers blast vulgar secular music in their car with their children present. They regularly watch demonic or sexually graphic movies. Their home is a safe haven for worldly culture, worldly conversations, and worldly entertainment. Rarely talking about or even thinking about spiritual matters, these sort of believers may live like Christians on Sunday and even avoid what we would label as the "big sins" throughout the week. But they lack such spiritual depth or awareness that one could not distinguish them from moral atheists. Their Christianity is more of a nice decoration that they wear, or a nice code of ethics by which they raise their kids, than it is an actual death to self or commitment to Christ. They may do such things out of ignorance or a misunderstanding of their *freedom in Christ*. Those who live this way very rarely think about spiritual warfare, and they gently mock those who do talk about it.

When guarding our eyes and ears, we must exercise a healthy awareness, while avoiding the immature extremes of superstitious fear and secular compromise. If you carry out a willful, consistent practice of allowing ungodly things into your mind through sights and sounds, then you most certainly will become more vulnerable to deception's power. By seeing and hearing that which is ungodly on a habitual basis, you gradually train yourself to think according to the patterns of deception. That way of thinking makes you vulnerable to any lie the enemy might want to push on you, and the resulting deception is what ultimately leads to bondage. Close the door. Lock the door. Trust the Holy Spirit to guard the door.

So when guarding your eyes and ears, how exactly do you avoid the extremes of paranoia and ignorance? Honestly, I don't think any true believer actually wants to be legalistic or apathetic, even though many are without realizing it. How can one keep the delicate balance? We want to be holy, but not religious or self-righteous or prideful or paranoid. We want to be sober-minded and grounded, but never worldly or compromising or passive toward spiritual battle.

Lest you toss up your hands in dismay, thinking it impossible or at best very difficult to properly guard your eyes and ears while also keeping a healthy balance, I need to remind you—the Holy Spirit has not left you alone to fight deception. To avoid the two unhealthy extremes of paranoia and apathy, we need only to adjust our perspective. If you focus on demons and their power, constantly giving them credit for everything and imagining that even one mistake can give them a "legal right" to have complete dominion in your life, then surely you'll fall into the trap of paranoia.

Conversely, if you focus solely on the pleasures of this world, believing that your freedom in Christ means that you can participate in anything and everything with no consequence, then you are a prime target for deception and, ultimately, spiritual bondage that you might not even recognize as bondage.

What's the solution? Consider the Holy Spirit. It's that simple. Don't be overcome by a fear of demons, nor by an apathy toward the spiritual realm. Instead, be overcome by a love of the Holy Spirit. Those who love the Holy Spirit fear only one thing—grieving Him.

> *And do not bring sorrow to God's Holy Spirit by the way you live. Remember, he has identified you as his own, guaranteeing that you will be saved on the day of redemption* (Ephesians 4:30 NLT).

Your body is the temple of the Holy Spirit. He dwells in you, with you, and around you. Your eyes are His eyes; your ears, His ears. So the Holy Spirit within you will help you to both recognize and then reject ungodly sights and sounds. In the believer, there is a divine discomfort that is felt whenever seeing or hearing an actual contradiction to God's nature. We can actually sense His grief over the ungodly visuals and messages.

The more mindful we are of the Holy Spirit's feelings, the more reactive we become to ungodly audio and visual experiences. The more considerate we become of the Holy Spirit's presence, the more natural it becomes to avert our eyes from ungodly sights or to keep our ears from ungodly sounds. Recoiling at sinful sights and sounds will become more and more instinctive. By surrendering to the Holy Spirit through obedience and an intentional mindfulness of His nearness, we train the body to live clean.

So then the key to freedom is not found in compiling an exhaustive list of "open doors" and then living the rest of your life with that list in hand. That list could take years to compile and still be incomplete. You can't systemize discernment. It's of the Holy Spirit. The real power is found in simply walking in the Spirit.

> *So I say, let the Holy Spirit guide your lives. Then you won't be doing what your sinful nature craves* (Galatians 5:16 NLT).

Your eyes are His eyes. What are you looking at with the Holy Spirit's eyes? Your ears are His ears. What are you listening to with the Holy Spirit's ears? Live in the awareness of the Holy Spirit's presence. Think about Him. Consider Him. Correct your behavior when you sense Him grieving over your actions. Respond appropriately when you feel His discomfort. Just love and honor His presence in your life. That will help you to keep your eyes and ears from becoming open doors to demonic deception. That's much better, more fruitful than the alternatives of obsessing over what could harm you or just completely ignoring open doors altogether.

Open Door #3: States of Being

There are sins of commission—the things we know we shouldn't do but do anyway (1 Corinthians 6:9-11). There are sins of omission—the things we know we should do but don't do anyway (James 4:17). Then there are states of being that make us more likely to sin or more likely to be deceived. Certain states of being pose huge risks for enemy influence. These states of being include but are not limited to pride, anger, apathy, exhaustion, and doubt.

Some states of being are not necessarily evil or sinful unto themselves, such as anger or exhaustion. However, like all other open doors, they can still place you in spiritual danger and make you more likely to fall under demonic deception.

For example, anger can cause a lot of problems for an otherwise lev-el-headed individual. People who have built stable and successful lives can destroy everything they've worked for in a single moment with just one decision made in anger.

> *Be ye angry, and sin not: let not the sun go down upon your wrath* (Ephesians 4:26 KJV).

Clearly, since it's possible to be angry without sinning, anger isn't sinful unto itself. Regardless, when you allow yourself to be controlled by your anger, with no restraint or discipline, you then become vulnerable to anger's harmful potential. In fully surrendering to anger, you may act, think, or speak in a way that gives a place of influence to the enemy.

> *Neither give place to the devil* (Ephesians 4:27 KJV).

This is not a reference to demon possession or demonic attachment to your being. The word *place* here isn't describing a literal, physical location. It's speaking of influence or "opportunity." When we become angry, we are more likely to do something regrettable. It's easier to say hurtful things, become violent, gossip, or criticize when you're angry. Out of anger, many accuse and tear down their fellow brothers and sisters in Christ, bringing up past sins and mistakes. In this way, they do the enemy's work for him. This is how anger can *"give place"* to the devil.

When you're angry, you're also more likely to believe the lies that best serve your ego. Especially when we're embarrassed by any lack of self-control displayed in a moment of anger, we grasp for anything that makes us feel validated in our rampage—even if this means grasping for a lie.

"I didn't do anything wrong. They're the ones who should apologize." "It's their fault I reacted that way." "If they didn't like the way I responded, they shouldn't have said that to me."

Anger's deception doesn't end at attempts to justify yourself for what was done in anger. This state of being makes us vulnerable to all kinds of other deceptions. When we're angry, we believe the worst about each other, about ourselves, and about life. "Things never work out for me. I'm done trying!" "I can't stand them. I don't need them anymore." "I hate the way I am."

In anger, some even blame God and hold bitter feelings against Him. Though anger may not itself be a sin, it sure does make you quite weak against the lies of the enemy. You've heard it said, "Don't speak when you're angry." I would add, "Be careful not to believe your own thoughts when you're angry."

Still, anger is only one example of a state of being that can incline us to believe the lies of the enemy. Think also of how we might act and think when we are very hungry, apathetic, doubtful, physically exhausted, cynical, prideful, and so forth. Be mindful of how you feel in any given moment, and then be even more mindful of how and what you think.

States of being can be open doors for the enemy's influence. Thankfully, we can at any moment retreat to the inner place of fellowship with the Holy Spirit.

> I pray that from his glorious, unlimited resources he will empower you with inner strength through his Spirit (Ephesians 3:16 NLT).

The Holy Spirit is the One who brings inner stability in moments of outer trouble. In moments when we are made weak by negative or unstable states of being, we can ground ourselves using the consistent strength of the Holy Spirit. We need only to pause and allow ourselves a moment to find our footing in Him. When you're angry, pause and reach for His patience. When you're tired, pause and remember who you are in Him. When you're feeling the intoxication of pride, pause and reflect on how much you need Him. Our feelings, our states of being, are so unpredictable and volatile. They shift up and down, back and forth, depending upon the circumstances in which we find ourselves. In contrast, the strength of the Holy Spirit, His character and nature, is consistent.

Close the door of compromised states of being by grabbing hold of the consistency of Christ's character by the Holy Spirit. How? You do this by pausing before you react or get carried away in ungodly thinking. That pause gives you a moment to retreat to the inner place and then surrender. Pause and surrender. Retreat to your inner self—for the inner you is stabilized by the Spirit. In so doing, you close the door of states of being.

Open Door #4: The Mouth

Finally, we look at the open door that is the mouth. Jesus said, *"It's not what goes into your mouth that defiles you; you are defiled by the words that come out of your mouth"* (Matthew 15:11 NLT). Here, Jesus was specifically referring to the strict dietary laws upon which the religious leaders of the day insisted. He didn't mean that no harm could come from what we consume or put into our bodies. He was simply emphasizing the condition of the heart as more important than strict religious rituals. With that in mind, we must acknowledge the fact that the Bible does, indeed, speak quite clearly on the matter of what our mouths consume.

For example, in the book of Proverbs, we can see that participating in gluttony and drunkenness is unwise.

My child, listen and be wise: Keep your heart on the right course. Do not carouse with drunkards or feast with gluttons, for they are on their way to poverty, and too much sleep clothes them in rags (Proverbs 23:19-21 NLT).

In the New Testament, we see drunkenness being condemned.

Don't you realize that those who do wrong will not inherit the Kingdom of God? Don't fool yourselves. Those who indulge in sexual sin, or who worship idols, or commit adultery, or are male prostitutes, or practice homosexuality, or are thieves, or greedy people, or drunkards, or are abusive, or cheat people—none of these will inherit the Kingdom of God. Some of you were once like that. But you were cleansed; you were made holy; you were made right with God by calling on the name of the Lord Jesus Christ and by the Spirit of our God (1 Corinthians 6:9-11 NLT).

Let's note that drug abuse is also condemned, as being high, like being drunk, robs you of sobriety. So the Bible condemns overeating, alcohol abuse, and, by way of principle, drug abuse.

How might these vices weaken us against the deceptive tactics of the enemy? Think of how overeating can lead to problems with your physical health, and then think of how health problems can cause states of being like depression, anxiety, and apathy. Then also think of how alcohol and drug abuse can increase anxiety, anger, and even pride. The state of your physical body can heavily affect the state of your feelings and thought life.

The Holy Spirit helps us to close the open door of the mouth by giving to us the fruit of self-control.

But the Holy Spirit produces this kind of fruit in our lives: love, joy, peace, patience, kindness, goodness, faithfulness, gentleness, and self-control. There is no law against these things! (Galatians 5:22-23 NLT)

Notice that the fruit is "self-control" not "Holy Spirit control." Leaving your free will perfectly intact, the Holy Spirit lets you choose control. He doesn't force you to choose control. This means that the Holy Spirit has given you what you need to make the right decision. The enemy wants you to believe that you have no power to choose, but you do. This doesn't mean that keeping or regaining self-control is easy, it just means it's possible.

Close the door of the mouth by making use of the self-control given by the Holy Spirit. God has given you the power to decide.

Note: I address addiction more thoroughly in Chapter 11.

6

IDENTIFYING STRONGHOLDS

So far, I've written to you about these important truths:

+ Strongholds are ungodly thought patterns that are built upon deception.

+ Those thought patterns become feelings and actions, which become habits, which become a way of living that we call "spiritual bondage."

+ The enemy's primary weapon against you is whatever lie you find most convincing. In getting you to believe the lie, he can cause you to live according to that lie under the power of a stronghold.

+ An "open door" is anything at all that causes you to become more susceptible to believing the lies of the enemy.

+ The Holy Spirit protects us from strongholds by speaking truth and by helping us to close open doors.

Let's now go deeper. What should you do if you're already living in bondage? Most of what I've written to you thus far has been about preventative spiritual measures. Now, I want to show you how to identify strongholds in your life so that you can begin to tear them down.

THE FATHER OF LIES

Ultimately, all deception comes from the father of lies.

> *For you are the children of your father the devil, and you love to do the evil things he does. He was a murderer from the beginning. He has always hated the truth, because there is no truth in him. When he lies, it is consistent with his character; for he is a liar and the father of lies* (John 8:44 NLT).

The first to fall for satan's lies were the angelic hosts who were persuaded to join in his rebellion against God.

> *This great dragon—the ancient serpent called the devil, or Satan, the one deceiving the whole world—was thrown down to the earth with all his angels* (Revelation 12:9 NLT).

Then, of course, Adam and Eve would later fall for temptation as a direct result of deception.

> *"You won't die!" the serpent replied to the woman. "God knows that your eyes will be opened as soon as you eat it, and you will be like God, knowing both good and evil."*
> *The woman was convinced. She saw that the tree was beautiful and its fruit looked delicious, and she wanted the wisdom*

*it would give her. So she took some of the fruit and ate it.
Then she gave some to her husband, who was with her, and
he ate it, too* (Genesis 3:4-6 NLT).

Deception exists in our world because of the work of satan. The devil spoke lies at the beginning, and his demons likewise are skilled deceivers. Every soldier in satan's army is armed with strategic and effective lies. This is why the Scripture gives us a clear warning to maintain spiritual vigilance.

*Stay alert! Watch out for your great enemy, the devil. He
prowls around like a roaring lion, looking for someone to
devour* (1 Peter 5:8 NLT).

The most effective way to identify the enemy's lies is to know the truth.

IDENTIFY THE STRONGHOLD

Especially if a stronghold has been in your life for an extended period of time, it can be rather difficult to identify the lies upon which it was built. We don't realize how many of the things we think and believe actually come from lies. That's the nature of deception. We have blind spots. We have deeply rooted beliefs that come from childhood, from life experiences, from family culture, and so forth. We just aren't aware of the lies we believe, and that's why they work.

Imagine you walk into a dark room, and you want to see. What would you do? Would you scream at the darkness? Would you try, through physical strength, to remove the darkness? Of course, not. You would simply turn on the light. Just as darkness is the absence of light, so deception is the absence of truth. You can't strike the darkness. Your only hope is to turn on the light.

> *Jesus said to the people who believed in him, "You are truly my disciples if you remain faithful to my teachings. And you will know the truth, and the truth will set you free"* (John 8:31-32 NLT).

The words of Christ, His teachings, the Scripture—that's truth. The more familiar you become with the truth, the more accurately you will be able to spot the lies. Lies begin to stand out, as you begin to know the truth.

Light reveals details. The more light you allow into your life, the more the lies will begin to reveal themselves. Beliefs you never knew were deceptive will be exposed for what they really were all along. You'll experience moments of clarity and breakthrough, as you begin to sharpen your spiritual sight. Layers upon layers of deception will be exposed. You'll start to learn things about yourself and begin to see how many of the things you thought and felt were actually based on deception.

The more aligned you become with truth, the more likely you are to catch what is out of line. Those who are consumed by truth become sensitive to even the lies that seem small. Living in the light will give you a zeal for the truth and a hyper-awareness of deception. To expose and identify the stronghold, let in more light. How do you allow more light into your life? How do you train yourself in truth?

GOD'S WORD

Begin with God's Word. The Word of God is the Source of light and truth.

Your word is a lamp to guide my feet and a light for my path (Psalm 119:105 NLT).

Don't tell me you're desperate for freedom but not devoted to reading God's Word. If we are to experience freedom, we must be committed to the Word. The Word of God is a precise leveler. By it, you can see even slight tilts toward deception. As you commit yourself to knowing the Scripture, you become more and more familiar with the truth. As you come to know the truth, your spiritual perception is trained to target and reject lies. Crooked lies are obvious against the straight truth. Deception stands out when measured against God's Word. The Word will reveal all of the lies you believe about God, yourself, the world around you, right and wrong—everything. You'll begin to realize how many of your long-held assumptions and ideas are actually based on lies.

THE HOLY SPIRIT'S VOICE

You also need to listen to the voice of the Holy Spirit. Every believer can hear the voice of the Holy Spirit.

My sheep listen to my voice; I know them, and they follow me (John 10:27 NLT).

He speaks through His Word.

All Scripture is inspired by God and is useful to teach us what is true and to make us realize what is wrong in our lives. It corrects us when we are wrong and teaches us to do what is right (2 Timothy 3:16 NLT).

The Word of God is the clearest way the Holy Spirit speaks to us. The Word is also the means by which we measure all truth. If you want to ensure that you're hearing from the Holy Spirit, compare what you hear to what the Scripture clearly teaches.

The Holy Spirit speaks through wisdom.

> *If you need wisdom, ask our generous God, and he will give it to you. He will not rebuke you for asking* (James 1:5 NLT).

Wisdom is the second most accurate means of hearing the Holy Spirit. The more familiar you become with the Word, the more your wisdom grows. Wisdom, though it may not always come in the form of specific instructions, is the divine reasoning of God in your spirit that allows you to navigate life. Wisdom is God's purposeful pull on you.

The Holy Spirit speaks through His whisper. What is the whisper of the Holy Spirit? This is when the Holy Spirit speaks specific and personal messages directly to you. For example, in moments of persecution and pressure, the Holy Spirit will give you the words to speak.

> *But when you are arrested and stand trial, don't worry in advance about what to say. Just say what God tells you at that time, for it is not you who will be speaking, but the Holy Spirit* (Mark 13:11 NLT).

The whisper is not as reliable as the Word and Wisdom, not because the Holy Spirit doesn't speak clearly, but because the whisper is so often muffled by the interference of our emotions and personal opinions. Still, this is one of the ways the Spirit speaks. Many believers try to live their lives by the whisper, when they should live by the Word and Wisdom. The Word of God and the Wisdom of the Spirit are the guiding references for hearing Him clearly. Prioritize the Word and Wisdom, and you'll more clearly and often hear His whisper.

Finally, the Holy Spirit speaks through wonders. This includes miracles and signs. An example of this is the prophetic ministry.

> *Do not scoff at prophecies, but test everything that is said. Hold on to what is good* (1 Thessalonians 5:20-21 NLT).

Wonders are the least reliable way we hear the Holy Spirit, because the enemy can perform false signs. This doesn't mean that we should reject God's wonders, signs, and miracles. This just means that signs and wonders cannot be the primary means we use to hear the Holy Spirit.

In order of reliability, it goes the Word, wisdom, the whisper, and then wonders. Build on the Word. It will give you wisdom. Wisdom will mature you as one who can accurately hear the whispers of the Spirit. Once you know the Holy Spirit for yourself, you can better discern wonders.

Growing in your ability to hear the Holy Spirit is as simple as knowing the Word, obeying the Word, and removing the distractions of the world.

Since you are already a Spirit-filled believer, you can hear the Holy Spirit. Just as you were born with the senses of hearing and seeing, so you were born again with spiritual sight and hearing. Hearing the Holy Spirit isn't a skill to be learned but a sense to be sharpened. You already have this ability.

Know the Word, and you will know God's voice and nature.

> *Study to shew thyself approved unto God, a workman that needeth not to be ashamed, rightly dividing the word of truth* (2 Timothy 2:15 KJV).

Obey the Word. Even if you don't know God's specific plan for your every moment, you can obey the general teachings of Scripture. Godly living invites the guidance of God.

> The Lord directs the steps of the godly. He delights in every detail of their lives (Psalm 37:23 NLT).

Finally, remove the distractions of sin, self, and satan.

> But when you pray, go away by yourself, shut the door behind you, and pray to your Father in private. Then your Father, who sees everything, will reward you (Matthew 6:6 NLT).

You can remove external distractions through practical means like setting aside time to pray privately, scheduling your day to include time devoted to just prayer, turning off your phone while praying, and even informing your loved ones of your prayer time so you're not disturbed.

You can also remove mental and emotional distractions through means like trusting that God hears you instead of begging Him to hear you, choosing to focus on thoughts that are true, worshipping the Lord in song, and placing your burdens on the Lord through prayer requests.

By clearing your life of both external and internal distractions, you become better positioned to hear the voice of the Holy Spirit, the voice of truth. In hearing His voice, you gain the advantage against the lies of the enemy.

SOUND TEACHERS

In addition to the Word and the voice of the Holy Spirit, God has given us teachers and preachers of the Word.

Now these are the gifts Christ gave to the church: the apostles, the prophets, the evangelists, and the pastors and teachers. Their responsibility is to equip God's people to do his work and build up the church, the body of Christ (Ephesians 4:11-12 NLT).

He must hold firm to the trustworthy word as taught, so that he may be able to give instruction in sound doctrine and also to rebuke those who contradict it (Titus 1:9 ESV).

So long as you know the Word and the voice of the Holy Spirit, you will have the discernment necessary to find solid teachers.

Teachers and preachers can point things out in the Word that we may have missed. They help to supplement our understanding of Scripture. Maybe the Holy Spirit is trying to speak to you about something in your life, and you're just not recognizing His instruction or correction. Perhaps you're not yet seeing it in Scripture either. That's when God will send preachers and teachers.

THE KNOWLEDGE OF TRUTH

The first key to tearing down any stronghold is identifying it. We identify strongholds through the knowledge of truth. We receive that knowledge through God's Word, the voice of the Holy Spirit, and anointed teachers and preachers. Once you receive it, compare the truth with everything you think and believe. If you find a contradiction between the two, you've found a lie. That lie could very well be contributing to a stronghold.

7

COMMANDING THE FORCES OF DARKNESS

Once you've identified the lies, it's time to deal with the liars themselves—the devil and his demons. That's what I cover in this chapter. I want to show you how to deal with the demonic aspects of a stronghold through the simple exercise of divine authority.

TWO KINGDOMS

There are only two kingdoms: the kingdom of darkness and the Kingdom of light. Those who do not belong to Christ are under the power of the kingdom of darkness. Those who belong to Christ have been rescued from the dominion of darkness and brought under the power of a new jurisdiction, the Kingdom of Heaven.

> *Once you were dead because of your disobedience and your many sins. You used to live in sin, just like the rest of the world, obeying the devil—the commander of the powers in the unseen world. He is the spirit at work in the hearts of those who refuse to obey God. All of us used to live that way, following the passionate desires and inclinations of our sinful nature. By our very nature we were subject to God's anger,*

just like everyone else. But God is so rich in mercy, and he loved us so much, that even though we were dead because of our sins, he gave us life when he raised Christ from the dead. (It is only by God's grace that you have been saved!) (Ephesians 2:1-5 NLT).

Clearly, you and I no longer belong to the enemy or his kingdom. The enemy can no longer touch us.

We know that God's children do not make a practice of sinning, for God's Son holds them securely, and the evil one cannot touch them (1 John 5:18 NLT).

The enemy can no longer own you, inhabit you, or have dominion over you. Still, the enemy can attack you. The way the enemy attacks the believer is quite different from the way he attacks the unbeliever. Spiritual warfare is different for the Christian from the way it is for the non-Christian. In fact, the unbeliever isn't even engaged in spiritual warfare. They aren't resisting the enemy or fighting against his will at all. They're just bound, totally under the enemy's power. The unbeliever is subject to the power of curses, demonic possession, and the worst forms of demonic assault. In severe cases of demonic influence, it's even possible for demons to directly physically harm the unbeliever. The enemy attacks the unbeliever from a place of authority.

By contrast, the enemy attacks the believer from the desperate position of defeat. Though deception might make it seem otherwise. Because you and I now belong to God, the enemy is quite limited on how he can attack us. This doesn't mean that we should be apathetic toward or ignorant of the devil's strategies. We must be engaged in combating demonic influence.

DEMONIC LIMITATIONS

In dealing with demons, there is a balance to be had. Some people are so obsessed with demons and demonic power that they minimize the Holy Spirit's power. Others are so skeptical of demonic power that they leave themselves wide open to attack. To help you find proper balance in dealing with demons, I want to show you, using Scripture, the limitations of demonic beings.

#1 Demons are not omnipresent.

> *When an evil spirit leaves a person, it goes into the desert, seeking rest but finding none* (Matthew 12:43 NLT).

Demons can only be in one place at one time. The verse from Matthew 12 illustrates the fact that demons travel, move about. The fact that they can move about is proof that they are not omnipresent. By definition, if someone is omnipresent, they are unable to move from one place to another since they are already everywhere at all times.

#2 Demons cannot read your mind.

Scripture clearly communicates that God alone can see into the human heart. Only God knows your thoughts.

> *Then hear from heaven where you live, and forgive. Give your people what their actions deserve, for you alone know each human heart* (1 Kings 8:39 NLT).

It may seem sometimes like the enemy can read your thoughts, but biblically speaking, this can never be the case. If someone thinks that demons are reading their mind, they have to consider at least two possibilities. The first possibility is that they may be mistaking their own negative thoughts for demonic voices. When a demon seems to reply to what you're thinking, it's possible this reply could actually be from your own voice of negativity.

The second possibility is that the demonic beings are simply reading exterior clues. It should be noted that demonic beings have been studying mankind for thousands of years. They are highly trained spiritual assassins. They know human nature. By simply looking at body language, listening to voice inflections, or observing your actions, they can get a pretty clear idea of what's going on within you.

For example, if I have something on my mind, my wife can tell what's running through my mind by just looking at me. She doesn't need to be able to read my mind in order to be able to read me. Likewise, those closest to me have learned to read me. In the same way, demons learn to read you very well, creating the illusion that they can see your thoughts.

Consider also the fact that demonic beings communicate with one another (Matthew 12:45). What one demon sees you do and say in secret can be communicated to another demonic being. They share your secrets with one another. They could use this intel to create the illusion that a demon or a demonically influenced person is reading your mind when they're actually just receiving intel from the demonic beings who observe you regularly.

Through careful observation, demons can see clues that tell them which lies affect you the most. They know when you're anxious, depressed, paranoid, angry, tempted, and so forth. For example, a demonic being might say something like, "God has rejected you." Then it waits to see if your heart rate rises, if you pace the room, or even if you jump online and run a search for Bible verses about God's rejection. From exterior clues alone, demons can learn to predict what you might be thinking in any given scenario. This is one way they exaggerate their power, but this isn't the same thing as them being able to read your mind.

#3 Demons cannot see the future.

> *Remember the former things of old: for I am God, and there is none else; I am God, and there is none like me, Declaring the end from the beginning, and from ancient times the things that are not yet done, saying, My counsel shall stand, and I will do all my pleasure* (Isaiah 46:9-10 KJV).

In the book of Isaiah, we see a definitive statement: *"there is none like me, Declaring the end from the beginning...."* It's rather straightforward here. One of the distinguishing abilities that God has is His exclusive power to see past, present, and future as one "picture."

Much in the same way that demons can read people without reading minds, so they can make educated guesses about the future. This would explain why some who operate under demonic power are seemingly able to predict certain things. As an economist can make an educated guess about the economy, so demons can make educated guesses about the future of any one individual or even society. They look for key indicators and trends. Additionally, it's also possible that demonic beings work to fulfill their own predictions.

We can conclude that demons cannot be omnipresent, read minds, or see the future. Those are their general limitations. In short, against the believer, demons can use their voices to lie and torment but hardly more than that.

NOT BY POWER OR MIGHT

Believe it or not, confronting the demonic aspect of a stronghold is the simplest part of tearing down strongholds. Though in this chapter I am not specifically addressing the topic of demonic possession, I am going to use examples of demonic possession from Scripture to show just how responsive demonic beings are to the Holy Spirit's power. By the power of the Spirit, you command absolute authority over demonic beings.

> *When the even was come, they brought unto him many that were possessed with devils: and he cast out the spirits with his word, and healed all that were sick* (Matthew 8:16 KJV).

It was with a simple word that Jesus expelled the forces of darkness. Demonic possession is the most severe form of demonic assault, yet Jesus vanquished this dark power with a simple command. What was at work? It was spiritual authority that came by the infilling of the Holy Spirit. Jesus Himself told us that He was driving out demons by the Holy Spirit.

> *But if I am casting out demons by the Spirit of God, then the Kingdom of God has arrived among you* (Matthew 12:28 NLT).

In contrast, we see that the seven sons of Sceva attempted to drive out demons through ritual—in a special prayer offered in the name of Jesus but through Paul's experience. Because they lacked the power that came from a connection with the Lord Himself, the demons overpowered them.

> *A group of Jews was traveling from town to town casting out evil spirits. They tried to use the name of the Lord Jesus*

in their incantation, saying, "I command you in the name of Jesus, whom Paul preaches, to come out!" Seven sons of Sceva, a leading priest, were doing this. But one time when they tried it, the evil spirit replied, "I know Jesus, and I know Paul, but who are you?" Then the man with the evil spirit leaped on them, overpowered them, and attacked them with such violence that they fled from the house, naked and battered (Acts 19:13-16 NLT).

Granted, the sons of Sceva were able to cast out some demons because the demons feared the name of Jesus. Still, they were limited when they attempted to practice exorcism by ritual instead of relationship.

When you confront demonic beings, you must remember that you are not confronting them in your own strength, power, or authority. They don't care about how much you think you know about them, what others consider to be your spiritual rank, or even how many years you've been engaged in spiritual warfare. They don't respond to your credentials—they respond to Christ. So it's not a matter of garnering techniques or of implementing learned protocols. It's simply the presence and power of the Holy Spirit. We are not the ones the demons fear.

In my first few years of ministry, I had begun to develop a reputation for how God was using me, and I'm ashamed to admit to you that I had developed a great deal of spiritual pride. I know the term "spiritual pride" might seem like an oxymoron. After all, pride is not spiritual. By this, I simply mean that I had begun to base my identity on my ministry accomplishments and how God was using me instead of who I was in Christ. When people needed healing, deliverance, or an encounter with God, they were often referred to me. I began to allow what God was doing through me to build up my ego.

It came to the point where my faith for healing miracles wasn't in God but in my "deep" prayer life. My confidence in my prophetic gifting wasn't in God's grace but in my "sharp" spiritual hearing. And my confidence in casting out demons wasn't in the authority of Christ but in my "expertise" about demons and the spiritual realm. In my mind, I was like a member of a spiritual special forces.

Whenever I would deal with demonic powers, I thought it was my knowledge of the spiritual realm that caused demons to submit. Because I believed the demons were responding to my own knowledge and experience, I thought it necessary to gather intel like the demon's name, type, rank, entry point, and so forth. Sure, people got delivered, but they were delivered despite my superstitious methods, not because of them.

I was limited in my understanding of divine authority. Casting out a single demon would take me hours. The exorcisms I conducted were more like interrogations than they were demonstrations of true authority. "What's your name? How did you get in? How many generations do you go back?" Don't ask me why I even trusted the intel I gathered from lying spirits. I would've told you, "They have to tell the truth because I carry authority, and I can command them to tell the truth." Yet I failed to see my own circular reasoning. After all, if I had the authority to make them tell the truth, I should have just used that authority to make them leave without an argument. Defending myself, I would have told you, "Jesus interrogated demons!"

Of course, I would have been referring to Jesus confronting the demoniac with a legion of demons in him. That was the one instance where Jesus asked for the name of a demon. But that wasn't an hours-long session in which Jesus conversed back-and-forth with the evil spirits. In fact, even after learning the name of the group of demons, Jesus didn't bother to use it.

> Then Jesus demanded, "What is your name?" And he replied,
> "My name is Legion, because there are many of us inside this

man." Then the evil spirits begged him again and again not to send them to some distant place. There happened to be a large herd of pigs feeding on the hillside nearby. "Send us into those pigs," the spirits begged. "Let us enter them." So Jesus gave them permission. The evil spirits came out of the man and entered the pigs, and the entire herd of about 2,000 pigs plunged down the steep hillside into the lake and drowned in the water (Mark 5:9-13 NLT).

So why did Jesus ask for the name of the demon? There are a couple possible explanations.

Obviously, Jesus knew the name of the demonic group before they told Him. So this could have simply been a demonstration of His power—to show that He had the authority to drive out even a whole legion of demons instantly.

Another thing to consider is the fact that in certain parts of the ancient world, it was believed that to learn someone's name was to gain power over them. The fact that Jesus didn't speak the name of the demon even after being given the name could have been Him demonstrating, "I know your name, but I don't need to use it to have authority over you." Truly, the only name you need to know when confronting a demonic power is the name of Jesus.

To conclude that Jesus would be unable to cast out the legion of demons without knowing its name would be to greatly underestimate the power of the Holy Spirit and to greatly overestimate the power of the demonic. How powerful our Christian myths have become! Just as old wives' tales become popular and then accepted as true, so many of the things we teach about spiritual warfare keep us from tapping into true power.

I was stuck in my ritualistic ways. Interrogations. Long deliverance sessions. Stabbing demons with angelic swords. Obsessing over demon types, ranks, and roots, I complicated the pure and simple power of the Holy Spirit.

Whenever anyone tried to lovingly correct my approach, I would arrogantly reply with spiritual-sounding yet very unbiblical defenses. I would say foolish things like: "Well, the Pharisees persecuted Jesus too, so I can see why you're coming against me." "You haven't dealt with real heavy demonic influence yet, so you don't understand how this works." "Maybe you need deliverance; that might be why you're coming against me." "You lack knowledge of the demonic realm and should stick to your area of expertise." "You just need to go deeper." "The only ones criticizing me are the ones not actually doing deliverance!" By that, I meant that they didn't use the methods I used. Because they weren't practicing the man-made rituals I had been taught, I incorrectly concluded that others weren't practicing deliverance ministry at all.

I had a hard time letting go of the man-made protocols that had become so popular. Many believers attach their identities to such methodologies. They may think their use and knowledge of these practices assigns to them a special rank or a greater effectiveness in spiritual battle. Those who become entangled in such things usually have the purest of intentions and motives. We all want to live free, help set people free, and train others to minister freedom. We all want to destroy the works of the devil, drive out demons, break strongholds, and utterly devastate the kingdom of darkness.

However, before we can learn the Holy Spirit's way, we must unlearn man's way. In order to do this, we must learn to not double down on what we've been taught just because it's familiar or validating. Letting go of old mindsets means rooting your identity in Christ, not in a set of doctrines or practices. Our power over demons isn't our source of identity or joy. Our connection with the Lord is.

But don't rejoice because evil spirits obey you; rejoice because your names are registered in heaven (Luke 10:20 NLT).

To be clear, I'm not saying these practices are bad, I'm saying they're not God's best. One may be able to defeat demonic power by use of these methods, but the victory comes despite these man-made rituals, not because of them. I mean, I can get from California to Florida by walking—but isn't it better to fly? The Holy Spirit can work through anything. This is not a matter of choosing between wrong or right, but of choosing between acceptable or most effective.

Dear reader, if we want to truly go deeper, we have to admit we're not at final depth. If we want to be more effective in spiritual warfare, we have to admit that we don't know it all. Don't allow your learned techniques to cause you to settle.

There are different levels of maturity and effectiveness in every single spiritual gift and ministry. Spiritual warfare is no different. When I first began to engage in spiritual warfare and deliverance, I took hours to cast out demons, screamed and yelled at demons as if they were intimidated by my raised voice, interrogated demons, and relied upon man-made techniques to get demons to leave. Because I operated in my own strength for a good portion of the spiritual battle, I would finish spiritual battles being absolutely exhausted. That was part of why I felt validated. In my heart I would say things like, *"I'm over here on the front lines helping people get free, while other pastors wouldn't dare be seen doing this."* I felt virtuous and validated by my own special form of martyrdom. *"I'm putting in the work. Others sit on the sidelines."*

Some may still be operating in this level of spiritual warfare. That's fine, as long as they don't get stuck there. There's a higher realm from which we can wage war. Those who walk deeply with the Holy Spirit and know what it is to carry His glory deal with demons like trainers deal with dogs. This isn't a back-and-forth showdown between demonic power and God's power; it's an extermination of pests. Man's way emphasizes demon power and special techniques—like ghostbusters. God's way emphasizes Holy Spirit power.

Before I was able to grow out of my ritualized approach to spiritual warfare, I first had to admit that I wasn't fully grown. Spiritual pride can keep people from growing. That's one of the most challenging aspects of growth—admitting you need to grow.

Thankfully, the Holy Spirit corrected me and began to show me a better way.

> Then he answered and spake unto me, saying, This is the word of the Lord unto Zerubbabel, saying, Not by might, nor by power, but by my spirit, saith the Lord of hosts (Zechariah 4:6 KJV).

That Scripture in Zechariah records a word spoken to Zerubbabel, but the core message is a truth that still applies today—it's not in our power but in the Holy Spirit's power. In fact, the Holy Spirit told me how grieved He is when believers give more credit to the power of demonic beings than to His power. We so often insult His power, and it stirs His holy jealousy.

> Or do you think that the Scripture says in vain, "The Spirit who dwells in us yearns jealously"? (James 4:5 NKJV)

The Holy Spirit is the Bondage Breaker, not me or you. Again, I'm not just writing about demonic possession and casting out demons. This is bigger than that. I am writing to you about the authority you carry by the Holy Spirit. Demons attack believers by speaking tormenting and confusing lies to us, but we can speak commands that silence them. The Holy Spirit has shown us, through the Word, how absolute His authority is over demonic beings.

> *Jesus and his companions went to the town of Capernaum. When the Sabbath day came, he went into the synagogue and began to teach. The people were amazed at his teaching, for he taught with real authority—quite unlike the teachers of religious law. Suddenly, a man in the synagogue who was possessed by an evil spirit cried out, "Why are you interfering with us, Jesus of Nazareth? Have you come to destroy us? I know who you are—the Holy One of God!" But Jesus reprimanded him. "Be quiet! Come out of the man," he ordered. At that, the evil spirit screamed, threw the man into a convulsion, and then came out of him. Amazement gripped the audience, and they began to discuss what had happened. "What sort of new teaching is this?" they asked excitedly. "It has such authority! Even evil spirits obey his orders!" (Mark 1:21-27 NLT)*

I want to point out several important things from that passage of Scripture in Mark 1. First, the people noticed the uniqueness of Jesus' authority. He taught with divine authority, unlike the religious leaders of His day. Second, Jesus drove out the demonic powers with a simple command. In several Gospel accounts, Jesus would drive out several demons from crowds of demoniacs, heal many who were sick, and all in one day. His method of ministry would only work if He was instantly driving out demons.

Finally, notice that the people were comparing Jesus to the religious leaders. This would have been a major pain to their egos. The Pharisees and Sadducees wanted to be seen, praised, looked to as spiritual, perceived as important, and generally esteemed by society. So when Jesus came onto the scene, His ability to teach like they couldn't teach and do what they couldn't do agitated their feelings of jealousy. The religious leaders practiced exorcism (Matthew 12:27), but not with the same kind of authority that Jesus had. History tells us that the religious leaders would use specific rituals and memorized prayers. The Bible tells us that Jesus, by contrast, drove out demons with a simple command (Matthew 8:16).

How upsetting it must have been for them when Jesus broke away from their traditions and performed exorcisms without having to jump through the same hoops they did. They likely were nowhere near as successful as Jesus in freeing people from demons.

The religious mindset hates the simplicity of God's power, because it takes the attention off of human performance and places it on God's ability. Few things frustrate the religious as much as when you don't obey their rules and regulations. When you truly walk in the power of the Holy Spirit, some might say you cast out demons "too quickly" or "too simply." Religious thinking will demand that you go through the proper steps and use the correct protocols. Religious thinking may even accuse you of leaving people in bondage, because religious minds cannot grasp the concept of such a power that could cause demons to instantly obey. But simply and quickly is how Jesus did it.

> *"My thoughts are nothing like your thoughts," says the Lord. "And my ways are far beyond anything you could imagine. For just as the heavens are higher than the earth, so my ways are higher than your ways and my thoughts higher than your thoughts"* (Isaiah 55:8-9 NLT).

Dear reader, a simple command from a child of God is all that's needed. When confronting demons, it's tempting to rely on theology and head knowledge, but Jesus shows us a better way, the Holy Spirit's way. Once you see that it's possible to command demons without the rituals, you'll never want to go back to the traditions of man. It's simply the presence and power of the Holy Spirit. That's what does it. Besides, Jesus healed on the Sabbath; so it's safe to say that it's okay to break from tradition now and then for the sake of the captives.

There is a beautiful deliverance movement happening in our generation, but it's not going to look anything like the days of old. This move belongs to the Holy Spirit. God is doing a new thing, a fresh thing. Don't miss the movement because of a memory or a methodology. No interrogations. No resistance. No rituals. Just pure power.

If this is challenging what you've been taught, you might feel uncomfortable. When I was first confronted with the truth of Scripture on these matters, because of what I had been taught and because of what everyone around me had so adamantly affirmed, I said within myself, *"I don't know. Something about this just doesn't sit right. This is confusing me."* Little did I know, the discomfort was the discomfort of God's correction. The confusion was coming from the traditions and teachings to which I was attempting to cling, not from the truth the Holy Spirit was introducing to me.

In this section, I referenced biblical examples of exorcism and possession. But remember, this is not just about casting out demons. I'm simply using exorcism as a reference. I'm wanting you to see how helpless demonic beings are against the sheer force of the Holy Spirit's power. If they're that helpless when it comes to full-on possession, then imagine how weak they are when it comes to a simple stronghold.

This does not mean we should be careless about or entirely dismissive of demonic beings. I'm just putting their power in proper perspective against the Holy Spirit's power.

KNOWING HIS AUTHORITY

Strongholds are built upon the lies of the enemy, and you have been given authority over the liars that attempt to deceive you. Don't hide in the corner with your hands over your ears. Stand up, and go on the offensive. Like a bully that is finally confronted, a demon that's confronted will reveal just how terrified it is of the power of the Holy Spirit. Demons scurry when God's people stand in faith instead of stressing over the fact that they're being attacked.

The Bible gives us clear insight on how we are to deal with these enemies—simply command them. This is not man's way, but the Holy Spirit's way. So how does that work? To help you understand the authority given to you, let's look back at the beginning.

Long ago, there was a conflict that took place in the heavenly realm. Satan persuaded angelic beings to join him in a rebellion against God. This was hardly a war, as satan and all his minions could not compare to God in strength and power. The devil, along with his rebellious ones, were banished to the earth.

> *This great dragon—the ancient serpent called the devil, or Satan, the one deceiving the whole world—was thrown down to the earth with all his angels* (Revelation 12:9 NLT).

Why did satan rebel? When did this occur? Let's look at the biblical timeline.

We know that God created the world and all life on earth during a six-day period (see Genesis 1:1-31). On days one through six, God created. On the seventh day, God rested.

Satan could not have fallen before the six days of creation, because when he rebelled, he was banished to the earth. Though it might be obvious, it should be noted that the earth had to be in existence in order for satan to be banished to it.

Here, some might assert the theory of the pre-adamic race, a civilization that existed before Adam and Eve were created. Some believe that this society existed and was destroyed before God "started over" with the six days of creation mentioned in Genesis. Aside from this theory standing on poor word translations, there are several reasons why we should reject the idea of a pre-Genesis civilization. I'll reference two. First, the Bible refers to Adam as the first man:

> *The Scriptures tell us, "The first man, Adam, became a living person." But the last Adam—that is, Christ—is a life-giving Spirit* (1 Corinthians 15:45 NLT).

If Adam was the first man, as the Bible clearly teaches, there could not have been a civilization in existence before Adam and Eve were created. Second, the Bible tells us that death came into the world by Adam's sin:

> *When Adam sinned, sin entered the world. Adam's sin brought death, so death spread to everyone, for everyone sinned* (Romans 5:12 NLT).

If we believe that a civilization was destroyed and that lives were taken before the creation of Adam and Eve, then we would have to conclude that death came before sin. That's a clear contradiction to Scripture. So we can biblically conclude that satan did not fall before the six days of creation.

What about during the six days of creation? Consider that satan had spent some time in Eden while he was still in his heavenly state.

Son of man, sing this funeral song for the king of Tyre. Give him this message from the Sovereign Lord: You were the model of perfection, full of wisdom and exquisite in beauty. You were in Eden, the garden of God. ...I ordained and anointed you as the mighty angelic guardian. You had access to the holy mountain of God and walked among the stones of fire. You were blameless in all you did from the day you were created until the day evil was found in you (Ezekiel 28:12-15 NLT).

In that passage, Ezekiel the prophet is giving a message to the king of Tyre. In that prophetic word, Ezekiel is drawing a parallel between the king of Tyre and satan. It's in that parallel that we catch a glimpse into satan's former state. Satan had at one point, in his heavenly form, spent some time in Eden. In order to have done so, satan must have fallen after the six days of creation.

So satan did not fall before the six days of creation, nor did he fall during the six days of creation. He rebelled sometime after the six days of creation. This is important because in establishing the "when," we begin to understand the "why." Why would satan have forfeited his heavenly nature, his position in God's Kingdom, or his nearness to God? What was it that caused satan to rebel against the God who formed Him? Looking to another prophetic parallel, we see a full picture beginning to form:

How art thou fallen from heaven, O Lucifer, son of the morning! how art thou cut down to the ground, which didst weaken the nations! For thou hast said in thine heart, I will ascend into heaven, I will exalt my throne above the stars of God: I will sit also upon the mount of the congregation, in the sides of the north: I will ascend above the heights of the clouds; I will be like the most High. Yet thou shalt be brought down to hell, to the sides of the pit. They that see thee shall narrowly look upon thee, and consider thee, saying, Is this the man that made the earth to tremble, that did shake kingdoms (Isaiah 14:12-16 KJV).

In Isaiah's prophetic parallel, we see that satan wanted to be like God. Satan wanted to ascend to the heights of the Father's throne. Was this all just a matter of pride? In part, yes. But there's more to it than that. From where did satan get this idea that he could be like God? The answer is shocking.

And God said, Let us make man in our image, after our likeness: and let them have dominion over the fish of the sea, and over the fowl of the air, and over the cattle, and over all the earth, and over every creeping thing that creepeth upon the earth (Genesis 1:26 KJV).

It wasn't just pride that tempted satan to rebel against God. It was satan's jealousy over what God gave to you. From the beginning, dominion was for man. And from the beginning, satan has been jealous of that dominion. Think about how humbling it must have been for satan when he was punished for his rebellion by being sent to the earth, the very place where man was in charge. Satan was placed under the dominion of man, against whom he burned with jealousy.

Knowing that he could not regain his heavenly status, satan made a plan. He knew that he couldn't ascend, so his plan was to get man to descend, to fall. Satan already knew the path to a lower state—sin, rebellion against God. Thus, satan tempted Eve. Man fell, lost dominion, and became subject to sin. Yet from the very beginning, it was God's intention to give you dominion.

Then God blessed them and said, "Be fruitful and multiply. Fill the earth and govern it. Reign over the fish in the sea, the birds in the sky, and all the animals that scurry along the ground" (Genesis 1:28 NLT).

When I look at the night sky and see the work of your fingers—the moon and the stars you set in place—what are mere mortals that you should think about them, human beings that you should care for them? Yet you made them only a little lower than God and crowned them with glory and honor. You gave them charge of everything you made, putting all things under their authority—the flocks and the herds and all the wild animals, the birds in the sky, the fish in the sea, and everything that swims the ocean currents (Psalm 8:3-8 NLT).

What was lost in Adam was gained in Christ. Adam took from a tree and brought forth death. Christ gave Himself on a tree and brought forth life.

Just as everyone dies because we all belong to Adam, everyone who belongs to Christ will be given new life (1 Corinthians 15:22 NLT).

Because of what Christ has done, we've been rescued from the kingdom of darkness.

Who hath delivered us from the power of darkness, and hath translated us into the kingdom of his dear Son (Colossians 1:13 KJV).

No longer under the dominion of the enemy, we are in Christ, restored to the place of the dominion God long ago intended for us.

This time, the dominion isn't *to* us but *through* us—not *from* us but from *Christ in us.* This time, dominion is secured in His sinless perfection, and we are secured in Him.

> *Therefore, God elevated him to the place of highest honor and gave him the name above all other names, that at the name of Jesus every knee should bow, in heaven and on earth and under the earth, and every tongue declare that Jesus Christ is Lord, to the glory of God the Father* (Philippians 2:9-11 NLT).

> *I also pray that you will understand the incredible greatness of God's power for us who believe him. This is the same mighty power that raised Christ from the dead and seated him in the place of honor at God's right hand in the heavenly realms. Now he is far above any ruler or authority or power or leader or anything else—not only in this world but also in the world to come. God has put all things under the authority of Christ and has made him head over all things for the benefit of the church. And the church is his body; it is made full and complete by Christ, who fills all things everywhere with himself* (Ephesians 1:19-23 NLT).

Christ is in power, and we are in Christ.

> *For he raised us from the dead along with Christ and seated us with him in the heavenly realms because we are united with Christ Jesus* (Ephesians 2:6 NLT).

This is why I'm perplexed by Christians who panic at the mere idea of being attacked by a demonic being. They're fighting from the wrong realm. They're attempting in their own strength. Dear reader, when you rebuke a demonic power, the rebuke comes from the very throne of Christ. When you confront a demonic being, Christ confronts that demonic being through you. Now that's power. That's true authority that must be recognized.

God can do whatever He wills. He reigns far above all. We're in charge because God says we are. In the earth, He has chosen to work through human beings. He created us in His image to steward His creation. He doesn't need us, but He chooses to use us. He has chosen to make us His ambassadors here in the earth. We are children of God, citizens of Heaven.

> But to all who believed him and accepted him, he gave the right to become children of God. They are reborn—not with a physical birth resulting from human passion or plan, but a birth that comes from God (John 1:12-13 NLT).

> But we are citizens of heaven, where the Lord Jesus Christ lives. And we are eagerly waiting for him to return as our Savior (Philippians 3:20 NLT).

As citizens of Heaven, we come in the name of Jesus.

> And then he told them, "Go into all the world and preach the Good News to everyone. Anyone who believes and is baptized will be saved. But anyone who refuses to believe will be condemned. These miraculous signs will accompany those who believe: They will cast out demons in my name, and they will speak in new languages. They will be able to handle snakes with safety, and if they drink anything poisonous, it

won't hurt them. They will be able to place their hands on the sick, and they will be healed" (Mark 16:15-18 NLT).

Here again we see it:

I tell you the truth, anyone who believes in me will do the same works I have done, and even greater works, because I am going to be with the Father. You can ask for anything in my name, and I will do it, so that the Son can bring glory to the Father. Yes, ask me for anything in my name, and I will do it! (John 14:12-14 NLT)

Much has been said and written about that particular portion of Scripture in John 14. While many debate the question of what Jesus meant by *"greater works,"* I just want to make a simple point by looking to the phrase *"will do the same works I have done."* Whatever you think Jesus meant when He said *"greater works"*—what they might be or how we could possibly do greater works than Christ—we definitely do know what *"same works"* means. It means healing the sick, raising the dead, and, yes, casting out demons. That same power over demons has been given to those who believe on the Lord Jesus.

ALIGNING WITH HIS AUTHORITY

To do something in the name of Jesus is to do something by His authority, on His behalf, for His glory, and very importantly, according to His will. If we want to act in Christ's authority, we must align ourselves with His will. If you want godly authority, you must have a godly lifestyle.

Granted, it's certainly possible to walk in a measure of power and still live in sin. This isn't an encouragement for anyone to sin. This is just an acknowledgment of the biblical reality that even hypocrites can operate in a degree of power.

> *Not everyone who calls out to me, "Lord! Lord!" will enter the Kingdom of Heaven. Only those who actually do the will of my Father in heaven will enter. On judgment day many will say to me, "Lord! Lord! We prophesied in your name and cast out demons in your name and performed many miracles in your name." But I will reply, "I never knew you. Get away from me, you who break God's laws"* (Matthew 7:21-23 NLT).

What a frightening reality. Fully confident that they would be accepted, these people strut up to the Lord. Yet they are rejected. Interestingly, the Lord doesn't deny that they moved in power. He denies that He ever knew them. There we see the proof that God will use you even if He doesn't know you.

Of course, that portion of Scripture is not about born-again believers. We know this because the Lord made it clear that He never knew them. Additionally, it's clear that they were relying upon their own works, so their faith was not in Christ's sacrifice.

The point I'm making here is that they prophesied, did miracles, and even drove out demons. Still, they were wicked people—*"you who break God's laws."* So there we see that it's possible to move in power and be a hypocrite. The Word of God and the name of Jesus are so powerful that they work, to some degree, even when a hypocrite uses them.

The seven sons of Sceva serve as another example of this.

> *A group of Jews was traveling from town to town casting out evil spirits. They tried to use the name of the Lord Jesus in their incantation, saying, "I command you in the name*

of Jesus, whom Paul preaches, to come out!" Seven sons of Sceva, a leading priest, were doing this. But one time when they tried it, the evil spirit replied, "I know Jesus, and I know Paul, but who are you?" Then the man with the evil spirit leaped on them, overpowered them, and attacked them with such violence that they fled from the house, naked and battered (Acts 19:13-16 NLT).

Thus, we know that even those who don't know the Lord and who live wicked lives can operate in at least a small measure of power.

However, it's still true that the more aligned we are with God's will and Word, the more accessible His authority becomes. The more consecrated we become, the more effectively His authority can flow through us. Again, it's not as though God needs us, but that is the order to the world He created. He wants us to be His vessels. While there are always exceptions, generally speaking, God has chosen, in His own wisdom, to work through us.

Only those aligned under God's authority can walk fully in God's authority. Only those who live by the Word can walk fully in the authority of the Word.

This actually explains why demons sometimes resist your commands to leave or to be silent. Rest assured, they're never resisting the Holy Spirit, and they're never resisting Christ's authority. They're resisting you. Sin takes us out of alignment with God's authority. Compromise takes us out of alignment with God's authority. But when you are living according to God's Word and you give a command, the demon has to immediately obey when you command it to stop lying to you, distracting you, or otherwise attacking you. When you live in Christ, you live in His authority.

Other than sinful disobedience, the only other limitation to the flow of divine authority through you is a lack of faith. When some of Jesus' disciples were unable to expel a demonic being from a little boy, Jesus expressed His frustration with their lack of faith:

> *One of the men in the crowd spoke up and said, "Teacher, I brought my son so you could heal him. He is possessed by an evil spirit that won't let him talk. And whenever this spirit seizes him, it throws him violently to the ground. Then he foams at the mouth and grinds his teeth and becomes rigid. So I asked your disciples to cast out the evil spirit, but they couldn't do it." Jesus said to them, "You faithless people! How long must I be with you? How long must I put up with you? Bring the boy to me"* (Mark 9:17-19 NLT).

The story then continues with Jesus expelling the demonic being from the boy's body. Later, when the disciples asked Jesus why they couldn't cast out the demon, He revealed this truth to them:

> *Jesus replied, "This kind can be cast out only by prayer"* (Mark 9:29 NLT).

Some manuscripts include the phrase *"and fasting"* in Mark 9:29. I believe it's correct to add that phrase, so that it reads, *"This kind can be cast out only by prayer and fasting."* Even so, the point I'm making here can stand in either case, with or without the phrase *"and fasting."*

Jesus made it clear that there were certain kinds of demons that could only be expelled by means of prayer (and fasting). Why is that the case? Jesus already gave us the answer: *"You faithless people!"* It was the lack of faith that made it difficult to confront that level of demonic power. Nothing in God's authority was lacking. The problem was the disciples' faith.

The solution Jesus gave was simply to go and pray (and fast). Why? Because prayer and fasting increase your faith. All demons are stubborn. The problem is never stubborn demons but doubtful Christians. So how do you deal with "stubborn" demons or demons that don't leave the instant you tell them to leave? Through special prayers? Through studying family bloodlines? Through finding out the demon's name, type, and point of entry? Through renouncing a list of generational sin or interrogation of the demon? No. You deal with stubborn demons through a simple increase in faith. This works because it's by faith that we access divine authority.

Costa Mesa, California. It was a Sunday evening service. Standing on the platform leading God's people in worship, I felt the wind of the Holy Spirit at my back. I could feel His mighty power pulsing up and down my body. As the congregation and I sang simple songs of worship, I sensed a divine boldness come over me. The Holy Spirit quickened me, and I spoke, "That's the presence of the Holy Ghost. He's here. Something has shifted in the heavenly realm." Then I was led to speak a simple prayer, "Every demonic power must go." Within seconds of that short and softly spoken prayer being released, screams could be heard from all over the packed venue. Demons had begun to manifest. Tempted to continue rebuking the demons, I raised the microphone to my mouth.

The Holy Spirit stopped me. "Just worship. I'll take care of it." So I obeyed Him. The people and I just continued to worship. Soon, the screams around the room stopped, and a great peace came over the atmosphere. The people had been delivered. The demonic powers had been forced out of the room, instantly.

Look, I have given you authority over all the power of the enemy, and you can walk among snakes and scorpions and crush them. Nothing will injure you (Luke 10:19 NLT).

It was as though a strong wind had blown leaves by the wayside, as though an ocean wave had dissolved a child's sand castle. It was that easy. The people had wanted freedom, and the Holy Spirit gave it to them. After a simple command, the work was done. In that moment, I couldn't help but think back to many years prior, to the old religious ways I had attempted to help people be free. What a difference!

We have the tendency to complicate spiritual warfare and then refer to that complication as "depth" or "special insight." However, true depth and power does not come and is not demonstrated in our ability to detail what we think we know about the spiritual realm or by inventing protocols never endorsed by the Holy Spirit. True depth is simple faith. It's strongly rooted, childlike, unshakable faith.

When a Spirit-filled believer gives a simple command against a demonic being, the demon has to obey it. That's truth. That's Bible. Powerful signs follow those who believe. Those who believe what? Those who believe the gospel. So if you believe the gospel, if you are a born-again Christian, then you've been given the ability to walk in these signs. I'm not saying that these signs are a demonstration of your salvation or that you can't be saved unless you perform miraculous signs. I'm simply saying that if you are born again, these abilities have been made available to you, though some born-again believers leave these abilities dormant and untouched.

Demons have to obey the commands of the born-again believer and instantly so, period. So the question should not be, "What gives a demon the legal right to disobey Christ's authority and stay in my life?" They can't disobey His authority. The question should be, "What prevents me from walking in the authority that Christ gave to me?" I promise you that it's never because the correct ritual wasn't performed or because the correct deliverance technique wasn't used or even because your "spiritual rank" wasn't high enough. It's simple. The only factors that can misalign you from God's flow of authority are sinful compromise and doubt. Ask the Holy Spirit to help you with these and then you're perfectly positioned to command the forces of darkness. Demons absolutely, positively, without exception, listen to what you command in Christ's authority.

Biblically speaking, we are given a clear revelation on how we ought to deal with demonic powers. Demons respond to the authority of Christ in us. When they don't respond, it isn't because the demon has overpowered Christ's authority or the Holy Spirit—it's simply because we're not walking in the authority that Christ gave to us. If the demon doesn't obey, it's not resisting Christ's authority; it's resisting you, because you're not aligned with Christ's authority. How do we walk in this authority? It's by simple obedience. It's by simple faith. That's why the disciples were told to fast and pray, to help their unbelief.

When we walk in faith, we walk in Christ's authority. When we walk in Christ's authority, demons must obey. It really is that simple. This isn't about using man's techniques but walking in God's truths. God's ways are better than our ways.

Even if the demon returns, as they're known to do, don't panic over the fact that it's trying to deceive you again. Just use the authority of Christ again.

WHAT IF THE DEMON STILL DOESN'T LISTEN?

Your success when confronting a demonic being depends upon the lifestyle you've been living long before the confrontation. You can't make up with rituals and incantations what you lack in lifestyle.

You can silence and take authority over a demon by commanding the demon to be silent, to stop harassing your mind, and to leave you alone.

That's it. If you're properly aligned with Christ's authority, there will be no issue there. The demon has to obey and instantaneously so. That's the power of faith and obedience. Anyone who tells you there's more to it is either unaware of what the Bible teaches or has other motives, likely to sell a solution to a problem they invented.

So what should you do if the demon doesn't seem to stop lying to and harassing you after all of that? Here's the biblical way to think about and approach the situation.

One: Be rid of sin and compromise. Sinful living pulls you out of alignment with Christ's authority.

Two: After you've ensured there's no sinful compromise in your life, you need to fast and pray. Fasting increases your faith. This is what Jesus said to do if the demon doesn't obey. This may need to be done a few times until your faith is strong. Keep in mind, this doesn't need to be perfected faith—just some faith.

> *"What do you mean, 'If I can'?" Jesus asked. "Anything is possible if a person believes." The father instantly cried out, "I do believe, but help me overcome my unbelief!" When Jesus saw that the crowd of onlookers was growing, he rebuked the evil spirit. "Listen, you spirit that makes this boy unable to hear and speak," he said. "I command you to come out of this child and never enter him again!" Then the spirit screamed and threw the boy into another violent convulsion and left him. The boy appeared to be dead. A murmur ran through the crowd as people said, "He's dead"* (Mark 9:23-26 NLT).

Faith aligns you with divine authority.

Three: And this one is difficult for some to accept—it's possible you've already properly and successfully defeated the demonic being, and now you need to deal with the mental and emotional aspects of the stronghold. It may not feel like it, but you'd be amazed at what our minds and emotions are capable of doing to us.

So let's summarize:

+ Address the demonic aspects of the stronghold.

+ Align with God's authority through faith and obedience. In doing so, you rely on the Holy Spirit's power, instead of man's powerless protocols.

+ Then exercise that authority through a simple command.

+ If the problem continues, fast and pray until you know your faith is strong. Strong faith is key to accessing Christ's authority. It's not that demons can resist the Holy Spirit's power and authority. Rather, it's that we aren't actually using the Holy Spirit's power and authority until we're properly aligned.

+ If the problem still persists after you've taken this simple biblical approach, recognize that the answer will not be found in strange superstitions or Christian myths about the spiritual realm.

So if after all of this the problem still persists, then you're no longer dealing with the demonic aspect but rather with the mental and emotional aspects of the stronghold.

Let's address these aspects in the next chapter.

8

STRONGHOLDS, THOUGHTS, AND EMOTIONS

Demons must submit to Christ's authority without delay, but the sin nature is a persistent problem. Demons leave when told. By contrast, the flesh doesn't come and go but shrinks and grows depending upon what thoughts and actions we choose. It's easier to defeat demons than it is to tame self. Demons can be commanded to go, but you can't cast you out of you. So once the demonic aspects of a stronghold have been dealt with through the exercise of authority, it's time to deal with the flesh. This can be a process.

Your mind is like a computer, and demonic beings are like computer hackers. They program your way of thinking through the persuasive ideas and ungodly thoughts that they suggest to you. Sure, you can get rid of the hacker through a simple exercise of spiritual authority, but are you addressing the programming they leave behind? Your mind and your emotions can be trained under a deceptive pattern. You can silence the liars, but do you allow them to leave behind their lies?

If a demonic being is allowed to lie to you for long enough, eventually you begin to repeat its lies to yourself. Self-deception is the eventual result of successful demonic deception. Once you begin to echo the lies of the demonic, that indicates that the stronghold's foundation has become deep enough to be mental and emotional. At this point, the deception is no longer just a repeat attack of the enemy but a way of thinking and feeling that you've embraced for yourself.

Whether the lies of the enemy came through culture, media, other people, negative experiences, or directly through a demonic being, if you believe the lies of the enemy for long enough, those lies become a part of your mindset. Most Christians aren't aware of the fact that they need to deal with demonic deception's lingering effects on their thoughts and emotions. They remove the bullet but never dress the wound. They rebuke the liars but never correct the leftover thought patterns from the lies.

This is precisely why some Christians think they need to "go in for deliverance" as often as one would get an adjustment from a chiropractor. Sure, get as much prayer as you need, but victory, not spiritual struggle, must eventually become your lifestyle. This is also why some bondages seem impossible to break—because the flesh is never dealt with. Most importantly, this is why demonic beings seem to so often be able to regain influence over some Christians, even after weeks or months of freedom. You need to address all aspects of the stronghold, not just the demonic being who attacks you with the lies.

To address the emotional and mental aspects of the stronghold, you must begin with the basics.

HONOR THE BASICS

What do successful athletes and soldiers have in common? They honor the basics. A soldier isn't trained on the battlefield, and an athlete isn't trained at the championship competition. A soldier goes through rigorous but basic training before deployment. An athlete spends years conditioning himself to be at peak performance. The moment of victory is won in the lifestyle that precedes it. It's the daily commitment to proper conditioning that ultimately brings success. If you want to avoid spiritual crisis, you must learn to practice the spiritual basics. If a believer is living as they should, strongholds will be broken, simply as a result of proper living.

Like athletes who want to cheat the system through use of drugs, so some Christians try to become spiritual warriors by reaching right for religious formulas and popular but unbiblical methods. They want to make up with superstitious ritual what they lack in spiritual routine.

Imagine someone undergoes a basic medical examination and tells their primary physician, "Doc, I'm not feeling well at all. Something just seems off." Their physician wouldn't immediately turn to the most deadly diseases as possible explanations for them not feeling well. What would he do? He would start with basic questions about their general health, and then he would go from there. He would ask, "How are you sleeping? How's your water intake? Are you getting any exercise? What's your diet look like? Do you have high amounts of stress?" Why do physicians start with basic questions to deduce the problem? It's because, more often than not, by simply doing the basics, you can avoid or heal most physical problems. The same goes for spiritual matters.

My social media inboxes are filled with messages from believers begging for relief from the sin nature. They often plead, "Please, pray for me! I just don't know how to break out of my bondage!" After praying with them, I almost always ask, "How's your prayer life? How's your devotion to the Word? Do you fellowship with other believers who can keep you accountable?"

Honestly, nine times out of ten, they reply by telling me that they rarely pray, very rarely ever read the Word, or are inconsistent in the Word, and rarely ever connect with other believers. These Christians deal with almost every kind of stronghold you can think of—temptation, accusation, torment of the mind, fear, depression, doubt—you name it. More than just sin problems, they deal with emotional and mental turmoil.

I think most Christians would be amazed at how many of their inner troubles would be resolved if they simply began to practice the basics of Christianity. I can't remember the last time I spoke to a tormented Christian who prayed consistently and for good portions at a time. I don't recall very many conversations with believers who faithfully devoted themselves to Scripture and also lived in confusion. This is not to say that Christians don't face trials, tragedies, and tests in life. Of course, the life of the believer is full of persecution and even problems. However, this doesn't mean that any believer has to ever settle for spiritual bondage. For the life of the true believer can be one of absolute spiritual victory.

To some, the basics are boring or take too long to bring results. The sad reality is that most don't want to practice the basics. They want to jump to the most extreme explanations for their sin problem. They want fast answers and fast solutions that require as little from them as possible. Itching ears want to be told they have no part in their own deception. Itching ears want to hear, "You're under a curse, so pray this quick prayer. You're demonized, so just undergo this quick process. You're dealing with a stubborn spirit, so let a spiritual guru handle your problem."

It's easier to have someone else lay hands on you than it is to develop spiritual discipline. This is why so many reach for the most drastic of explanations for their problems. We want to keep blaming demons, even after they've been rendered powerless, so that we don't have to implement spiritual disciplines. Yes, confront the demons. Then after you've dealt with the demons, it's time to face yourself. It's time to take responsibility for some of the things happening in your life. Sometimes, the chaos and heaviness come from the thoughts and actions that you choose.

Mature believers honor the basics. All believers must know the Word.

> *Study to shew thyself approved unto God, a workman that needeth not to be ashamed, rightly dividing the word of truth* (2 Timothy 2:15 KJV).

All believers must live lifestyles of prayer.

> *Rejoice always, pray without ceasing, give thanks in all circumstances; for this is the will of God in Christ Jesus for you* (1 Thessalonians 5:16-18 ESV).

All believers must worship God in Spirit (John 4:24), live holy (1 Peter 1:16), and fellowship with other believers (Hebrews 10:25). These practices, among a few others, are God's basic prescribed maintainers of spiritual health.

If I wasn't sleeping, eating, exercising, or drinking water and I began to feel ill, my first response wouldn't be assuming I have some terminal illness. My first response would be to check the basics of my lifestyle. Yet when Christians neglect the spiritual basics and then reap the consequences of their lack of discipline, many times their first response is to blame a generational curse, a demon, or a soul tie.

Dear reader, though it might be difficult to accept, the mental and emotional effects of a stronghold come about as the result of the decisions we make in our thoughts and actions. We choose what we allow into our minds. We choose to neglect the Word, making ourselves vulnerable to belief in the lies. These choices we make yield actual results.

The flesh is either weakened or strengthened depending upon the choices you make. Some decisions you make will strengthen your flesh, while others strengthen your spirit. Whatever strengthens my spirit weakens my flesh. Whatever strengthens my flesh weakens the influence of the spirit in my life.

> But I discipline my body and bring it into subjection, lest, when I have preached to others, I myself should become disqualified (1 Corinthians 9:27 NKJV).

The body is not sinful unto itself (1 Corinthians 6:19). Still, the body can become an instrument of the sin nature. So Paul, in order to keep his body from becoming an instrument of the sin nature, chose a lifestyle of spiritual discipline. Deliverance should lead to discipline. Discipline brings dominion.

God didn't create you to live in depression, with anxiety, or under torment. God didn't design you to live in the frustration of habitual sin or the aimlessness of confusion. His ways work. I don't write this to shame you. I write this so you might know that you don't have to settle and you can choose this victory. Though it may not feel like it, God gave you the power to choose victory. Yes, spiritual victory is a choice.

Troubles and tragedies? Yes, that's part of life. Spiritual bondage? Demonic deception? Internal defeat? Absolutely never. That's not God's intention for you. In order to live in God's freedom, you must submit your life to God's order. That's done through the basics.

I don't mean that you just practice the basics for a week and then quit because it doesn't seem to be working. I'm not talking about an inconsistent commitment to the things of God. Many Christians claim that spiritual discipline doesn't work for them, because it didn't work fast enough. But if you're going to commit to the basics, you need to commit to the long term. This isn't a quick fix. This is a whole new way of living.

This, of course, begs the questions: Isn't that the problem in the first place? Aren't those with strongholds struggling with the basics because of the strongholds? To some degree, yes. However, as you commit your ways to God's will, the strongholds in your life will lose more and more power. Just because you're being spiritually attacked or deceived doesn't mean you lose your free will. You can choose to begin acting according to the Spirit, even if only incrementally.

> *So I say, let the Holy Spirit guide your lives. Then you won't be doing what your sinful nature craves. The sinful nature wants to do evil, which is just the opposite of what the Spirit wants. And the Spirit gives us desires that are the opposite of what the sinful nature desires. These two forces are constantly fighting each other, so you are not free to carry out your good intentions. But when you are directed by the Spirit, you are not under obligation to the law of Moses* (Galatians 5:16-18 NLT).

We have to turn our focus to what the Holy Spirit can do through us. We may not begin where we want to begin, but if we practice daily obedience, we will eventually be where we want to be. Each small victory will train you to think victoriously. Each win against the stronghold will condition you to be a spiritual winner. Focus on what God is doing, even if it seems small. Focus on the progress, not on the presence of problems or the absence of perfection.

This is why I'm sometimes a bit frustrated with preaching that makes people obsessed with demons. It turns the focus of the listener to demons and demonic power, instead of the Holy Spirit and His power. If a person truly lives in the Spirit, can any stronghold or demonic attack work on them? Of course not! So why not just teach people to live in the Spirit?

I'm not saying that we shouldn't be aware of how demonic attacks work. We covered much of that in previous chapters of this book. Sure we should know our enemy. I'm merely addressing the problems that arise when we teach Christians mostly about darkness—how to identify darkness, how to know you're in darkness, how to avoid darkness, how darkness is taking over the world, how darkness is coming for our children, how darkness can sneak its way into your life, and so on. Darkness, darkness, darkness. Demons, demons, demons. What about the light? What about the Holy Spirit?

Live in the light, and you won't live in darkness. Walk in the Spirit, and you won't walk under the power of a stronghold. How do we live in the light of the Holy Spirit? Honor the basics. Obey God. Obey when it costs you. Obey when you want to and when you don't want to. Demonic strongholds and attacks can only succeed if we have some form of disobedience in our actions or disorder in our thinking. That's the not-so-popular truth, but it is the truth.

Again, I'm not talking about trials. Trials happen. Things that we wish wouldn't happen will happen. Things that break our hearts happen. Loss and chaos abound in this world. I'm talking about that internal defeat, spiritual defeat. Spiritual defeat comes from believing a lie or from living in disorder.

I know that's not what sells books or gets views. I know to some that's not as exciting as special prayers, demonology, or complicated spiritual warfare tactics. Still, it's the truth, and only in the truth do we find freedom. That's where the real power is, because that's the work of the Holy Spirit—truth.

When you walk in the Spirit, it's difficult for the enemy to lie to you. When you live as you should, you simply don't live out the works of the flesh. What are the works of the flesh?

When you follow the desires of your sinful nature, the results are very clear: sexual immorality, impurity, lustful pleasures, idolatry, sorcery, hostility, quarreling, jealousy, outbursts of anger, selfish ambition, dissension, division, envy, drunkenness, wild parties, and other sins like these. Let me tell you again, as I have before, that anyone living that sort of life will not inherit the Kingdom of God (Galatians 5:19-21 NLT).

So much of what we blame on demons is actually a result of an undisciplined flesh. Yes, demons can attack and affect you. Yes, demons can create powerful deceptions or strongholds in your life. But the flesh is a problem too.

So many say, "I'm dealing with a spirit of lust!" or, "I can't help myself. I'm dealing with a spirit of anger." Yes, demonic beings can influence you in these areas, but the harsh reality is that lust and anger are simply works of the flesh. Demons don't do the sinning for you. This is why surrender and obedience to the Holy Spirit is so liberating:

But the Holy Spirit produces this kind of fruit in our lives: love, joy, peace, patience, kindness, goodness, faithfulness, gentleness, and self-control. There is no law against these things! (Galatians 5:22-23 NLT)

You would be amazed at how many of your mental and emotional problems would cease to be issues if you committed yourself to walking in the Spirit, to doing the basics. This again raises the issue of what seems like a catch-22. I need to live right in order to be free, but I have to be free in order to live right? But that's the great lie. The lie is that you have no choice. The lie is that it's all to be blamed on demons. The lie is that you have no self-control. It's time to stop believing the lie that your choices had nothing to do with the bondage you're in.

You can blame people putting word curses on you, or you can realize that as a Spirit-filled believer you have the power to live in victory. You can blame former generations for their sins of the past, or you can decide to obey God in your present. You can blame demonic beings for bringing you down, or you can believe the truth that sets your mind on the things above. You can live in fear thinking that the enemy is waiting around every corner, or you can live aware of the greater reality—the truth that even if the weapons are formed, they won't prosper. When you live in the Holy Spirit, you live in freedom.

It's time to choose to believe the truth.

CHOOSE TO BELIEVE THE TRUTH

The thoughts you think can either be in agreement with God's truth or in agreement with lies. The alignment of your thoughts is a prediction of the alignment of your actions. This is why it's of utmost importance that we filter our thoughts through the truths of God's Word. The Bible tells us to choose what we think about, to choose the ideas we allow to dominate the mind.

> *Since you have been raised to new life with Christ, set your sights on the realities of heaven, where Christ sits in the place of honor at God's right hand. Think about the things of heaven, not the things of earth* (Colossians 3:1-2 NLT).

A similar instruction is given in Philippians.

> *Finally, brethren, whatsoever things are true, whatsoever things are honest, whatsoever things are just, whatsoever things are pure, whatsoever things are lovely, whatsoever*

things are of good report; if there be any virtue, and if there be any praise, think on these things (Philippians 4:8 KJV).

The Bible wouldn't command us to do something that was impossible for us to do. God wouldn't say, *"think on these things"* or choose your thoughts, if thoughts could not be chosen. Though it may not feel like it, though you might find it difficult to believe, you can choose your thoughts. However, after years or even decades of thinking in a certain pattern of thought, we become so used to certain thought patterns, so trained in our own ways, that we may find it rather difficult to choose otherwise. Thoughts can become habitual, just like physical actions can become habitual.

Imagine that your thoughts were like explorers, slashing their way through the leaves and plants of a dense jungle. As these explorers make their way through the land, their steps and movements begin to form paths in the wilderness. After years of activity, these explorers form clear paths and smooth walkways. Naturally, the travelers who come along after them will choose to walk the already-cleared trails. The routes formed by previous explorers become the preferred means of travel for the ones who come after them.

That's how your thoughts work. Your mind is that jungle. Those "explorers" are formative thoughts. Once you allow those thoughts to create a certain path, it becomes easier for the thoughts that come after them to follow the same path. For some, these paths have been traveled for years. So when they attempt to think according to the truth, they have to veer off into the brush to form new paths. But forming a new path is very difficult and uncomfortable, especially if an easier and previously formed path is so readily available. Like explorers struggling through a wild brush, so your thoughts will be tempted to just get back on the previously traveled path instead of going through the trouble of creating a new one.

So this pattern of thinking can make it seem as though your thoughts are out of your control. However, it's not that your thoughts are out of control; it's just the opposite. Your thoughts are taking the paths you've formed throughout the years. It's time to choose a new path, no matter how easy it might be to take the old roads. It's not that choosing to believe the truth is impossible; it's just that choosing the old deceptive thoughts is easier. Yet the Bible tells us to control our thoughts, thus defeating any excuse we might have. In controlling our thoughts, we experience true transformation.

> *And so, dear brothers and sisters, I plead with you to give your bodies to God because of all he has done for you. Let them be a living and holy sacrifice—the kind he will find acceptable. This is truly the way to worship him. Don't copy the behavior and customs of this world, but let God transform you into a new person by changing the way you think. Then you will learn to know God's will for you, which is good and pleasing and perfect* (Romans 12:1-2 NLT).

Right thinking always works, eventually.

It's worth noting that I don't mean this in the "New Age" sense. Unfortunately, New Age teachings about the universe, attraction, and the power of positive human thinking have added confusion to this subject. This isn't just a matter of thinking positively, but truthfully—and that only happens when the Word of God is received by the Holy Spirit. No one on their own can think their way to freedom, but we can cooperate with the Holy Spirit by thinking according to truth. We need the help of the Holy Spirit.

> *When the Spirit of truth comes, he will guide you into all truth. He will not speak on his own but will tell you what*

he has heard. He will tell you about the future (John 16:13 NLT).

Because of the patterns we develop in our thinking, it can be challenging to "catch" ourselves in the act of an untruthful thought. We lie to ourselves so frequently that we have trouble even spotting the lies on our own. I can't tell you how many times I've allowed my worry to get so out of control that I become just completely convinced that something terrible is going to happen and immediately so.

We all have the tendency to default to our old thought patterns, and this is when the Holy Spirit speaks. In those moments, if you pause for even just a split second, you'll hear His loving voice. He's that stable, truthful whisper who speaks against all the lies we tell ourselves. In the moments when your flesh seems the strongest, it becomes the most difficult but also the most crucial time to listen to the Holy Spirit. Right when you're the angriest, the most distraught, the most afraid, the most lustful, the most tormented—right then and there, you must listen to Him. He is most certainly speaking. He's always speaking.

FIGHT REINFORCING LIES

It's at this point that the ungodly thought pattern will show resistance to the voice of the Holy Spirit. You see, strongholds are self-defending. Within each stronghold is a set of back-up lies that prevent you from even beginning to pursue truth. So the moment the truth is presented, the stronghold will present another lie that's designed to deter you from embracing the truth.

For example, the stronghold of fear seeks to preserve itself through back-up lies. It would look something like this:

- Primary lie: "Something bad is going to happen to you!"
- Truth: "God will protect me. I can let my guard down."
- Back-up lie: "When you finally let your guard down, something bad will happen."

Another example could be the accusation of the enemy. Here's how that might look:

- Primary lie: "God has rejected you because of your past."
- Truth: "I'm a forgiven new creation. My past is gone."
- Back-up lie: "But this might not apply to you and your specific, very vile sin."

Here's how the stronghold of temptation might defend itself:

- Primary lie: "This sin will fulfill you."
- Truth: "True fulfillment is only found in God."
- Back-up lie: "But why live holy now? You're eventually going to fall into sin again anyway."

For good measure, here's one more example. Let's look at depression.

- Primary lie: "I'll never be free from this."
- Truth: "You can be free from depression by renewing your mind with God's Word."
- Back-up lie: "I've tried it so many times before. That won't work for me."

No matter the stronghold, it's possible that you will have to combat a series of lies in order to break through to belief in the truth. That's why you have to make up your mind ahead of time to commit to truth. You must have a serious determination to side with truth. Loyalty to what God says means choosing to believe what He says even when you feel like falling back on old thought patterns. To remove a stronghold, you need to fight a war, not just one battle.

Once you have the truth, you must allow yourself to believe the truth. Your belief in the truth is the shield of faith.

> *In addition to all of these, hold up the shield of faith to stop the fiery arrows of the devil. Put on salvation as your helmet, and take the sword of the Spirit, which is the word of God. Pray in the Spirit at all times and on every occasion. Stay alert and be persistent in your prayers for all believers everywhere* (Ephesians 6:16-18 NLT).

Every lie the enemy tells you is a fiery arrow, and faith is the shield that blocks it. You must train to block the lies with your faith. Your belief in what God has declared is your guard against what the lie says. Typically, this is where the battle is most difficult. Sometimes it's hard to make that switch. But what good does it do to identify the lie if you're just going to keep believing it?

When the enemy shoots arrows of accusation, shield yourself with trust in God's forgiveness. When your mind has become conditioned by rejection, cling to the shield by believing in God's acceptance. When the enemy is tormenting your mind, raise the shield by choosing to believe that God has given you power over the enemy. Let yourself believe God. Let yourself trust His goodness.

Could it be that you're afraid of believing the truth because you don't want to be disappointed? Is it possible that you're afraid it won't work?

Or do you fear loosening your grip on what you think is control? Is that what's preventing you from trusting God?

You need to allow yourself to trust what God's Word says. The shield will work. Belief is a choice, because trust is a choice. If you trust God, you will believe the truth. The fiery darts can be scary, but the shield will hold. You can relax in the truth. You can relinquish the doubt. Don't be afraid to believe the truth. Yes, it applies to you too. Yes, it applies to your situation too.

When the fiery lies are raining down upon you, raise your trust in what God has said. Pick up the shield of faith.

First, we identify the lie. Then, we deflect the lie by believing the truth. And then we destroy the source of the lie by using the sword of the Spirit. First, it's recon. Next, it's defense. Then, it's offense. Take up the sword of the Spirit. To use the sword of the Spirit is to take the truth on the offensive, to actively combat the source of any lie.

When the fiery arrow is launched, that's the lie being spoken. When I raise my shield to deflect the arrow, I am choosing to believe God's Word. That's protection. But when I wield my sword, I am actively attacking the liar. That's advancement.

"God will never forgive your past!" Arrow launched.

"If I confess my sins, He is faithful and just to forgive me." Shield raised.

"I am the righteousness of God in Christ!" Enemy defeated.

"You should look at pornography right now. Nobody will know. It will satisfy." Arrow launched.

"I will set no wicked thing before my eyes." Shield raised.

"Walk in the Spirit and you will not fulfill the lust of the flesh." Enemy destroyed.

Shield and sword. Defense and offense. Belief and declaration. Trust God and resist the devil. Accept the Word and then rebuke the enemy with the Word. This means that you may have to work through several lies to see victory—shield, sword, shield, sword.

FLESHLY RESISTANCE

There are countless lies that the enemy can use to reinforce a stronghold in your life. Additionally, there are fleshly problems that can make it more difficult to fight the reinforcing lies. I'll list four.

#1 - Being Addicted to Chaos

This factor is the addiction to chaos that many don't realize they have. This doesn't mean that you enjoy being bound or that you don't desire to be free. It's much deeper than that. In ministering deliverance from strongholds to believers, I've discovered that some have grown so accustomed to their bound, chaotic, and destructive way of living that they are hesitant to embrace a life without chaos. It's uncomfortable to them because it's so unfamiliar. They almost don't know what to do with themselves once they begin to experience some level of freedom. They feel tension, bracing for the impact of something that they feel must go wrong eventually.

Here are some signs that you may be addicted to the chaos of a stronghold:

1. When people try to encourage you, you find
   a way to deflect the encouragements.

2. When people encourage you, you end up debating them
   instead of considering the biblical truth they minister.

3. When someone presents a solution that seems too
   simple, you reject their explanation and insist that your
   issues are more complicated than they understand.

4. When you begin to experience some kind of freedom, you can't
   enjoy it, because you're anticipating things going wrong again.

5. When things begin to become less chaotic, you insist that it's
   too good to be true and that nothing ever goes right for you.

6. You dismiss small victories and progress as "temporary."

7. When you experience victory and some troubles return,
   you hyper-focus on the returning issues and see the
   returning issues as "proof" that "it didn't work" or that
   "it was never going to work in the first place."

8. From the perspective of another, it seems almost as if you're
   trying to convince yourself to stay in your old way of thinking.

9. You don't see yourself as someone who could ever be free.

It's possible to want freedom yet still be addicted to bondage. I can't tell you how many Christians I've talked to who tell me of some of the most horrific and complex mind battles and demonic attacks. Yet they reject the truth by telling themselves that the solutions work for everyone else but them, or that the solutions in God's Word will only work temporarily. Because of how they were raised, family dynamics, or just years of struggle, they are simply uncomfortable without chaos.

They are seemingly addicted to their stress. What they don't realize is that this is the flesh's way of partnering with the stronghold in helping to ensure that they won't do what's necessary to tear it down.

#2 - Basing Identity on Struggles

Some believers base their identity on their struggles. When one experiences trauma or tragedy, such experiences can sometimes lead to deep and long-lasting strongholds. These sort of strongholds bury themselves so deeply that their very identity becomes viewed through the lens of what was experienced. So it's not just that they think, *This is what happened to me*, or, *This is what I went through.* No, the stronghold roots itself so effectively as to cause them to think, *This is who I am*, or, *I'm just the one who suffers, who always goes through it, the one to whom no good could ever happen.*

Even still, this can go beyond just viewing yourself as the one who struggles. In some cases, a very subtle form of pride is developed around this stronghold, a pride that makes us feel a false sense of security. This subtle pride can manifest itself in statements like, "The devil messes with me so often because he knows how much of a threat I am," or, "I'm always under spiritual attack because the enemy knows how much damage I can do to his kingdom." And while it may be true that you're a potential threat to the kingdom of hell, as all believers are, if you're not careful, you may get a sense of validation from the fact that you struggle so much.

Keep in mind that spiritual defeat is not a trait of the Christian life. Trials, yes. Defeat, no. We shouldn't seek validation in anything apart from our relationship with the Lord Himself. That sense of validation is part of what causes you to see your identity through the lens of your struggle. Don't wear defeat like a spiritual badge of honor. Spiritual defeat doesn't glorify God. That sense of validation is part of what makes your flesh resist the tearing down of a stronghold.

#3 - Enjoying the Attention Struggles Bring

In very rare cases, some believers get validation from the attention they receive because they are always "under attack" or always "going through it." They feel valued or loved because others are constantly there to pray for them, counsel them, or pat them on the back and say things like, "I'm sorry you're always going through this." Now let me be perfectly clear: this is not the case with every believer who struggles. Additionally, we absolutely should go to our brothers and sisters for help, and they should pray for us and encourage us. And we should feel loved and encouraged when others demonstrate this sort of kindness. There's great comfort in having people there for us. There's nothing wrong with that. It's biblical to be there for one another in difficult times.

Yet this is also where we must be careful. Some of us have felt so discouraged and unloved for so long that we become addicted to the attention that our struggles gain for us. So it's possible to lose motivation to tear down a stronghold, since the stronghold can be the reason why we get the attention we sometimes crave. The stronghold can become the excuse we use for needing the comfort of others. Some hesitate to tear down a stronghold because the tearing down of that stronghold would mean they would no longer have a reason to be pitied, rescued, or attended to by others. The stronghold is the reason others pay attention to them, and some would rather not lose that attention. Some don't want to be delivered because their bondage gains them attention. This is not the case with every believer, so just do an honest self-evaluation to make sure it isn't the case with you.

#4 - Insisting That it Must Be "Deeper"

Some insist that their means of freedom must be as complicated as the stronghold itself. I've seen Christians literally pout when they are presented with the simplicity of the Holy Spirit's power and the Word of God. They tell long and intense stories involving word curses, generational curses, demonic displays of power, various attacks being brought against them, tragedies, mind battles, nightmares, betrayals—you name it. They seem disappointed to hear that their solution is the same as anyone else's solution: simply, the power of the Holy Spirit. It's almost as if they want the solution to be difficult.

Far too many Christians reject the truth, because they think that the solutions sound too simple. That freedom can only come through a complicated process is yet another reinforcing lie that keeps a stronghold in place. The insistence upon rituals and man-made protocols is partially what keeps believers bound. They either don't believe God's Word will work for them, or they hope that their solution will be more "deep." Many confuse "complicated" for "deep." This desire for deliverance to be complicated or more interesting blocks the way to freedom. Some want it to be complicated because it feels more effective than just simple obedience and faith. Others want it to be complicated because that complication would feel more validating for them having had to struggle with such complicated spiritual bondage.

In some cases, these believers who insist on ritualized freedom were rescued from the occult, New Age practices, or witchcraft. Though now saved, they expect that their solution will be as complicated or as ritualized as their former way of thinking trained them to believe. In that way, they cling to their old way of thinking and try to force it upon the Scriptures. I've noticed this deception most effectively at work in newly converted Christians with former backgrounds involving New

Age practices, the occult, or witchcraft. They take teachings from their old beliefs as souvenirs.

People who come from such backgrounds were taught by their former belief systems that the spiritual realm is transactional. That may be the case for unbelievers who have to deal with demons in their own strength. But this is not the case for the born-again believer. There's a great powerlessness in trying to force old beliefs into biblical truth.

Don't fall for this deception of the enemy. The enemy is so subtle. Many believers fall into powerless religion, while thinking it to be spiritual. How can this be? This may upset the religious establishment, but I'm going to tell you the truth. We have to stop getting our spiritual warfare teachings from the occult and from the New Age movement. If you want true power, then what you know of the spiritual realm must come from the Word of God. It's wonderful when believers get rescued and saved from the occult or the New Age. My family was saved from the occult—and we have to leave our former way of thinking there. We can't borrow ideas from systems founded upon demonic deception and call it "intel." We can't embrace the complicated transactional approach of witchcraft and then try to weave it into ministry practice. Go after the truth of the Word, not the traditions of the world. The teachings from those systems are based on lies. God doesn't hide our freedom behind ancient secrets and demonic mysteries that need to be uncovered. Everything we need to know about the demonic realm is written in Scripture.

When you come to Christ, you're not just switching teams while holding on to old protocols. You're under an entirely different system. Deliverance doesn't work according to the teachings and protocols of those former belief systems. You can't fight curses with incantations, strongholds with rituals, or demonic power with specialized prayers and hidden knowledge. Those belief systems will teach you that defeating demonic power is like solving a riddle or uncovering a mystery. For the believer, the battle isn't like in the movies where the protagonist has to discover a demon's hidden weakness or find its origins to know exactly how to defeat it.

If one is not satisfied with the biblical solutions we are given for strongholds and spiritual attacks, then that could only be because of a lack of faith in God's Word and power.

THE HOLY SPIRIT GROUNDS YOU

If you want to tear down a stronghold of deception in your life, you need to be prepared to not only deal with the primary lie upon which it is built, you have to be prepared to deal with all of the lies that help to reinforce that primary lie. We also need to address the fleshly complications that cause believers to be addicted to the chaos of a stronghold, to base their identity on their struggles, to become too dependent upon pity or attention, and to insist that the answers to their problems be complex. The Holy Spirit helps us defeat these fleshly complications by keeping us grounded in our true identity.

> So you have not received a spirit that makes you fearful slaves. Instead, you received God's Spirit when he adopted you as his own children. Now we call him, "Abba, Father." For his Spirit joins with our spirit to affirm that we are God's children (Romans 8:15-16 NLT).

The Holy Spirit reminds you of who you are. When you know your identity, you overcome addiction to chaos, you know you're not the "one who will always struggle," you no longer have to rely on others to feel valuable, and you know that God's simple truths will work for you too.

Every step of the way, the Holy Spirit is involved in the process of tearing down strongholds. When reinforcing lies complicate the path to freedom, the Holy Spirit speaks simplifying truths. He counters the series of lies that keep you from choosing to believe the truth. And by grounding you in your identity, He untangles you from fleshly complications that make it harder to address both primary and reinforcing lies.

RENEW THE MIND

After you have begun to practice the basics of spiritual disciplines, and once you have made the commitment to choose to believe the truth, even in the face of reinforcing lies, you have one more core biblical principle to implement. You must also learn to renew the mind. In doing all these things, you will become successful in both identifying and tearing down strongholds.

So what is the renewing of the mind? Mind renewal is the biblical way to experience true and lasting transformation:

> And be not conformed to this world: but be ye transformed by the renewing of your mind, that ye may prove what is that good, and acceptable, and perfect, will of God (Romans 12:2 KJV).

The transformed mind is the key to permanent deliverance. Referring back to the jungle analogy I used, we could say that breaking free of a stronghold is like taking a new path, but renewing the mind is like regrowing plant life as to erase old paths. Renewing the mind helps to ensure that you will not go back to your former ways of thinking.

Renewing the mind is like reprogramming a computer. Reprogramming your thoughts takes time. Many frustrated Christians attempt to better control their own thoughts, only to be met with the resistance of past patterns. When these patterns make it difficult for us to form new ways of thinking, we have to persist. Yet instead of persisting in their new way of thinking, many just quit and say things like, "I already tried that. It doesn't work for me." But the renewal of the mind is a process. Like any discipline, the discipline of the mind takes practice and persistence. The good news is that it works.

The Word of God is the standard against which we measure the progress of our being perfected.

> *All scripture is given by inspiration of God, and is profitable for doctrine, for reproof, for correction, for instruction in righteousness: That the man of God may be perfect, thoroughly furnished unto all good works* (2 Timothy 3:16-17 KJV).

The receiving of Scripture is the key to renewing your mind. As you receive God's Word, transformation begins to take place. The transformation might, at first, seem slow and subtle, but rest assured, you are being changed as you consume the Scripture. It's impossible to read God's Word and not be transformed in some way, even if that transformation is not immediately apparent.

The Word of God is a spiritual mirror in which we can see the thought patterns in us that need changing.

> *But don't just listen to God's word. You must do what it says. Otherwise, you are only fooling yourselves. For if you listen to the word and don't obey, it is like glancing at your face in a mirror. You see yourself, walk away, and forget what you look like. But if you look carefully into the perfect law*

that sets you free, and if you do what it says and don't forget what you heard, then God will bless you for doing it (James 1:22-25 NLT).

So often I read God's Word and realize, "I could improve here. I need to change that. That's a flaw in me I need to correct." While reading the Scripture, I often say, "Father, there's so many ways I need to be more like Jesus. Please, help me to be more like Jesus." It's not a matter of condemnation but correction. The Word of God is a mirror. It allows you to see your spiritual reflection. As you look to the Word, not only will the Word correct your actions, attitudes, and character flaws—it will correct your thinking.

The Word of God is the substance of our meditation.

Oh, the joys of those who do not follow the advice of the wicked, or stand around with sinners, or join in with mockers. But they delight in the law of the Lord, meditating on it day and night. They are like trees planted along the riverbank, bearing fruit each season. Their leaves never wither, and they prosper in all they do (Psalm 1:1-3 NLT).

Meditation is simply repetition in thought. Ungodly meditation demands that we empty the mind, but godly meditation instructs us to fill the mind with God's Word. As you repeat the truths of God in your mind, continually apply them to any given circumstance, and persistently choose to believe those truths, you begin to form a biblical mindset. Truths begin to form paths in your mind, and these paths become the preferred routes for your thoughts. Strongholds call your attention to what causes fear, depression, doubt, torment, and the like. But the Word calls our attention to the truths that produce holiness, faith, boldness, peace, joy, and love.

As we meditate on God's Word, we renew our thought life. The renewal of our thought life is one of the ways in which we throw off the sin nature—the sin nature is what gives a foundation to the mental or emotional aspects of a stronghold.

> *Throw off your old sinful nature and your former way of life, which is corrupted by lust and deception. Instead, let the Spirit renew your thoughts and attitudes. Put on your new nature, created to be like God—truly righteous and holy* (Ephesians 4:22-24 NLT).

9

HELP ME, HOLY SPIRIT

There's a lie that works for everyone. So what was the lie that was working on me? What was at the root of my severe anxiety? I was determined to find out. I considered a few things.

Never really fitting in, I had been teased as a kid. Maybe that had something to do with it? Then there was the seemingly obvious explanation. Maybe I had to sever some tie, renounce some spiritual affiliation with my great-great grandfather, the warlock from Mexico. I started analyzing the shows I had watched as a kid. Perhaps there were some hidden demonic messages in there. I even became suspicious of others, going so far as to think that someone might have been unintentionally cursing me with their jealousy or their "ungodly prayers."

In one instance, I remember there was a guest speaker from Ghana, Africa, visiting the church I was attending. He talked a lot about spiritual warfare. So I asked him to pray for me. The moment I went up to receive prayer, he interrupted me. He pointed to his own forehead as he glared at me and declared, "Torment of the mind! I see it." He placed his hands on my head and rebuked the demonic attacks. I felt God's power and fell to the floor. I truly believe that was an encounter in God's presence, but just weeks later I was right back where I started. I even had intercessory prayer teams do hours-long "sessions" over me. Same story. I would feel good for a few weeks and, after opening no demonic doors, would go right back to feeling attacked again.

I think what frustrated me the most was the thought that no matter how many times I had attempted to be free, I just wasn't freed.

My prayer was simple, "Help me, Holy Spirit."

Then I surrendered. I stopped trying to be the spiritual warfare expert. I stopped looking for the right person to pray for me. I stopped obsessing over the bondage itself. The Holy Spirit told me something that didn't sound spiritual to me at all. His instructions were simple: "Relax."

You see, I had become so worked up by the mere fact that I was struggling. My walk with the Lord had become about overcoming an issue rather than drawing closer to Him. I was seeking deliverance when I should have been seeking Jesus.

Now upon hearing this, the struggling one might protest, "But I am seeking God. I am trying. I'm doing my best. But He ignores me. He doesn't help me. Nothing good ever happens for me. It's one battle after another. I just can't catch a break."

> *But we all, with open face beholding as in a glass the glory of the Lord, are changed into the same image from glory to glory, even as by the Spirit of the Lord* (2 Corinthians 3:18 KJV).

It is focusing on the Lord that brings victory. It's abiding in Him that brings transformation. As you look unto Jesus, you are changed in the same image. God did not call you to go from deliverance to deliverance, but from glory to glory. This is what the Holy Spirit began to teach me.

For me, my breakthrough came in a series of encounters with God. There wasn't one single moment when I became completely free of anxiety and depression. There was a timeline of key moments that led up to the freedom in which I now live. Remember, the demonic aspect of a stronghold can be dealt with instantly, but dealing with the mental and emotional aspects (the flesh), can sometimes be a process.

One very key instance occurred on a ministry trip I took to North Carolina. At that time in my life, my depression and anxiety had become especially intense. I was navigating life as a newlywed. Some of my key friendships had become strained because of my anxiety and distrust. The ministry wasn't very "successful" by the metrics that most people would measure success. I felt like I was failing on all fronts.

I remember waking up the morning I was to go to the airport. I didn't feel at all like getting up. I didn't want to deal with the traffic, the airport, the time away from Jess. Honestly, I didn't feel like preaching either.

On the way to the airport, I felt anxious about the future and depressed about my present. I felt hollow inside. I was sitting in the front passenger seat. One of my friends was driving. Another friend was sitting in the back. Trying to keep my mind clear, I began to watch the traffic around our car. Then I noticed that a car ahead of us in the far left lane began to swerve to the right and cut across several lanes, all in one swoop. We were in the far right lane, transitioning to another freeway. The car cut us off, hit the center divider, and flipped over. A loud thud, followed by a high-pitched scraping shrieked across the freeway. I watched in horror as I noticed the passenger in that car flailing around. Sparks flew as the car slid within mere feet of our car. My friend who was driving us swerved and was able to avoid any impact.

We called 911 and made sure the driver was helped. For the sake of the privacy of the one in the other car, I can't say much else other than things didn't look good for him. Because I didn't know him personally, I was never given an update. We were shaken, and my anxiety devoured me.

While I was checking in at the airport, my hands were still shaking. I felt a strong sense of doom. Then I began to imagine my plane crashing and burning. I got on the plane with my team, and everything was a blur.

To this day, I only remember waking up the next day in my hotel room. I stared at the ceiling. Waves of terror, depression, anxiety, hopelessness, emptiness, and numbness kept washing over me. I was done. I remember thinking, *I don't think I've ever felt worse than this, right here and now.*

I had hit bottom mentally and emotionally. You know, that's when the Holy Spirit shows up. There, in the low point when I felt my weakest, the Holy Spirit was finally able to get through to me. I had done everything I knew to do. I had exhausted my own strength and effort. The Spirit of Truth went to work. He revealed something to me so simple yet so liberating. The Holy Spirit spoke, and it changed my life. Our conversation went something like this:

"Do you remember when you were a little boy, and you were afraid of the demonic faces that would visit you at night?"

"Yes, I remember."

"Do you remember how that consumed your thoughts?"

"Yes, Holy Spirit, I do."

"And do you remember in kindergarten being afraid of how the other kids treated you?"

"Yes."

"Do you remember how, as a boy, you were afraid of the rides at theme parks? Do you remember how excited you would be to go to theme parks with your mom and dad? And do you remember how your worries would darken your whole day? Do you remember how convinced you were that you would be killed?"

"..."

"Do you remember how as a teenager, you couldn't get your license because you were afraid of being in a car accident? Do you remember how difficult it was for you to make friends because you were afraid of being rejected?"

At this point, something began to break in me. Tears began to fall down my face. The Holy Spirit continued.

"Do you remember how afraid of hell you were, even after I saved you? Do you remember how afraid you were of being predestined for damnation? Do you remember how each and every one of these fears consumed your mind for months and even years at a time?"

"Yes."

"What do you fear now?"

"I'm afraid of failing as a husband. I'm afraid of failing in ministry. I'm afraid of being alone. I'm afraid of everything falling apart."

And then He asked me a question that illuminated my mind. It was a major shift.

"Why don't you believe that I love you and that I intend to do good things in your life?"

I absolutely broke. For the first time in a long time, I could see the light breaking up the shadows.

> There is no fear in love; but perfect love casteth out fear: because fear hath torment. He that feareth is not made perfect in love (1 John 4:18 KJV).

In that moment, I realized something. That anxiety had followed me for my entire life. It showed itself in different forms in each stage of my life, and it manifested in a variety of so many different lies. It affected me in more ways, both large and small, than I had known. Yet, it was all the same fear. It had always been that same fear.

I knew God loved me, but I knew it intellectually, as an idea, as a fact. I hadn't allowed the implications and effects of that revelation to change me. You see, deep down, I believed the lie that I was alone, unwanted, and unloved. I truly believed that God was angry with me and that He intended to harm me. I know that to some this may sound generic or too simple. Especially those who have struggled extensively become cynical when hearing things like this. Dear reader, it really was that simple. It really was just light versus darkness.

I looked back at my life again. Only this time I could see the lie. I watched it work through every stage of my life. It was so convincing, so believable. The enemy used every hurt, every trial, every disappointment, every negative emotion to reinforce that lie. I could finally see how it robbed me of joy and peace. I could see just how deceived I had been. This subtle lie lingered in the back of my mind, like a hidden parasite. It had influenced everything about me.

I actually believed the lie that God would reject me. I never said that out loud or even that clearly—but I still believed it. Because of that fear of rejection, I didn't feel protected. Because I didn't feel His protection, I was afraid. I realized that it ultimately all stemmed from one lie. One simple but somewhat believable lie.

My tears of dismay turned into tears of joy. The powerful illusion that satan had projected over my mind was gone in an instant.

Everything in the kingdom of hell is a shifting shadow. A shadow is merely a projection that causes its substance to appear much bigger than it actually is. Shadows can be scary. But shadows can do no harm outside of your belief in their power. Every demonic stronghold is built with shadows. The gates of hell—even its walls and structures—are built with bricks of darkness. The weapons are smoky illusions. The arrows are sharp silhouettes. But the moment you turn on the light, the shadows simply cease to be. Everything about the kingdom of hell dissolves in the light of the Holy Spirit's truth.

That was a key moment for me. In that one important instant, I identified the lie. That was a huge factor in my freedom. Still, as I stated, the ultimate breakthrough in my life came progressively. To this day, I still have to remain vigilant against that lie. The enemy still attempts that lie on me, presenting it in various forms and through various sources—and in my varying mental and emotional states. Just because I still have a battle doesn't mean I'm still in bondage. I fight from the seat of authority, from the place of victory.

Not only did the Holy Spirit help me to identify the lies, but to this day, He still reminds me of the truth. And every time He does, I sense the warmth of His love, the safety of His acceptance, and the joy of freedom. I cried, "Help me, Holy Spirit!" And He helped me. As I write this, I am still living in the permanence of that freedom.

IMPORTANT NOTE: NOW IT'S YOUR TURN

So what's the lie that works for you? Is there more than one lie? What's the stronghold that has a foundation in your mind? Let's now take everything we've learned on this subject and apply it specifically to the various kinds of strongholds.

This is a very important note: In the following chapters, I write to you about the different kinds of strongholds that can keep you bound. Because we've already gone over the basics of overcoming strongholds in general, I won't be repeating these basics in every chapter. Instead, I'm going to use most of the following chapters to touch on the unique aspects of each specific stronghold.

In addition to the specific strategies I will give you concerning each kind of stronghold, these basics that we've already covered should be applied to all strongholds:

Dealing with Deception and Open Doors

+ Put on the Armor of God (Chapter 2)
+ Rely on the Spirit of Truth (Chapter 4)
+ Close Open Doors (Chapter 5)
+ Identify Strongholds Through God's Word, the Spirit's Voice, and Sound Teachers (Chapter 6)

Dealing with the Demonic (Chapter 7)

+ Know God's Authority
+ Align with God's Authority
+ Give a Command
+ Fast and Pray to Increase Faith

Dealing with the Mental and Emotional (Chapter 8)

+ Honor the Basics
+ Choose to Believe the Truth
+ Fight Reinforcing Lies
+ Renew the Mind

So that you can remember to apply the basics to each battle, I will add this reminder in each chapter:

REMINDER

10

THE STRONGHOLD
OF TEMPTATION

Lust, greed, power, and more. The world is full of temptations, and some believers have fallen into cycles of repeat sin. They do what they don't want to do, again and again. These cycles of habitual sin can last for months or even years. Believers who battle besetting sins become filled with frustration, fear, guilt, and desperation. They may experience a few days or weeks of victory, only to be pulled back into the cycle. Some begin to wonder if they can ever be free. They lose hope. Even worse, some begin to doubt their own salvation or that God's forgiveness still applies to them.

REMINDER

Don't forget to apply these basics in your fight against the stronghold of temptation.

Dealing with Deception and Open Doors

- Put on the Armor of God (Chapter 2)
- Rely on the Spirit of Truth (Chapter 4)

+ Close Open Doors (Chapter 5)
+ Identify Strongholds Through God's Word, the Spirit's Voice, and Sound Teachers (Chapter 6)

Dealing with the Demonic (Chapter 7)

+ Know God's Authority
+ Align with God's Authority
+ Give a Command
+ Fast and Pray to Increase Faith

Dealing with the Mental and Emotional (Chapter 8)

+ Honor the Basics
+ Choose to Believe the Truth
+ Fight Reinforcing Lies
+ Renew the Mind

WHY WE SIN

Make no mistake. We are drawn into sin by our own lusts and desires.

> *But every man is tempted, when he is drawn away of his own lust, and enticed* (James 1:14 KJV).

We are ultimately the ones who choose to sin. But demons encourage us in our temptations. This is why Jesus told us to pray for deliverance from the temptations of the evil one.

> *And lead us not into temptation, but deliver us from evil: For thine is the kingdom, and the power, and the glory, for ever. Amen* (Matthew 6:13 KJV).

Satan tempted Adam and Eve. Satan tempted Jesus. Satan tempts you and I through his lying demons. The stronghold of temptation is based on various forms of the same lie:

+ "This sin will fulfill you."
+ "This sin is worth it."
+ "This sin will be more fulfilling than God's presence."
+ "This sin has no consequence."

Now you may say, "But I don't believe any of those lies! I know that sin won't fulfill me, but I do it anyway." I would say that our actions tell us what we truly believe. You may know intellectually that sin doesn't fulfill, but do you know that truly and deeply? Does every part of you agree with the truth, or is there some part of you that is deceived enough to believe in exceptions?

The lies we believe about sin and its ability to satisfy become the deception under which we think and feel. Of course, actions follow, and we choose sin. Once sin is chosen, we become more prone to deception. Then the cycle repeats, and as the cycle repeats, the bondage is strengthened.

If sin were a product, demons would be salesmen. Demons lie constantly to you about sin. Every act of sin begins with the belief in a lie.

THE NATURE OF TEMPTATION

Look, for example, at the first temptation. Notice how the enemy contradicts the truth of what God says before he lures Adam and Eve into sin:

> *The serpent was the shrewdest of all the wild animals the Lord God had made. One day he asked the woman, "Did God really say you must not eat the fruit from any of the trees in the garden?" "Of course we may eat fruit from the trees in the garden," the woman replied. "It's only the fruit from the tree in the middle of the garden that we are not allowed to eat. God said, 'You must not eat it or even touch it; if you do, you will die.'" "You won't die!" the serpent replied to the woman. "God knows that your eyes will be opened as soon as you eat it, and you will be like God, knowing both good and evil." The woman was convinced. She saw that the tree was beautiful and its fruit looked delicious, and she wanted the wisdom it would give her. So she took some of the fruit and ate it. Then she gave some to her husband, who was with her, and he ate it, too. At that moment their eyes were opened, and they suddenly felt shame at their nakedness. So they sewed fig leaves together to cover themselves (Genesis 3:1-7 NLT).*

First the enemy questioned the Word: *"Did God really say you must not eat the fruit from any of the trees in the garden?"* Then the enemy contradicted the Word: *"You won't die!"* Deception is never obvious. Eve likely wouldn't have believed the lie if she was certain that it directly contradicted what God said. However, because she had become unsure about what God had actually said, she eventually believed the lie. Questioning the Word leads to contradicting the Word.

The Bible tells us, "*She saw that the tree was beautiful and its fruit looked delicious, and she wanted the wisdom it would give her.*" There, we are seeing all three components of temptation.

> *For all that is in the world, the lust of the flesh, and the lust of the eyes, and the pride of life, is not of the Father, but is of the world* (1 John 2:16 KJV).

+ She saw—lust of the eyes.
+ Fruit looked delicious—lust of the flesh.
+ She wanted the wisdom—pride of life.

When she looked at the fruit, she was tempted by what she saw. When she noticed that the fruit looked delicious, she became hungry for it. That was the craving of the flesh. It was the lust of the flesh. When she desired the wisdom, she desired to be like God. Her desire to be like God, in that instance, was a desire born of pride. That was the pride of life. Every sin you will ever be tempted with will fall under one of these three categories of temptation: 1) lust of the eyes; 2) lust of the flesh; 3) pride of life.

HOW JESUS HANDLED TEMPTATION

In fact, Jesus Himself was tempted in all three of these points. Pay attention to how He overcame the deceptive lure of temptation.

> *Then Jesus was led by the Spirit into the wilderness to be tempted there by the devil. For forty days and forty nights he*

fasted and became very hungry. During that time the devil came and said to him, "If you are the Son of God, tell these stones to become loaves of bread." But Jesus told him, "No! The Scriptures say, 'People do not live by bread alone, but by every word that comes from the mouth of God.'" Then the devil took him to the holy city, Jerusalem, to the highest point of the Temple, and said, "If you are the Son of God, jump off! For the Scriptures say, 'He will order his angels to protect you. And they will hold you up with their hands so you won't even hurt your foot on a stone.'" Jesus responded, "The Scriptures also say, 'You must not test the Lord your God.'" Next the devil took him to the peak of a very high mountain and showed him all the kingdoms of the world and their glory. "I will give it all to you," he said, "if you will kneel down and worship me." "Get out of here, Satan," Jesus told him. "For the Scriptures say, 'You must worship the Lord your God and serve only him.'" Then the devil went away, and angels came and took care of Jesus (Matthew 4:1-11 NLT).

The enemy is more cunning than most realize. His strategy against the Lord Jesus wasn't as simple as it appears. In total, I count four angles of attack the enemy used. The first attack was to use Jesus' hunger against Him. There, we see the enemy taking advantage of the Lord's vulnerable state of hunger. Remember, states of being can be open doors to deception. The second angle of attack was to twist the Scripture and tell Jesus, *"He will order his angels to protect you."* The third attack was to tempt Jesus by offering Him all the kingdoms of the world. Here, the enemy was offering Jesus a cross-less, seemingly painless path to rulership over the nations. The fourth angle of attack was actually threaded through the first two angles of attack. In each of those instances, what was the underlying method? It was to challenge the identity of the Lord—*"if you are the Son of God."* The enemy was challenging the truth about who Jesus was.

In the story of Jesus' temptation, we see the three components of temptation. The lust of the eyes (kingdoms of the world), lust of the flesh (bread to eat), and the pride of life (prove yourself by throwing yourself from atop the temple.) Still, ultimately, the underlying lie, the big push the enemy was using to tempt Jesus was the challenge of His identity. That was the lie the enemy used in an attempt to reinforce the power of the temptation.

How did Jesus respond? It is written! He used truth to combat the underlying deception. The deception wasn't just about bread and hunger, demonstration of power, or the kingdoms of the world. The deception was about identity. Jesus cut to the root of the lie using the Word of God.

No, Jesus did not use His experience, as some attempt to do. He used the Word. Some are under the impression that their power against the enemy comes from their own "depth" in the Spirit or their many years of experience in dealing with demons. The enemy finds that laughable. If anyone could have used their experience, it would have been Jesus. But He didn't use His experience. He used the Word of truth. Jesus could've pointed to His own baptism. He could have said, "Devil, what do you mean if I'm the Son of God? Weren't you there at the Jordan River on the day I was baptized? It wasn't long ago, you know! When I came out of the water, the Holy Spirit descended upon me like a dove. Many witnessed this! And didn't you hear My Father's strong voice speaking clearly from the heavens? Weren't you there when He spoke? He said, 'This is My beloved Son, in whom I am well pleased.'"

No, Jesus didn't do that. Rather, He fought the deception of the enemy with the written Word. That's where we begin in the tearing down of every stronghold—with the truth of the Word. Before you can resist sin, you need to hide God's Word in your heart.

I have hidden your word in my heart, that I might not sin against you (Psalm 119:11 NLT).

REPENT AND RENOUNCE

Why is the truth of the Word the key to overcoming temptation? Because temptation ultimately gets its power from deception. If you're tempted with lust, the lie could be that the sexual act will fulfill you. If you're tempted with bitterness, the lie could be that you're entitled to not forgive. If you're tempted with power, the lie could be that you need it. To break free from the act of a sin, we must be free from the lies we believe about that sin.

If you want to be free from sin, you need to repent of and then renounce your sin. There's a lot of misunderstanding surrounding these two words—*repent* and *renounce*. Many are under the impression that *repent* means to "turn away from" or to "go in the opposite direction." Don't get me wrong; we should absolutely turn away from our sin, but that's not what the word *repent* means.

Additionally, many are confused about the word *renounce*. When we think of the word *renounce*, most of us will imagine reciting a list of past sins or generational wickedness. We may think of phrases like, "I renounce the witchcraft of former generations," or, "I renounce all bitterness and unforgiveness." While there's nothing wrong with verbally rejecting evil, that's not what renouncing is. Not biblically, anyway. If we're not careful, renouncing can just become a religious act or ritual. Some imagine that God can't set them free unless they list everything they did wrong. However, we know the Holy Spirit's power is not limited to our memory of past sins or of specialized prayers.

Now, I'm not just being picky about terminology. It's important to understand what it means to both repent and renounce.

The Greek word for *repentance (metanoia)* literally means "a change of mind." This means that we should come into agreement with what God says and thinks about our sin. That's what it means to repent of sin—to change your mind about sin.

What does it mean to renounce? Almost anytime you see the word *renounce* in Scripture, it means to "turn from" or "forsake." Look at Titus 2:12 in both the New Living Translation and then the English Standard Version of the Bible:

> *And we are instructed to turn from godless living and sinful pleasures. We should live in this evil world with wisdom, righteousness, and devotion to God* (Titus 2:12 NLT).

> *Training us to renounce ungodliness and worldly passions, and to live self-controlled, upright, and godly lives in the present age* (Titus 2:12 ESV).

True renouncing is action, not speech.

So to repent is to change your mind, and to renounce is to change your behavior. Repentance brings me into agreement with God. Renouncing is the forsaking of my evil ways. True repentance is a change in mind that results in a change in direction. Here in Acts, we see that repentance results in a turning to God.

> *Now repent of your sins and turn to God, so that your sins may be wiped away* (Acts 3:19 NLT).

Far too many believers try to renounce sin before they repent of sin. They try to change their behavior before they have changed their mind. This causes frustration. If you are attempting to produce new actions from an old mindset, you'll end up angry at yourself. Am I saying we shouldn't turn from sin? By no means! I'm saying that your attempts to turn from sin will fail until you also repent, change your mind about sin.

Furthermore, don't mistake regret for repentance. Sure, godly sorrow leads to repentance (2 Corinthians 7:10). So some healthy form of regret might lead to repentance. Still, regret itself is not the same as repentance. Many Christians think that feeling bad for sin is the same as repenting of that sin. Just because you feel shame over sin doesn't mean you've actually changed your mind about it.

Here's the reality: many don't necessarily want to be set free from sin but from the shame, guilt, and consequences of sin. We say things like, "I'm sorry, Lord! I don't ever want to do that again!" All the while, we can be lying to ourselves. That may be what we pray out loud, but the flesh is self-deceiving. You will lie to you. As you shout, "No more sin," the part of you that still craves sin will whisper, "for now." The sin nature always intends to go back to sin. Don't give it any influence.

If you leave allowance for your sin somewhere in the back of your mind or intend to do well until the craving arises again, then you'll remain stuck. The flesh is so deceptive that it will tell itself things like, "Well, if I only sin once in a while, then technically it won't count as a sinful lifestyle, just a mistake." The flesh will try to make compromises with you, saying, "We'll live holy for 90 percent of the time. We'll be clean for five days out of the week. Just give me something, anything. As long as you do mostly well, it still counts as 'trying' to live holy." You need to make up your mind about the truth before the temptation ever occurs, so that when temptation comes, you've already determined to deny it. You need to make up your mind that sin will not be tolerated, not one bit. There's no relief coming for the flesh's cravings, and you need to be determined to leave it that way.

In fact, the enemy may even have you convinced that it's not really possible to be free of sin. He may say, "Oh, you've tried so many times and for so many years. You've had so many people pray for you, and you've prayed yourself." If he can't absolutely convince you that you can't live holy, he'll at least try to make you believe that freedom is somewhere off in the distance, years and years from now.

To repent means to come into agreement with God. It is to agree with God that the sin is wrong. It is to agree with God that the sin must go, not just for now or for a few weeks or until you can't hold up under temptation anymore. To repent is to agree with God, in the core of your being, that what you're doing is wrong and that it must go, immediately, permanently, and completely. It is to commit to never allowing it back in your life again, even in a "smaller" form. Once you've become totally convinced about the truth of your sin and of God's power to make you holy, then and only then will you begin to see real progress.

Once you have truly repented—changed your mind—then the deception of temptation loses its power. Repent, change your mind about sin. Then you can renounce, forsake the sin. After dispelling the deception about sin, then it's just a matter of staying ahead of self and satan.

SATAN AND SELF

You have two enemies: self and satan. You don't fight self in the same way you fight satan. This is where most believers become confused, discouraged, and stuck.

We know we are in a spiritual battle against the devil and his demons.

> *For we wrestle not against flesh and blood, but against prin-*
> *cipalities, against powers, against the rulers of the darkness*
> *of this world, against spiritual wickedness in high places*
> (Ephesians 6:12 KJV).

> *Stay alert! Watch out for your great enemy, the devil. He*
> *prowls around like a roaring lion, looking for someone to*
> *devour* (1 Peter 5:8 NLT).

We also understand that the enemy's primary weapon against the believer is deception. That deception can ultimately produce bondage. Still, there's another enemy we have, and this enemy sometimes cooperates with demonic powers. It's the enemy of self.

> *For the flesh lusteth against the Spirit, and the Spirit against*
> *the flesh: and these are contrary the one to the other: so that*
> *ye cannot do the things that ye would* (Galatians 5:17 KJV).

At first glance, this may appear to be a contradiction. The Bible says we don't fight against flesh and blood but then also tells us that the flesh fights against the Spirit.

In the famous Ephesians verse, when we are told that we do not fight against flesh and blood enemies, we are simply being told that we aren't waging war with other human beings. Therefore, our weapons are not carnal but spiritual. So we are given the armor of God, rather than armor produced with human hands. Some have misapplied the meaning of Ephesians to imply that everything that comes against us is demonic. They neglect the other truths of Scripture regarding the sin nature.

In Galatians, where the Scripture talks about the "flesh" warring against the Spirit, it is ultimately talking about the sin nature. The sin nature is simply what results when we use our God-given free will to decide for something that contradicts the nature of God. Demons can influence us to function in the sin nature, but the sin nature is not itself a demon. If the sin nature was just a demon, we wouldn't be held personally accountable for our sins. So we have to deal with both enemies.

DEALING WITH SATAN

Demons can use their lies to influence you to act according to the sin nature, so we deal with demonic beings by resisting their temptations.

> *So humble yourselves before God. Resist the devil, and he will flee from you* (James 4:7 NLT).

It's interesting to me that we speak of stubborn demons who argue to keep their influence or who delay their submission. They aren't that strong. Any influence they have over you is so weak that even just resistance, let alone confrontation, is enough to cause them to flee.

As in the case of Jesus, the enemy was resisted three times before he fled. When you resist the enemy, he eventually flees. Jesus resisted the enemy with the truth of the Word. We must do the same. We resist the enemy by simply saying, "No." We resist the enemy by choosing to not act upon the temptations he presents. We resist the temptations of the enemy by declaring God's Word.

The believer's authority comes from the Word of God. If God promised it, you can enforce it. Using sexual sin as an example, in practical application, the battle might look something like this:

The enemy reminds you of a pornographic image that you saw. That's the lust of the eyes. In response, your body begins to crave what it sees. That's the lust of the flesh, the craving. Instead of allowing yourself to debate with the enemy, you immediately reply, *"I made a covenant with my eyes not to look with lust at a young woman"* (Job 31:1 NLT). You then immediately reject the thought and begin asking the Holy Spirit for strength.

Then the enemy comes back, "But it will be just this one more time," or, "You've been living clean for a few weeks. The Lord will understand." Addressing the invitation to compromise, you fire back, *"But among you there must not be even a hint of sexual immorality, or of any kind of impurity, or of greed, because these are improper for God's holy people"* (Ephesians 5:3 NIV). You press into prayer. You cry out for the Holy Spirit to rescue you.

The temptations in your life are no different from what others experience. And God is faithful. He will not allow the temptation to be more than you can stand. When you are tempted, He will show you a way out so that you can endure (1 Corinthians 10:13 NLT).

Persistent, the enemy tries once more: "This won't hurt you, as long as you don't make it a habit. What harm will it do?" Mindful of your friend the Holy Spirit, you declare, *"And do not bring sorrow to God's Holy Spirit by the way you live. Remember, he has identified you as his own, guaranteeing that you will be saved on the day of redemption"* (Ephesians 4:30 NLT).

Now I'm not giving you an exact script to follow. That would be a religious approach, and religion always gives way to legalism. Legalism never leads to freedom. What I'm giving you here is only an example of how the battle might play out. The main takeaway is to engage the enemy biblically—that is to resist immediately and use the truth of God's Word to combat the lies that make temptation harder to resist.

Demons are highly intelligent beings. You're not going to win in a debate with them. So you need to avoid the back-and-forth of temptation. This is why the Bible teaches us to flee, to run away from temptation.

> *Run from anything that stimulates youthful lusts. Instead, pursue righteous living, faithfulness, love, and peace. Enjoy the companionship of those who call on the Lord with pure hearts* (2 Timothy 2:22 NLT).

There needs to be an immediate resistance. The enemy already has you if you get trapped in, "Should I or shouldn't I?" By debating, considering, or weighing the options you've already fallen for a lie. The lie being, "I'm strong enough to only take this so far." Sin is not under your control. By getting stuck in contemplation, you fall for the illusion of "resisting" sin. Contemplation isn't the resistance of sin—it's giving in to sin at a slower pace. So instead of contemplating, flee! *Immediately* resist. Don't debate with the devil, defeat him by immediately resisting the temptation.

Add to your resistance the Word of God.

> *But when the Father sends the Advocate as my representative—that is, the Holy Spirit—he will teach you everything and will remind you of everything I have told you* (John 14:26 NLT).

When you're full of the Word, the influence of the Spirit is strong upon your life. Ask Him to remind you of the truth in times of temptation. Then be quick to listen for His voice when the temptation comes. Cry out, "Help me, Holy Spirit!" And don't stop calling upon Him until you're rescued. Drown out the tempting lies of the enemy with calls for the Holy Spirit's help.

Temptation is not an event, it is a process. Most of the battle is won or lost long before the opportunity of sin is presented. By living a lifestyle of receiving and living the Word, you're prepping yourself to stand against sin long before the temptation comes across your path.

So that's how you deal with the demonic aspect of the stronghold of temptation—you immediately resist and use the Word to counter the lies that make temptation more difficult to overcome. This makes the enemy flee. Then you need to deal with self.

DEALING WITH SELF

We already know how demons are involved in the stronghold of temptation. They tell you lies that tempt you to sin. Demons don't do the sinning for you. You do that on your own free will. You may be asking for deliverance when what you really need is discipline. We need to stop blaming our sin problems on demons instead of taking responsibility for an undisciplined flesh. In fact, the Bible makes it clear that the only reason that demonic beings can tempt us in the first place is precisely because of a lack of discipline and self-control. I'll show you.

Do not deprive each other of sexual relations, unless you both agree to refrain from sexual intimacy for a limited time so you can give yourselves more completely to prayer. Afterward, you should come together again so that Satan won't be able to tempt you because of your lack of self-control (1 Corinthians 7:5 NLT).

"So that Satan won't be able to tempt you because of your lack of self-control." It's our lack of self-control that gives the enemy the power to tempt us in the first place.

Now I'm not saying that Christians never need deliverance. Of course, we at times do need deliverance. This whole book is about experiencing deliverance from strongholds. But the only way the enemy can keep believers bound in the stronghold of temptation is if they refuse to take responsibility for their lack of self-control.

But the Holy Spirit produces this kind of fruit in our lives: love, joy, peace, patience, kindness, goodness, faithfulness, gentleness, and self-control... (Galatians 5:22-23 NLT).

Though it might seem obvious, many of us miss the fact that self-control is the ability that the Holy Spirit gives you to control yourself. He won't control you, but He's given you the ability to control you.

Stop blaming demons. We give them too much credit. Our lack of discipline is the only reason their temptations work. How is it that we can choose to spend hours thinking about what tempts us and then turn around and blame demonic oppression for our failure to live holy? This isn't a message of condemnation but of truth. And only truth sets us free. I know some blame demons for their poor choices. However, ultimately, we are the ones choosing to sin.

The only way to deal with the sin nature is to keep it weak. Don't allow it an opportunity to get what it craves. Rearrange your whole life around holiness. Make whatever changes needed, even if they're drastic.

But put ye on the Lord Jesus Christ, and make not provision for the flesh, to fulfil the lusts thereof (Romans 13:14 KJV).

The sin nature is dealt with throughout your lifetime.

But I keep under my body, and bring it into subjection: lest that by any means, when I have preached to others, I myself should be a castaway (1 Corinthians 9:27 KJV).

Paul the apostle here is not saying that the body is the sin nature. He's saying that the body can become an instrument of the sin nature if it isn't kept in check.

Rebuke and resist the enemy. Make up your mind about sin. Then ask the Holy Spirit to expose the lies you believe about sin, to remind you of the truth when you're tempted, and to help you keep the sin nature weak.

11

THE STRONGHOLD
OF ADDICTION

THE NATURE OF ADDICTION

D rug addiction. Alcohol addiction. Porn addiction. Food addiction. Those are just some of the many kinds of addictions that can dramatically alter and utterly ruin the lives of those under their power. An addiction is more than a habit or a constant choosing of a vice. What makes addiction such a powerful stronghold is not just the demonic, mental, and emotional aspects but its additional physical aspect. At first, addictions are formed by foolish decisions but eventually go on to develop a physiological element. The body eventually aches for what it was trained to desire.

Whenever I write of the physical aspects of addiction, some cry out, "Brother David, you're missing the spiritual aspect! It's demonic!" Whenever I write of the demonic aspects of addiction, some cry out, "David, not everything is a demon. Addiction affects both brain and body!"

Why can't it be both? Both the demonic realm and the physical realm exist. God created both the spiritual and the material world. There is cause and effect in the natural and the supernatural. This "either or" mentality is precisely why so many are still in bondage. Those who speak of the demonic are labeled as "crazy." Those who speak of the physiological are labeled as "not deep enough." Both extremes deny some aspect of God's Word. Both extremes deny some aspect of the reality God formed. The Word clearly speaks of both deliverance and discipline, temptation and free will, soul and body, demons and the sin nature. Dear reader, it's "both…and" not "either…or." Addiction is both demonic and physiological.

We must learn to acknowledge and address the physical and practical needs of those bound by addiction, in addition to their spiritual needs.

A dear friend of mine was telling me of her terrible struggle with trying to overcome a heroin addiction. She told me of a "deliverance" retreat that she had attended. Because those operating the retreat were so fixated on only the demonic aspects of the bondage, that event mentally and emotionally scarred my friend and actually made her problem much worse. Her story confirmed to me that some believers actually need deliverance from their so-called deliverance.

Her voice shook, as she told me of how the retreat had attracted people who were dealing with severe drug addictions. Because the retreat took place in the mountains, the retreat attendees had to rely upon the retreat hosts for food and lodging. The people were subjected to long periods without food, sleep deprivation in the guise of prayer meetings, and hours of strange teachings. So these people were dealing with drug addictions, being deprived of food, being deprived of sleep, and then they were told they couldn't leave the meeting until they were believed to be completely delivered. Unfortunately, they weren't considered completely delivered until they vomited, something rather difficult to do on an empty stomach.

On a side note, we don't see in Scripture that vomiting is a prerequisite for deliverance. I used to insist on this when ministering deliverance but noticed it stopped happening the moment I stopped suggesting it. With what I see in Scripture and what I've seen in my experience of ministering deliverance, I've concluded that people can still be set free without having to vomit. If it happens when someone is set free, I take no issue. It's insisting upon it as a prerequisite to freedom that's the problem—especially since Scripture doesn't require it.

So these desperate people were basically being held hostage until they threw up in a bucket. That was their ticket out of there. It was as if the retreat hosts had become frustrated with not being able to deliver the addicts and required them to play along so that they could tell success stories about their retreat.

The abuse my friend had to endure is indicative of the sort of religious behavior that can result when we don't acknowledge all of the factors that are involved with spiritual bondage. Well-meaning believers may try to help, but then become frustrated when their methods don't seem to work. Instead of approaching it biblically, with real power, some simply up the intensity of their man-made protocols. So we need to deal with both the demonic and the material facets of addiction if we want to operate in true power.

REMINDER

Don't forget to apply these basics in your fight against the stronghold of addiction.

Dealing with Deception and Open Doors

+ Put on the Armor of God (Chapter 2)
+ Rely on the Spirit of Truth (Chapter 4)
+ Close Open Doors (Chapter 5)

+ Identify Strongholds Through God's Word, the
Spirit's Voice, and Sound Teachers (Chapter 6)

Dealing with the Demonic (Chapter 7)

+ Know God's Authority

+ Align with God's Authority

+ Give a Command

+ Fast and Pray to Increase Faith

Dealing with the Mental and Emotional (Chapter 8)

+ Honor the Basics

+ Choose to Believe the Truth

+ Fight Reinforcing Lies

+ Renew the Mind

THE ROLE DEMONS PLAY IN ADDICTION

The role that demons play in the stronghold of addiction is simple: they use deception to lure you into temptation—and that temptation, if yielded to often enough, becomes addiction.

Paul the apostle instructed the married Corinthian couples to not deprive one another of sex. Even though Paul is specifically speaking of sex in the following verse, we see something quite insightful regarding the strategy of satan:

> *Do not deprive each other of sexual relations, unless you both agree to refrain from sexual intimacy for a limited time so you can give yourselves more completely to prayer. Afterward, you should come together again so that Satan won't be able to tempt you because of your lack of self-control* (1 Corinthians 7:5 NLT).

Paul warned the Church that satan could take a short season of sexual abstinence as an opportunity to tempt the married couples with sexual sin. Satan would seize upon an opportunity for effective temptation. The takeaway is simple: satan tempts us when we're most vulnerable, in the area we are most likely to yield.

That's the role of the demonic when it comes to addiction: deception unto temptation. Once someone yields to a temptation for long enough, the physical problem of addiction can result. So it could be said that the root of addiction—deception and temptation—is spiritual, while the addiction itself—the strong craving—is physical. This is why we say that addiction is both a spiritual and a physical problem.

THE ROLE THE SIN NATURE PLAYS IN ADDICTION

Now I'm going to write something to you that isn't popular teaching, but it's the truth: demons may feed you the lies, but you feed yourself what you crave. Demons may tempt you, but you choose to sin. Demons don't do the drinking for you. Demons don't stick the needle in your arm for you. Demons don't run an internet search for you. Granted, they sometimes do play a very central role in the temptations you face, but they do not do the sinning for you.

I know this seems harsh, especially when the addiction can become so powerful that it seems as though there is another person in your body working against you. But if you're a born-again believer, this "other person" that causes you to stumble is simply the sin nature. The sin nature consists of your old patterns. The Bible reveals that the body can be "programmed" under the sin nature:

> Do not let sin control the way you live; do not give in to sinful desires. Do not let any part of your body become an instrument of evil to serve sin. Instead, give yourselves completely to God, for you were dead, but now you have new life. So use your whole body as an instrument to do what is right for the glory of God. Sin is no longer your master, for you no longer live under the requirements of the law. Instead, you live under the freedom of God's grace (Romans 6:12-14 NLT).

Your body is like hardware; your thinking is like software. Under the old programming, your body was an instrument of sin. Under the new programming, your body can be free of addiction.

> So letting your sinful nature control your mind leads to death. But letting the Spirit control your mind leads to life and peace. For the sinful nature is always hostile to God. It never did obey God's laws, and it never will. That's why those who are still under the control of their sinful nature can never please God (Romans 8:6-8 NLT).

This is what addiction does. It gives strength to the "old programming" through the physical body.

I want to do what is good, but I don't. I don't want to do what is wrong, but I do it anyway. But if I do what I don't want to do, I am not really the one doing wrong; it is sin living in me that does it. I have discovered this principle of life—that when I want to do what is right, I inevitably do what is wrong. I love God's law with all my heart. But there is another power within me that is at war with my mind. This power makes me a slave to the sin that is still within me. Oh, what a miserable person I am! Who will free me from this life that is dominated by sin and death? Thank God! The answer is in Jesus Christ our Lord. So you see how it is: In my mind I really want to obey God's law, but because of my sinful nature I am a slave to sin (Romans 7:19-25 NLT).

We can't downplay just how crucial the sin nature is to any addiction.

Here's how addiction works:

Deception > Temptation > Sin > Habitual Sin > Addiction

So though demonic deception can tempt us to sin, it's only when we respond to that temptation that an addiction can be formed. It is the yielding to the sin nature that leads us into the trap of addiction.

THE ROLE THE BODY PLAYS IN ADDICTION

Once the physical body has been "programmed" to ache for the sinful pleasures it has been routinely fed, we call that "addiction." This can be food, sex, alcohol, drugs, porn—anything that the body and brain can adapt to fiercely crave. It's a fact that the body and the brain can be altered, restructured to the point where its sinful cravings can be as strong as hunger, if not stronger. In the case of drugs and alcohol, your body becomes dependent upon the substance. At that point, in extreme cases, the body's need for its vice can even become life-threatening.

Once the addiction has reached this point, willpower and discipline alone begin to lose their strength. The body begins to act on what it's been trained to do and crave. Sadly, these cravings are so strong that men and women give up all they love to fulfill them. I've seen parents abandon children, spouses abandon spouses, and people give up everything they've worked to achieve for just "one more" taste of what they crave.

So the nature of addiction is thus—it begins in deception. That deception makes you more vulnerable to temptation. You choose to yield to that temptation. That yielding to temptation becomes a habit. That habit affects the brain and body profoundly enough to become an addiction. By the time the bondage has become an addiction, there are physical elements to it. Addiction is the physical consequence of a constant yielding to temptation.

ADDRESSING ADDICTION

We should remember that God can do anything He wants. I've seen addicts of all sorts instantaneously delivered, never to touch or even crave their preferred vice again. Then there are times when I've seen addicts progressively delivered, losing their cravings over time, as they surrender more and more to the Lord. However freedom may come, there are layers to this stronghold that must be considered.

This is a huge topic. Especially when it comes to substance addiction, the subject would require a book unto itself. I'm not a medical professional, so I won't be able to cover every aspect of addiction. However, I am a teacher of the Word, so I want to equip you with some biblical truth that can act as a spiritual foundation for freedom.

Let's look to Scripture.

DEAL WITH IT EARLY

At a certain point, some addictions, like drug addictions, affect the body and brain to such a degree that discipline and willpower alone lose their effectiveness. In speaking with many who have struggled with drug or alcohol addiction, I have discovered that the pull of a full-on addiction can be so powerful that they sacrifice everything they love in order to feed it. So, as with any problem, it's best to address it as early as possible.

Perhaps you have not yet moved beyond the stronghold of temptation and come under the stronghold of addiction. Perhaps your habits are truly still just habits, cycles of willful disobedience. Stop it there while you can, lest the habits profoundly influence the body and brain.

Scripture speaks of a progressively increasing effect of sin that begins in desire but ends in death.

> *Temptation comes from our own desires, which entice us and drag us away. These desires give birth to sinful actions. And when sin is allowed to grow, it gives birth to death* (James 1:14-15 NLT).

What begins as a desire for pleasure or relief or escape will eventually become lethal. Like lighting the fuse of an explosive device, giving in to temptation begins a process that continues to develop, whether you like it or not. For as long as you are giving in to sin, you are strengthening the chains of sinful habits. Sin makes no exceptions. What you sow is what you reap.

> Don't be misled—you cannot mock the justice of God. You will always harvest what you plant (Galatians 6:7 NLT).

Given enough time, sin always destroys.

> Catch all the foxes, those little foxes, before they ruin the vineyard of love, for the grapevines are blossoming! (Song of Solomon 2:15 NLT)

Song of Solomon is about two lovers coming together. The vineyard represents their love for one another. The little foxes represent those little things that bring destruction if they aren't dealt with right away.

"Just a sip" quickly becomes "one more drink." "One more drink" quickly becomes a lifestyle of drunkenness. "Just a glance" quickly becomes "one more video." "Just a friend" quickly becomes "I hope they don't find out." The earlier you address an addiction of any kind, the better.

DEAL WITH IT PRACTICALLY

> He forgives all my sins and heals all my diseases (Psalm 103:3 NLT).

God can heal your addiction miraculously, instantaneously. We know that. That's what we should believe for, in each and every instance of addiction. But while we hope for a miracle, we should also take practical measures to work against the addiction. Just as a sick person believes for their healing but also takes practical health measures, so one suffering from addiction should believe for their instant miracle while also taking practical measures to combat their addiction. This isn't a lack of faith. Quite the contrary, this is faith in action.

If your deliverance from addiction isn't instantaneous, don't fret or think yourself abandoned. Far too many Christians give up on a miracle simply because it didn't come in the way they hoped it would come or when they hoped it would happen.

On a side note, I wrote a great deal on how demons must respond immediately to the authority of Christ in you. So at this point, some readers may wonder, *Why doesn't God just heal the physical aspects of the addiction instantly as well?* First of all, sometimes He does. And we should believe for that each time we pray against addiction. I'm simply addressing what we should do if the miracle doesn't occur as quickly as we'd like. Second, I'm not saying that demons themselves can linger to harass you after you've commanded them to stop attacking you. I'm saying that the physical effects of the addiction itself can linger and need to be dealt with if God doesn't instantly remove those physical effects. The physical effects of addiction can be likened unto sickness. And biblically speaking, demons and sickness are not the same thing. There are many biblical examples of Christians battling lingering sicknesses but never lingering demonic bondage. You can read more about sickness in Chapter 12.

To my main point, we should approach everything in faith. Believe for an instant miracle in faith. If that doesn't happen when you think it should, then continue to take practical measures, in faith. And remember that you're not fighting addiction alone. The Holy Spirit is involved with the overcoming of your addiction. In fact, the Bible clearly tells us that the Holy Spirit helps our physical bodies.

But you are not controlled by your sinful nature. You are controlled by the Spirit if you have the Spirit of God living in you. (And remember that those who do not have the Spirit of Christ living in them do not belong to him at all.) And Christ lives within you, so even though your body will die because of sin, the Spirit gives you life because you have been made right with God. The Spirit of God, who raised Jesus from the dead, lives in you. And just as God raised Christ Jesus from the dead, he will give life to your mortal bodies by this same Spirit living within you (Romans 8:9-11 NLT).

The Holy Spirit quickens our physical bodies. He empowers them unto holiness. The same resurrection power that brought life back to the body of Christ works in you, empowering you to resist the sin nature's programming. There is a tangible, physical touch of God's power on you. You can't do this without that power. Use that power as you take daily practical steps toward freedom.

Daily, you should make use of anything that aligns itself with God's will for your life. We know that the Lord doesn't want you living with addiction, so medical treatments that work to heal that addiction and that don't contradict teachings of Scripture should be embraced. Now, there are some philosophies, treatments, and practices that can worsen the problem. This is why we should primarily be grounded in the truth of God's Word. Avoid such things as New Age practices and humanism.

But generally speaking, God is not against the idea of helpful medical treatment, nor is seeking legitimate medical treatment somehow a demonstration of a lack of faith. In fact, there are Christian treatment clinics for all sorts of addictions.

Think of the fact that Jesus spoke of medical practice in a positive context.

But when Jesus heard that, he said unto them, They that be whole need not a physician, but they that are sick (Matthew 9:12 KJV).

Jesus would not have used medical practice in a positive light in His analogy if He thought it to be unholy. He would not have used what He thought to be an evil practice as a parable of His ministry to sinners.

Whenever medical treatment or counseling is suggested, zealous but misguided Christians might tell you, "You're counseling it out because you can't cast it out!" Now, I don't have an issue with that phrase itself. Sometimes I think it's used appropriately, because sometimes Christians deny and avoid the reality of spiritual warfare. I agree that many times people tend to forget about spiritual realities. However, many say such things as if there's never anything but demonic elements to consider. Yet even after dealing with the demonic, which is relatively straightforward, there's still the need to address our thinking, our habits, and in the case of addiction, the physical aspects of the stronghold. This can be dealt with miraculously instantly, but if that doesn't happen, we shouldn't just sit back and allow the addiction to remain without resistance.

Rely upon the power of the Holy Spirit, that your body might be quickened unto the exercise of holy living. And at the same time, don't be ashamed of also applying biblically consistent material solutions such as medical treatment, rehab, and yes, even counseling. Demons must go instantly, but physical problems can linger. Don't fight the progressive miracle while you continue to believe for the instant miracle.

DEAL WITH IT AGGRESSIVELY

Imagine two friends standing along the sides of a deep dark pit, peering down into the drop. They can't see the bottom, but they know it must be a long way down. Nervous, one friend warns, "Don't stand too close! You could fall." Confident, the other brags, "I'm pretty careful." He begins to walk the very edge of the drop-off, balancing his body with his arms. "This isn't a good idea. Please, get away from the edge. You're making me nervous!" His friend pleads with him. "I got it. I'll be fine." Just as he speaks of his ability to maintain his balance, he slips and then slides down into the opening. All his friend can do is watch in horror—unsure if his friend will survive.

That's addiction. People make choices that bring them close to the edge, because they are either totally convinced of their ability to maintain control or they don't care if they fall in. Either way, though it was their choice to step up to the edge, once they begin to fall, it becomes less of a choice and more of a consequence. They're the ones who walked up to the edge, but once they fall in the hole, they need help to get out.

> *The sinful nature wants to do evil, which is just the opposite of what the Spirit wants. And the Spirit gives us desires that are the opposite of what the sinful nature desires. These two forces are constantly fighting each other, so you are not free to carry out your good intentions* (Galatians 5:17 NLT).

You have to treat the sin nature like it's another person working against you. It takes a lot to subject it. Start by admitting that you, indeed, have an issue. Then don't let the man of sin have a chance.

> *But put ye on the Lord Jesus Christ, and make not provision for the flesh, to fulfil the lusts thereof* (Romans 13:14 KJV).

Attack this issue from all angles. Don't give the man of sin an opportunity to grow in strength or to indulge in his cravings. Say "no" to the flesh.

If one person falls, the other can reach out and help. But someone who falls alone is in real trouble (Ecclesiastes 4:10 NLT).

Set up accountability with other believers. Don't let shame keep you from reaching out for help. Be honest with them and give them access to a true and meaningful connection with you. Respect their role in challenging you and checking up on you. Addiction only grows stronger in isolation.

Run from anything that stimulates youthful lusts. Instead, pursue righteous living, faithfulness, love, and peace. Enjoy the companionship of those who call on the Lord with pure hearts (2 Timothy 2:22 NLT).

If you truly want to be free and you're truly done with addiction, then even though your body is "programmed" to temporarily work against you, you need to exercise your will in whatever capacity possible. This means that if you're desperate enough, you'll make major changes to starve the man of sin. Don't let him get an opportunity. Delete your contacts. Get a new phone. Move away if you must. Disconnect completely from ungodly influence. Stop lying to yourself about how capable you are of handling your addiction. Run from temptation or even the opportunity to be tempted. Get serious about this.

And then don't let your guard down.

If you think you are standing strong, be careful not to fall (1 Corinthians 10:12 NLT).

Once you start doing well, you need to realize that the man of sin is waiting for the opportunity to regain strength. When you were born again, you were freed from the penalty of sin—this is the position of justification (Romans 5:1). As a believer, you are continually freed from the power of sin—this is the process of sanctification (Philippians 1:6). But not until you receive your heavenly body will you be freed from the presence of sin—that will be the promise of glorification fulfilled (Philippians 3:20-21).

Watch for the rise of the flesh. Be aware of the situations in which you choose to place yourself, the people around whom you choose to be, and the thoughts you allow yourself to entertain. Examine relapses, and keep going. Victory over self isn't a one-time event—it's a lifestyle of vigilance.

Resist the demonic powers. Deal with the deception behind the temptation. And then weaken the man of sin by addressing the physical aspects of addiction through both prayerful and practical means. Treat the man of sin like a different person. Take from him every opportunity to fulfill his cravings. Take aggressive actions against him. He's deceitful, manipulative, pushy, and selfish. Don't give him what he wants.

Instead, take bold and aggressive steps in the Spirit.

12

THE ATTACK OF SICKNESS

The problems of sickness and disease can't be classified as a stronghold, because they aren't necessarily always the result of deception. Still, I wanted to address the problem of sickness because I know that many wonder about the potentially demonic aspects of sickness. Sickness can be demonic, but not all sickness is demonic. The attack of sickness is similar to the stronghold of addiction in that it affects the physical body. Unlike addiction, it doesn't always result from the choices we make. Sure, many of the health and dietary choices we make can cause us to be more vulnerable to sickness. But sickness can also come at random. Sickness can be a demonic attack, but it can also be of natural origin. So it's important to understand the nuances between sickness that is completely a demonic attack and sickness that comes about as a result of simply existing in the natural world.

DEMONIC ATTACK

Demons cannot physically harm born-again believers, except for in two ways. Demons can physically attack the believer with sickness, and demons can physically attack the believer by means of a demonically influenced individual. In either case, in order to physically attack a Christian, a demon must use something that physically exists in this world. Demons cannot directly touch the believer, like in the case of demonic possession. If they want to bring harm to our physical bodies, demons must use one of these two extensions—sickness or a person who is demonically influenced.

First, let's look at how demons can use sickness. Sickness is a reality of the fallen world. Though not every sickness is directly brought about by a specific sin, sickness only exists in the first place because sin has come into this world. Demons can use the existence of sickness in this world to come against a believer's physical body. Though an Old Testament example, Job's sickness illustrates how this might look.

> Satan replied to the Lord, "Skin for skin! A man will give up everything he has to save his life. But reach out and take away his health, and he will surely curse you to your face!" "All right, do with him as you please," the Lord said to Satan. "But spare his life." So Satan left the Lord's presence, and he struck Job with terrible boils from head to foot (Job 2:4-7 NLT).

We should note that though demons can use sickness against believers, a sickness is different from a demon. The Bible draws a clear distinction between the two. Demons are sentient beings, while sickness is simply a disorder of the body. Possession is when a demonic being takes up residence in your body and takes over some of your physical capacities—like a parasite. When someone is possessed, the person is said to have a demon inside. On the other hand, when someone is sick, the person is said to have a sickness. So a sickness is not the same thing as a demon.

Additionally, a demon doesn't need to possess, oppress, or enter a believer to cause sickness in a believer. Sickness is an attack that can be used against you from the outside. Sickness can be sent into the body, but this doesn't mean that the demon enters with it.

Second, let's look at how demons can use a demonically influenced person. To illustrate this, I simply need to point out the various martyrs in Scripture. Stephen was stoned. John was beheaded. Jesus was crucified. These murderous acts were carried out by people who were under the influence of demonic power. Christians are not immune to violence, unless God miraculously intervenes, as He sovereignly does in some instances.

In conclusion, if a demon wants to physically harm a Christian, it must use its influence over a demonically bound individual or use a sickness. Both of these are things which exist in the physical world. Neither being attacked by a violent demoniac nor being sick is the equivalent of being possessed.

WHAT ABOUT SLEEP PARALYSIS?

So if demonic beings can only physically harm believers indirectly through sickness and demonically influenced people, what about sleep paralysis? Many believers report similar accounts of resting in bed and then suddenly being held down or even choked by a demon—only to be released when declaring the name of Jesus. There are countless reports like these, so we can't just dismiss this shocking reality. What we can do is describe it in a way that's consistent with Scripture.

First, don't you think it's odd that if demons can physically harm or grab Spirit-filled Christians that they always seem to do so in the exact same way, over and over again? Why do they only choke the believer? Why don't they ever finish the job? Why do they seem to wait until the believer is in bed? Why wouldn't they attack the body of the believer in other ways? I mean, if demons truly had the power to directly harm the born-again believer's physical body, then why do they only seem to do so while the believer is in a half-asleep state?

Here's why: sleep paralysis is part demonic, part biological. I know that doesn't sound right but allow me to explain. I'm going to show you just how deceptive and sneaky the enemy is.

Let's first address the biological aspect. To keep you from moving while you dream, your body actually paralyzes itself every single night. You can research this fact. This isn't always completely successful, as you might know from twitching or kicking in your sleep. But this is your body's natural attempt at keeping you from disturbing yourself while you sleep—so that when you dream of running, jumping, fighting or something like that, you don't thrash about and wake yourself up. Yes, every night your body paralyzes itself while you sleep.

Sometimes, your brain thinks you're still asleep even when you're waking up. It's at this moment that you become aware while still being unable to move.

A study done by Texas A&M University explained that "Sleep paralysis is an episode where your brain tells the body that you're still in the rapid eye movement (REM) stage of sleep in which the limbs are temporarily paralyzed (to prevent physically acting out dreams), heart rate and blood pressure rise, and breathing becomes more irregular and shallow. This is the stage of sleep where your most vivid dreams occur, which can explain why some people may hallucinate during sleep paralysis."[1]

When you wake up before your body can switch out of REM sleep mode, the paralysis stays in place, and you are left consciously suffering through the terror of it. Since this is the sleep phase, you are very likely to see things around you that are not actually in the physical realm.

So the paralysis itself, along with the increased heart rate and shallow breath, are biological. This occurs simply because you've become awake and alert while your body is still in deep sleep mode.

This is when the demonic attacks begin. Remember, demons love to exaggerate their power over you, and they wait to attack until you are in a vulnerable state. When you're experiencing sleep paralysis, your mind is awake, but your body is still asleep. It's at this point that the enemy can speak lies, causing deceptive projections and sounds. It's in this terrifying moment that the enemy can cause you to see and hear demonic entities. So even though you're being "held down" by your body's own natural sleep state, the enemy can make it seem as though you're being held down by a demonic being, thus exaggerating its power. So the biological aspect is the paralysis itself, but the demonic aspect is found in the projections the enemy creates during sleep paralysis.

I know this isn't the popular explanation for sleep paralysis, but it is the biblically consistent one.

Consider this too: one of the known ways to break out of sleep paralysis is to take control of your breathing. Because breathing is both a voluntary and involuntary bodily function, when you take control of your breathing, your body receives the signal that you're awake. This is partly why the paralysis is broken the moment you are finally able to open your mouth to pray.

Then the devil laughs at us for believing it was all him. It was partly him, but only the fear part. The demons that lie to you celebrate the fact that you now believe they have more power than they actually do. Then you become worried. You think, *Oh no! The devil physically attacked me! His power is increasing over me. What door did I open? Where did I go wrong? Did God lift His protection from me?*

And then what happens? You worry. You obsess over the idea that you've become more susceptible to attack. You go looking at click-bait YouTube videos and reading fearmongering articles on how the devil has more power over you now. Because of the fear, you become more exhausted, and exhaustion is a major contributing factor to sleep paralysis. So the cycle continues. You go down deeper and deeper into the rabbit hole. This is a perfect example of how the devil *actually* does attack Christians—he uses deception.

Because of my severe anxiety, there was a season of my life when I was experiencing sleep paralysis almost every night. I found that exhaustion, eating too close to bedtime, and sleeping on my back were natural factors. I also found that fear and believing the lies of the enemy were spiritual factors. I actually overcame the demonic aspect before I was able to overcome the physical aspect. Once I realized that the enemy couldn't touch me, the demonic visuals and sounds no longer accompanied my sleep paralysis episodes. In fact, toward the end of the struggle, I would experience sleep paralysis with no fear or demonic visuals. I recall just lying in bed frozen, thinking to myself, *Well, here we go again. Time to take control of my breathing.* I didn't fight the paralysis or try to move, which actually just makes it worse. Instead, I stood calm, thanked the Lord for His protection, and slowly began to take control of my breath. Peace and faith caused the paralysis to lift. Eventually it stopped altogether, as I was no longer exhausted due to the fear of the sleep paralysis itself. So while the enemy can use sleep paralysis as an opportunity to exagerate his power, sleep paralysis is not an example of a demonic being actually being able to harm you or even touch you physically. It is a biological occurence that the enemy seizes upon with frightening visuals and sounds—projections without a punch. Your body is the Holy Spirit's temple.

NATURAL AND DEMONIC

So sickness is one of the enemy's only options for attacking the physical body of the believer. We know that sickness can be the result of demonic attack, but are there any biblical examples of sickness being of natural origin? Consider Epaphroditus.

Meanwhile, I thought I should send Epaphroditus back to you. He is a true brother, co-worker, and fellow soldier. And he was your messenger to help me in my need. I am sending him because he has been longing to see you, and he was very distressed that you heard he was ill. And he certainly was ill; in fact, he almost died. But God had mercy on him—and also on me, so that I would not have one sorrow after another (Philippians 2:25-27 NLT).

Epaphroditus didn't fully recover immediately, even though it's likely that Paul himself prayed for him. Epaphroditus actually came close to death before he was healed. Timothy likewise suffered from a natural sickness. Paul wrote to Timothy about help for his stomach problem.

Don't drink only water. You ought to drink a little wine for the sake of your stomach because you are sick so often (1 Timothy 5:23 NLT).

So in Timothy's case, there was no divine healing. Paul instead told him to use a medicinal approach. Paul didn't get on Timothy's case telling him to get rid of a demonic influence in his life; he instructed him to use a natural remedy for a sickness that was of natural origin. So obviously, the sickness was not demonic in nature.

This raises the question, "How can I know the difference between a sickness that is demonic in nature and a sickness that is of natural origin?" Discerning the difference between demonic sickness and natural sickness is as simple as addressing the sickness from both angles. Here's how to do that:

DEALING WITH DEMONIC SICKNESS

We know that demons must obey the authority of Christ in you, and if they don't obey immediately, the remedy the Scripture gives to us is prayer and fasting.

> *Howbeit this kind goeth not out but by prayer and fasting* (Matthew 17:21 KJV).

So if you suspect a sickness is demonic in nature, speak a faith-filled command against the demonic entity. No rituals, tricks, or techniques can expel the demon—it's simply the authority of Christ in you.

If the sickness remains, fast and pray. Then rebuke the demonic attack again. Now you may not like what I'm about to tell you, but that's really all there is to dealing with demonically rooted sickness. If you want to be sure, you can fast and pray a few more times, but don't allow yourself to get stuck in the frustration of believing that the enemy is winning.

Because sickness can sometimes linger even after you've rebuked the enemy, it's tempting to label that sickness as "demonic." But the sickness's ability to linger is actually evidence that it's of natural origin. Why? Because demons have to obey the authority of Christ exercised through you. That doesn't mean you need to give up on the miracle, but it does mean that you can be free of the burdensome idea that you're doing something to allow the enemy to win. Of course, if you're living in sin, that's a different story. However, if you're a faith-filled, Spirit-filled believer who is walking with God and you rebuke a demon, the demon has to obey. So whatever remains at that point cannot be demonic.

Especially when you seem to have one health issue after another, it can become frustrating. Be careful that in your vulnerable and desperate state that you don't go delving into religious and powerless methods that end up doing more harm than good. You're a child of God. A simple word against spiritual attack will do.

Again, if you're living in sin, dabbling in occult superstitions, or implementing New Agism, you're opening yourself to attack. Nevertheless, the moment you repent of sin and rebuke the enemy, that's all there is to it. At that point you're living right. If you're living right and exercising Christ's authority, then demonic attacks absolutely have to cease. If, at that point, the sickness doesn't cease, then it can't possibly be demonic. It comes back to the basics: live right, exercise authority, and then fast and pray. After you've done those things, if the sickness goes, then it was a demonic attack. On the other hand, after you've done those things, if it remains, you can conclude that the sickness is of natural origin.

How then do we deal with sickness of natural origin?

DEALING WITH NATURAL SICKNESS

So how should we go about receiving our healing, once the possibility of it being demonic has been addressed? Biblically speaking, there are a few things that can block your healing. You already know that one of those blockages can be demonic attack. The Bible also teaches that disobedience can, in some but not all cases, cause sickness.

> *For if you eat the bread or drink the cup without honoring the body of Christ, you are eating and drinking God's judgment upon yourself. That is why many of you are weak and sick and some have even died (1 Corinthians 11:29-30 NLT).*

Does this mean that every sickness is always a direct result of personal sin? By no means.

"Rabbi," his disciples asked him, "why was this man born blind? Was it because of his own sins or his parents' sins?" "It was not because of his sins or his parents' sins," Jesus answered. "This happened so the power of God could be seen in him" (John 9:2-3 NLT).

The Bible also demonstrates clearly that doubt can prevent healing. That was the case, even with people who Jesus wanted to heal:

And because of their unbelief, he couldn't do any miracles among them except to place his hands on a few sick people and heal them (Mark 6:5 NLT).

Time and time again, we see that faith plays a part in receiving healing.

And he said to her, "Daughter, your faith has made you well. Go in peace. Your suffering is over" (Mark 5:34 NLT).

And Jesus said to the man, "Stand up and go. Your faith has healed you" (Luke 17:19 NLT).

And Jesus said, "All right, receive your sight! Your faith has healed you" (Luke 18:42 NLT).

Now this of course does not mean that in every instance people aren't healed that it's because of their lack of faith. This just means that sometimes doubt is what's blocking the miracle. Those who minister healing are often accused of cruelty and accused of blaming the sick in order to save face when a healing doesn't occur. That may be true in some instances. But we also can't ignore the clear truths we see in

Scripture. So though a lack of faith isn't always the reason someone isn't healed, we at least have to consider it as a possible factor.

So, biblically speaking, demons, disobedience, and doubt can in some cases prevent someone from receiving healing. So if you're honestly looking for biblical answers, there you go. According to Scripture, those can be reasons as to why some aren't healed.

As you may know, I believe in healing. I passionately preach healing. Every time I pray for someone who is sick, I fully believe that God will heal them. But that doesn't mean healing will always happen. That's not a statement of doubt. That's the reality. We must remember that having faith for a miracle doesn't negate the sovereignty of God. We must learn to trust His timing and His will.

So always pray and believe as if the miracle will happen, and then trust God's timing no matter the result. Approach the request for the miracle with faith—approach the result with trust in God. What should you think if you have faith, you rebuke all demons, and repent of sin, but you still aren't healed? Well, all we can do is pray and believe and then trust God with the results. This isn't the answer many want to hear but it's reality. We aren't the healers. We do the possible. God does the impossible.

Why did Paul allow his friend to go to the brink of death if he was able to heal him by his own will? Why didn't he heal whatever Timothy's sickness was? There again, we see God's sovereignty as a factor. Think also of Lazarus. The people begged Jesus to heal him, but the timing wasn't right. Jesus waited until he was dead to work a miracle.

Yes, God indeed wants to heal. I wouldn't be in the healing ministry if I didn't think that miracles could result from putting faith in God's power. However, God's timing is a factor rarely considered. And even if His timing is considered, it's rarely embraced with hopefulness. These truths might not be emotionally satisfying, but they are the realities of Scripture.

I'm often approached by angry or worried Christians who are emotionally distraught and mentally conflicted about their requests not being granted. "David, I don't get it," they'll often explain. "I believed God for my healing, and I'm still sick! I have faith. I repented of sin. I rid myself of all demonic influence. What's going on? Why hasn't God done what He's supposed to do? I'm disappointed. I put my faith in His Word and it didn't work."

Such a response comes about as a result of a fundamental misunderstanding of how God works. Such a view of God treats Him like a vending machine: "If I put the right amount of faith in, then I should get the miracle I want out." In fact, many have left the faith or even the Spirit-filled movement as a result of this misunderstanding. This misunderstanding makes people feel lied to, ignored, or rejected by God. This is part of the reason why I'm so passionate about not only ministering healing but also biblical teaching around the subject.

Yes, faith in God's power can result in healing, but that doesn't mean we can control God.

So why aren't some healed? For the same reasons that people weren't healed, even in the days of Jesus and the apostles. Sometimes it's demonic. Sometimes it's disobedience. Sometimes it's doubt. Once you address and rule out those factors, you're left with God's timing and sovereignty. So does that mean we shouldn't believe for healing? By no means! Continue to believe for your healing with great hope and expectation. Trust while you wait.

> *Keep on asking, and you will receive what you ask for. Keep on seeking, and you will find. Keep on knocking, and the door will be opened to you. For everyone who asks, receives.*

Everyone who seeks, finds. And to everyone who knocks, the door will be opened (Matthew 7:7-8 NLT).

Treat every day as if it could be the day the miracle happens, and if it doesn't happen, then thank God that the miracle could come tomorrow. I'd rather go the rest of my life in a state of hopefulness. I'd rather continue to believe for the rest of my days than to give up a moment too soon. This, by the way, is one of the great hopes of Heaven, which we also must look forward to while we continue to believe for healing.

In conclusion, it's a matter of faith-filled, Bible-based deduction. Sickness can be a demonic attack, it can be of natural origin, and it can be a combination of the two. If you suspect your sickness might be a demonic attack, command the demonic power to leave and the sickness will leave with it. If the sickness doesn't leave at that point, then fast and pray. If the sickness doesn't leave at that point, then it's time to address it as if it's of natural origins. Treating it as a sickness of natural origins, you would address the potential problems of doubt and disobedience.

You could also, at the same time, seek to improve your health through earthly means, as Paul instructed Timothy. This isn't a lack of faith. And if you address the possible issues of doubt and disobedience and the sickness still doesn't leave, then trust in God's timing while continuing to believe. But don't fall into the mentally and emotionally anguishing trap of obsessing over unbiblical solutions. Yes, the Holy Spirit may instruct you with something that's very specific to your situation, but if He does, He will make it absolutely clear.

After you've done what the Bible prescribes, then it all comes down to trust and hope. Trust while you wait.

ENDNOTE

1. Texas A&M University. "Sleep paralysis: Fully awake and unable to move," *ScienceDaily*, September 19, 2016; www.sciencedaily .com/releases/2016/09/160919151320.htm; accessed December 19, 2022.

13

CHRISTIANS AND DEMON POSSESSION

In Chapter 14, we will look at the stronghold of torment. Of all the strongholds a believer can be under, torment is the one that most closely resembles demonic possession. Because of this, many believers address the stronghold of torment as if it were demonic possession. In applying the wrong diagnosis, the believer never implements the proper spiritual cure. This explains why the tormented are the ones who often get stuck in cycles. They may experience freedom for days, months, or even years at a time only to again be afflicted in the mind. Before we can focus on the proper solution, we need to have clarity on the actual problem. You need to know what torment is not. Accurate diagnosis is necessary if you want to find the proper cure. To properly diagnose the problem, we need truth.

So, in this chapter, we address the popular and powerful deception that Christians can be demon possessed. This, more than most other misconceptions about spiritual warfare, keeps believers in perpetual bondage. This fringe idea that Christians can be demon possessed isn't believed by most serious Bible teachers and Christians, but it's popular enough to be a problem in a very small sub-sect of a sub-sect of Christianity. It is for the sake of that one that I write a chapter that may not apply to the ninety-nine. Usually, it's those who are most desperate and vulnerable who fall prey to this powerful lie.

Thankfully, this doctrine is losing ground, but I write this chapter to help make sure that remains the trend. The next generation must be equipped with solid, foundational doctrines of spiritual warfare and deliverance. I do this because I love God's people and the deliverance ministry. The deliverance ministry is sacred and beautiful. We must keep it completely pure if we are to keep it truly powerful. May this chapter serve as an eye-opener to those who are bound by this powerful lie of the enemy, and may this serve as a reference to those who desire to know and propagate the truth.

We're going to look at the biblical truths that reveal that Christians cannot be demon possessed, and we're even going to address some of the most often misapplied Scriptures on this topic. We will look at the explanation for why we sometimes see Christians seeming to manifest demons. Bottom line—we're going to seek biblical truth.

And after dealing with this myth, we will then deal with the stronghold of torment in the next chapter.

TRUTH CONFRONTS

When confronted with truth, we are forced into making a decision. This is why hearing the truth is uncomfortable—especially when the truth contradicts what we've been told often, loudly, adamantly, and over long periods of time. When the truth contradicts our deeply held beliefs, we immediately become defensive. So I want you to make a commitment right now. Make a commitment that you'll believe what the Bible says over what people say. Make a commitment that you'll believe the Scripture over stories, truth over tradition. Remember that strongholds have reinforcing lies, so be careful that in your attempt to defend your own beliefs that you aren't falling for satan's subtle tactics and actually defending your bondage. To argue with God's Word is to argue against freedom. Don't argue against your deliverance.

Because of its intense nature, torment is the stronghold most often confused for demonic possession, but the enemy does not have to possess you to torment you. In the case of the born-again believer, the enemy must torment you from the outside. Many believers spend far too much time seeking exorcism for what they think is demonic possession when they should be pursuing deliverance from a stronghold, which is powerful deception.

To establish this truth, we need to explore the big question, "Can Christians be demon possessed?" We know demon possession is real. We know that unbelievers can be demon possessed. Additionally, we know Christians can be attacked, affected, influenced, and deceived by demons. But can Christians be demon possessed? Can demons literally dwell in or attach to the believer's being? Christians need deliverance, but do Christians ever need exorcism?

There are only two approaches to answering this question. One way to answer this question is to look at your experience or the experiences of others. Here's the only issue with looking to experience as the primary means of authority. Different people have different experiences that contradict one another. So some may say, "In my experience, I've found that everyone who has ever been demon possessed wasn't truly born again." And others might say, "Oh, I've seen Christians manifest!" They might even say, "As a Christian, I myself was delivered from demon possession." Now experience does count, so we mustn't discount experience entirely. The question becomes, "How do you interpret your experiences in light of the Word?" It's possible that some mistake an intense deliverance from a spiritual bondage or stronghold for deliverance from demonic possession.

So to avoid confusion, we look to a better way of answering the question of Christian demon possession: We must first look to God's

Word. Scripture holds more authority than our stories. We have to remember that the Bible is our ultimate authority. Don't get me wrong. Experiences count, and experiences can be very good, but experiences must be interpreted through the truths of Scripture. So we must first answer this question based on Scripture and then seek to explain our experiences through what the Bible clearly teaches.

There's a lot riding on the answer to this question. If Christians can be demon possessed, then Spirit-filled living alone isn't enough to keep us in freedom. If Christians can be demon possessed, then we now need a whole new set of approaches to living in liberty. This is precisely why many become angry if you even question that idea, because entire sub-cultures of Christianity have been formed on this notion.

On whatever side of the question you currently stand, be encouraged to know that your identity is found in Christ, not in what you believe about spiritual warfare doctrines.

> *But don't rejoice because evil spirits obey you; rejoice because your names are registered in heaven* (Luke 10:20 NLT).

If you believe that Christians can be demon possessed, then when you hear the truth from Scripture, your first response may be to defend what you believe, to explain your point of view based on some experience you had, to label the one who tells you the truth as someone who needs to "go deeper" or "learn more" about spiritual warfare.

I know this because that's how I used to be. You see, I used to teach that Christians can be demon possessed. I taught that along with several other unbiblical spiritual warfare doctrines. Whenever someone tried to correct me, I would arrogantly argue, "But that's because they're religious. They lack power. I have experience, they don't. They haven't cast out as many demons as me." Or I would say, "Well, the Pharisees attacked Jesus too!"

"You're keeping people in bondage."

"Spiritual warfare isn't your area of expertise."

"Maybe you need deliverance from a demon!"

Those were the attacks I used against people who wanted to help me find the truth. I had to attack the person telling me the truth, because I knew I had nothing against the truth itself. I would tell people, "Spiritual warfare isn't your area of expertise. Leave it to those who specialize in deliverance." But think about the flaw in such a response. In this kind of response, bias is revealed. In other words, I was saying, "You're only an expert if you agree with me," or, "You can't be right if you don't tell me what I've already been told." Just because we've been given information doesn't mean that information was true. Just because we've been given Scriptures that seem to back an idea doesn't mean that those Scriptures were used properly. If everyone who disagrees with us is immediately discredited as "ignorant," then how exactly would we ever receive correction if wrong?

The change came for me when I started to study the Scriptures specifically on spiritual warfare and follow the actual leading of the Holy Spirit. I was confronted and corrected. Instead of trying to hang on to unnecessary and inaccurate doctrines, I bowed to the truth of God's Word. I repented from religion and the traditions of man.

DEMONIZATION ALWAYS MEANS POSSESSION

First, we need to define what we mean by "demon possession." To be demon possessed is to be overtaken in body by a demonic being. In cases of possession, demons attach themselves to a host and torment the person. They even have control over some of the individual's physical capacities. To be demon possessed is to be claimed as a host, to have your body owned and inhabited by a demonic being. The Bible has a word to describe this state: demonization. It's used here:

> When evening had come, they brought to Him many who were demon-possessed. And He cast out the spirits with a word, and healed all who were sick (Matthew 8:16 NKJV).

In that verse in Matthew 8, the Greek word for *demon-possessed* is *daimonizomai*. *Daimonizomai* or *demonization* is never used to describe the condition of a born-again believer, and it literally means "to be possessed by a demon." You can look this up in the Strong's Interlinear New Testament under "definition." In A Greek-English Lexicon of the New Testament and Other Early Christian Literature, the definition given for *demonization* is to "be possessed by a hostile spirit." This is why nearly every translation of the Bible uses the phrase "demon possessed" when it comes to the word *demonized*. Because that's what it means. Simply put, *demonization* is always a reference to full-on possession.

Sometimes the word *demonization* is translated as "under the power of a demon." But the phrase "under the power of a demon" is simply another way of saying "demon possessed." They are synonymous. Bottom line: there's only one word for "demon possession" in the New Testament, and that one word never means anything else but full-on demonic possession, no matter how its phrased.

I've heard some clever word play that is often used in an attempt to create debate around the word's meaning. You'll often hear people say things like, "Well, the word *possessed* isn't even used in the original language; it's actually *demonized*. And demonized doesn't always mean 'possessed.'"

The problem with that reasoning is that it's just not true. The word *demonized* is the Greek equivalent for our term *demon possessed*. And there is no spectrum of being demonized, at least not in biblical terms. You are either demonized as in "possessed" or not. Demonization is possession, it's ownership. Again, the word *demonization* is always a reference to full-on possession. It never means anything else but that.

Furthermore, some cause confusion by attempting to create new phrases for possession such as "having demons," "having a spiritual spouse" (which is a New Age teaching), "being oppressed," or, "having demonic attachments." This confusion is solved by sticking with God's Word. If anyone uses any phrase to mean that someone has a demon in them or attached to them, then they are describing possession. And possession is always ownership.

You've possibly heard the phrase, "a Christian can have whatever they want." There's some truth to that, though the idea doesn't exactly make a strong case for Christian demon possession. Dear reader, a Christian can have whatever they want, but can a demon ever have what belongs to God?

A MATTER OF OWNERSHIP

So if possession is ownership, the question then becomes, "Who owns the believer?" Let's look at what the Bible says:

> The Spirit is the guarantee [the first installment, the pledge, a foretaste] of our inheritance until the redemption of God's own [purchased] possession [His believers], to the praise of His glory (Ephesians 1:14 Amplified Bible).

> But you are not like that, for you are a chosen people. You are royal priests, a holy nation, God's very own possession. As a

result, you can show others the goodness of God, for he called you out of the darkness into his wonderful light (1 Peter 2:9 NLT).

And you belong to Christ, and Christ belongs to God (1 Corinthians 3:23 NLT).

It's perfectly clear that the believer belongs to God. That's not even debated among serious Bible believers. You then have to ask yourself, "Can a believer be both owned by God and a demon at the same time?" That is, can the believer have both the Holy Spirit and a demon dwelling them? Here's what the Bible says:

But you belong to God, my dear children. You have already won a victory over those people, because the Spirit who lives in you is greater than the spirit who lives in the world (1 John 4:4 NLT).

Notice that the Scripture makes a distinction between God in you and a spirit in the world. It clearly teaches that one is in you and then clearly states that the other is not. So it's perfectly clear that a Christian cannot be owned or possessed. If someone ever says, "The Bible doesn't say outright that Christians can't have demons," we know that verse blatantly states otherwise.

If someone is truly demon possessed, their demons will manifest as they receive salvation. But after someone is born again, possession is simply off the table. Other forms of attack can still affect the believer, but possession is simply out of the question, at least according to the teachings of Scripture. Demonization is possession. Possession is ownership. And the believer is owned by God, not by a demon.

Now at this point someone might say, "Well, Christians can't be possessed but they can be oppressed." If by "oppressed" you simply mean that a Christian can be attacked or deceived, then you're right on track. That we have already seen in the Scripture. But if by "oppressed" you mean a "Christian version of demon possession," that is inaccurate.

WHAT ABOUT THE BODY?

Furthermore, the body of the believer cannot be inhabited by a demon because the body is the dwelling place of the Holy Spirit:

> Don't you realize that your body is the temple of the Holy Spirit, who lives in you and was given to you by God? You do not belong to yourself, for God bought you with a high price. So you must honor God with your body (1 Corinthians 6:19-20 NLT).

WHAT ABOUT THE SOUL?

Once it's become clear that demons can't dwell in the spirit or in the body of the believer, it seems that demons run out of spaces to hide. It's at this point that some might interject, "But man is a body, soul, and spirit. Demons may not dwell in the body, where the Holy Spirit dwells. And demons may not dwell in the spirit, but they can dwell in the soul if the believer gives them a legal right."

No doubt, if a believer lives in sin and compromise, there are profound consequences. I've already covered how open doors might affect the believer in Chapter 5.

However, aside from the fact that this idea of "soul possession" was never taught in the New Testament, consider what the implications of such a reality would be. The soul is the dwelling place of the will. Not even God will take control of the will, let alone allow a demon to take control of the will. Can demons take control over man's free will? Let's look at the demoniac in Mark 5.

> *When Jesus climbed out of the boat, a man possessed by an evil spirit came out from the tombs to meet him* (Mark 5:2 NLT).

What demon would will its captive toward freedom? Do we really imagine that this was the exercise of demonic will? The man was drawn to Jesus and approached the Lord by his own will. Clearly, the man's will was intact, so it was not his soul that was possessed.

Demons, by nature, are parasites. They look for hosts. They are rather uncomfortable outside of a physical being. This is why they begged Jesus to allow them access to a herd of pigs:

> *"Send us into those pigs," the spirits begged. "Let us enter them"* (Mark 5:12 NLT).

Demons tire when they are expelled from their physical host body:

> *When an evil spirit leaves a person, it goes into the desert, seeking rest but finding none* (Matthew 12:43 NLT).

So this notion that demons can hide in the soul is just not biblical. Demons possess bodies, not wills. Consider also the fact that every case of demonic possession in Scripture came with severe and obvious signs and symptoms. The Bible doesn't give us any examples of hidden demons or asymptomatic demoniacs. I know that some might have experiences that would seem to contradict this point, but we'll address that a bit later in this chapter.

ADDRESSING MISAPPLIED BIBLE VERSES

So far we've seen that:

+ The word *demonized* and all of its secondary phrases is always a reference to full-on demon possession.

+ The word *demonized* is never used to describe a born-again believer.

+ Christians can be attacked and deceived; but this must not be confused for possession.

+ Believers cannot be owned by a demon, because they are God's possessions.

+ The believer's spirit cannot be inhabited by demons.

+ The believer's body cannot be inhabited by demons.

+ Demons do not possess souls, only bodies.

When we hold to the truths of Scripture, the boundaries created by those truths draw us to an inescapable conclusion: Christians absolutely cannot be demon possessed, "demonized." Mark 16 shows us that the believers are the ones doing the exorcisms, not receiving them.

If someone wants you to believe that a Christian can be demon possessed, the burden of proof is on that person. The individual will have to demonstrate, with Scripture, that this is the reality. So far, we've seen that the Scripture teaches just the opposite—clearly teaching that we are God's possession. So is there any good reason to believe that a Christian can be demon possessed or demonized? Here are some common attempts at proving this unbiblical notion.

What about Judas?

There's no doubt that satan himself possessed Judas Iscariot. That's the frightening reality.

> *When Judas had eaten the bread, Satan entered into him…* (John 13:27 NLT).

If you look at what the Bible reveals about Judas, it becomes clear that Judas was not a true believer but rather a wolf among sheep. Just because Judas was a disciple of Christ doesn't mean that he was fully committed in his heart. Think of those in Matthew 7:

> *Not everyone who calls out to me, "Lord! Lord!" will enter the Kingdom of Heaven. Only those who actually do the will of my Father in heaven will enter. On judgment day many will say to me, "Lord! Lord! We prophesied in your name and cast out demons in your name and performed many miracles in your name." But I will reply, "I never knew you. Get away from me, you who break God's laws"* (Matthew 7:21-23 NLT).

In fact, several of Jesus' disciples abandoned Him when His teachings became too difficult to receive.

> *"But some of you do not believe me." (For Jesus knew from the beginning which ones didn't believe, and he knew who would betray him.) Then he said, "That is why I said that people can't come to me unless the Father gives them to me."*

At this point many of his disciples turned away and deserted him (John 6:64-66 NLT).

Whether you believe Judas was backslidden when he was possessed or you believe that he was never born again to begin with, the fact of the matter is that Judas was most certainly not a born-again believer at the time of his possession.

These people left our churches, but they never really belonged with us; otherwise they would have stayed with us. When they left, it proved that they did not belong with us (1 John 2:19 NLT).

Additionally, Jesus didn't refer to Judas as a son of God but as a son of *perdition*, which means "loss" or "destruction."

While I was with them in the world, I kept them in thy name: those that thou gavest me I have kept, and none of them is lost, but the son of perdition; that the scripture might be fulfilled (John 17:12 KJV).

Judas was an unrepentant thief who followed Jesus because of greed. This greed is what would ultimately cause Judas to betray Jesus.

Not that he cared for the poor—he was a thief, and since he was in charge of the disciples' money, he often stole some for himself (John 12:6 NLT).

Jesus knew from the beginning that Judas was not a true follower.

Then Jesus said, "I chose the twelve of you, but one is a devil" (John 6:70 NLT).

In fact, Jesus very plainly declared that Judas was not truly clean, not truly born again. Jesus made it clear that even though all of the disciples needed *some* cleaning, Judas was *entirely* unclean.

> Jesus replied, "A person who has bathed all over does not need to wash, except for the feet, to be entirely clean. And you disciples are clean, but not all of you." For Jesus knew who would betray him. That is what he meant when he said, "Not all of you are clean" (John 13:10-11 NLT).

So, no, Judas is not an example of a Christian being demon possessed.

Didn't Jesus call Peter satan?

Jesus revealed to His disciples that He would be crucified.

> From then on Jesus began to tell his disciples plainly that it was necessary for him to go to Jerusalem, and that he would suffer many terrible things at the hands of the elders, the leading priests, and the teachers of religious law. He would be killed, but on the third day he would be raised from the dead (Matthew 16:21 NLT).

Up to this point, it had been believed by many that Jesus would usher in a new era of earthly victory. When Jesus spoke plainly about what would actually happen, Peter resisted.

> But Peter took him aside and began to reprimand him for saying such things. "Heaven forbid, Lord," he said. "This will never happen to you!" (Matthew 16:22 NLT)

Peter was speaking against God's will. This is why Jesus was so harsh with him.

> *Jesus turned to Peter and said, "Get away from me, Satan! You are a dangerous trap to me. You are seeing things merely from a human point of view, not from God's."* (Matthew 16:23 NLT).

Did Jesus call Peter satan because satan had possessed him? Actually, Jesus clearly explained why he called Peter satan: *"You are seeing things merely from a human point of view, not from God's."* Jesus was correcting Peter's perspective. Unwittingly, Peter had spoken on behalf of the will of the enemy which is why Jesus referred to Peter as an adversary. This verse says nothing about possession, as it clearly did in the case of Judas.

Furthermore, and this is the conclusive piece of evidence, we never see Peter later having to go through an exorcism. This portion of Scripture is widely known to simply be about how Peter had been influenced by his worldly perspective to ultimately speak on behalf of the enem which is why Jesus referred to him as an "adversary." This is influence but most certainly not possession. Especially since we know that the Bible teaches truths that contradict the idea of a believer being demon possessed, we can dismiss the claim that Peter was demon possessed.

What about Ananias and Sapphira?

Much like with the case of Peter, the story of Ananias and Sapphira is often used as a supposed example of Christians being demon possessed. Ananias and Sapphira had sold some property, kept some of the money for themselves, but then intentionally gave the impression that they were donating the entire amount to the work of the apostles. Their sin wasn't keeping some of the money for themselves. Their sin was lying about giving the full amount.

But there was a certain man named Ananias who, with his wife, Sapphira, sold some property. He brought part of the money to the apostles, claiming it was the full amount. With his wife's consent, he kept the rest. Then Peter said, "Ananias, why have you let Satan fill your heart? You lied to the Holy Spirit, and you kept some of the money for yourself. The property was yours to sell or not sell, as you wished. And after selling it, the money was also yours to give away. How could you do a thing like this? You weren't lying to us but to God!" (Acts 5:1-4 NLT)

We don't know for sure whether or not Ananias and Sapphira were actually born-again believers. In previous chapters, we know that many were saved and filled with the Holy Spirit; but it's not known for certain whether Ananias and Sapphira were among those being saved or if they just casually affiliated with the true believers. In Acts chapter 4, there's a record about the unity of the true believers and how they shared all things. Note the phrasing in the beginning of Acts 5: *"But there was a certain man named Ananias."* The phrasing seems to be drawing a contrast between Ananias and the believers mentioned in the previous chapter. Acts 4 describes true believers selflessly sharing all things; Acts 5 describes a man and a woman who lied about their commitment to the Church. This phrasing, this contrast being drawn, seems to indicate that Ananias and Sapphira were not truly counted among the true believers.

Ananias and Sapphira were likely imposters. They could have just been people of the world who were trying to impress others with their giving or perhaps curious about what was happening with the new movement. We just don't know. I've even heard it suggested that Ananias and Sapphira selling their property and then giving money to the Church was somehow proof of their salvation. I disagree. True believers give, but not everyone who gives is a true believer. I reject the notion that you can purchase godly devotion. I reject the idea that you can purchase your salvation with a cash offering. In fact, I myself have seen worldly people give finances toward godly causes.

Nevertheless, for the sake of answering the question about whether or not they were demon possessed, we will assume for now they were born-again believers.

As a consequence of their lies, they were struck dead.

> As soon as Ananias heard these words, he fell to the floor and died. Everyone who heard about it was terrified. Then some young men got up, wrapped him in a sheet, and took him out and buried him. About three hours later his wife came in, not knowing what had happened. Peter asked her, "Was this the price you and your husband received for your land?" "Yes," she replied, "that was the price." And Peter said, "How could the two of you even think of conspiring to test the Spirit of the Lord like this? The young men who buried your husband are just outside the door, and they will carry you out, too" (Acts 5:5-9 NLT).

The word for *filled* in the text is *pléroó*, which means "to make full" or "to complete." This is not the word for *demonization*, which means to be "possessed by an evil spirit." Had this been a case of demonic possession, the word for "demonization" would have been used. Also, had satan literally entered them, the Scripture would use a flagrant description of demonic or satanic entry, as it did in the case of Judas. In this case, what's being described is satan bringing his influence to fullness through the choice that Ananias and Sapphira made to deceive.

If I say, "David filled the glass cup," you don't picture me standing in a small glass cup. You would rightfully picture me filling the glass cup with water, perhaps from a pitcher. In the same way, satan filled the hearts of Ananias and Sapphira, but this doesn't necessarily mean he filled their hearts literally with himself. So with what did satan fill their hearts? The Scripture tells us he filled their hearts with deceit "to lie." They allowed their hearts to be filled with deceit, not necessarily with satan himself. Thus, satan's work was "made full" or "completed" through their rebellious act of lying to the Holy Spirit.

The word *pléroó* is used in another Scripture, and this solidifies the point. It's the same word used in Ephesians to describe the Holy Spirit's ongoing influence in the life of the believer, as opposed to the initial infilling.

> *Don't be drunk with wine, because that will ruin your life. Instead, be filled with the Holy Spirit, singing psalms and hymns and spiritual songs among yourselves, and making music to the Lord in your hearts* (Ephesians 5:18-19 NLT).

Ephesians 5 refers to a believer who has already been filled with the Holy Spirit at salvation (Romans 8, Ephesians 1). So it speaks of the ongoing influence, not the initial infilling. In the same way, with the same word *pléroó*, we see that the story of Ananias and Sapphira speaks of satan's influence yet doesn't involve any original language that even so much as hints at possession or habitation.

Furthermore, if Ananias and Sapphira were possessed, why didn't Peter conduct an exorcism? Why weren't they given an opportunity for repentance? Why doesn't the Scripture use language that's descriptive of ownership or possession? And most importantly, why were they struck dead instead of delivered?

If Ananias and Sapphira are examples of Christian demon possession, then this doesn't bode well. That would mean that death, not deliverance, is the result of this unbiblical notion of Christian demon possession. Let's thank God that Ananias and Sapphira are most certainly not examples of this. Let's thank God that death is never God's plan for the demon-possessed person.

The fact that Ananias and Sapphira aren't even confirmed as born-again believers coupled with the fact that the original language doesn't describe ownership or possession and considered with the reality that the Scripture was describing influence in the phrase "fill your heart," we can safely conclude that Ananias and Sapphira are most certainly not examples of Christians being demon possessed.

Didn't Jesus tell us to pray for deliverance?

To be delivered simply means to be set free. We can be freed from all sorts of deceptions, bondages, and attacks. Exorcism, however, is a more specific kind of deliverance. It is specifically to be set free from demon possession. This subtle but very important distinction is what causes so much confusion. Not every time the word *deliverance* is used does it mean "exorcism." Deliverance and deliverance ministry cover far more than just exorcism.

Yes, Jesus told us to pray for deliverance, but this deliverance isn't deliverance from demon possession. Look at the verse:

> *And lead us not into temptation, but deliver us from evil: For thine is the kingdom, and the power, and the glory, for ever. Amen* (Matthew 6:13 KJV).

Here, Jesus is talking about deliverance from the evil one who tempts us. This is deliverance from temptation, not possession. Christians often need deliverance because they can be deceived and attacked. But Christians never need exorcism, because they cannot be inhabited by or possessed by demonic beings. Christians often need deliverance, never exorcism.

What about the Samarians in Acts 8?

Some point to the Samarians in Acts chapter 8 as an example of Christians undergoing exorcism. Is this really the case?

> *Philip, for example, went to the city of Samaria and told the people there about the Messiah. Crowds listened intently to Philip because they were eager to hear his message and see the miraculous signs he did. Many evil spirits were cast out, screaming as they left their victims. And many who had been paralyzed or lame were healed* (Acts 8:5-7 NLT).

Unless someone has already been exposed to a forced interpretation of Acts 8, they wouldn't see anything in this portion of Acts that could support the unbiblical idea that Christians can be demon possessed. So how is it used to support the claim?

The explanation goes something like this: "The Samarians listened intently to Philip's message, so they must have been born again. And after they were born again, they had evil spirits cast out of them. So that's an example of Christians having demons cast out of them."

However, the Bible doesn't tell us that the Samarians were all born again, just that they "listened intently" or "paid attention" to what was being said. Just because someone listens intently to what you're saying doesn't mean they believe it or will embrace it. For example, we are told to "beware" of false teachings.

> *"Why can't you understand that I'm not talking about bread? So again I say, 'Beware of the yeast of the Pharisees and Sadducees.'" Then at last they understood that he wasn't speaking about the yeast in bread, but about the deceptive teaching of the Pharisees and Sadducees* (Matthew 16:11-12 NLT).

In that portion of Scripture, the Greek word *beware* is the exact same word for the phrase "listened intently" used in Acts 8. Was Jesus telling us to embrace and commit ourselves to the false teachings of the Pharisees and Sadducees? No. He's telling us to watch out for it—to pay attention to it. This proves that "listening intently" doesn't equate to acceptance and belief.

Furthermore, even if some of the Samarians were born again, there would still be no indication that everyone present was born again. Thus, there is no reason to assume that it was the born-again Samarians who received exorcism, as opposed to those who weren't born again. So even stretched to an unstable extreme, this portion of Scripture doesn't even come close to indicating that Spirit-filled believers were having demons cast out of them.

What about the demon-possessed people in the synagogue?

So he traveled throughout the region of Galilee, preaching in the synagogues and casting out demons (Mark 1:39 NLT).

This question has a simple answer. Just because the people were in the synagogue doesn't mean that they were born again. Sadly, not everyone who steps foot in a church building or who regularly attends church is truly born again. So the demoniacs in the synagogue aren't examples of Christians being demon possessed.

Isn't this like saying Christians can't have sickness?

Isn't saying that Christians can't be demon possessed or have demons the same as saying that Christians can't be sick? No, because we see examples in the New Testament of Christians being sick. We even see instructions for how to minister healing to fellow believers:

> And the prayer of faith shall save the sick, and the Lord shall raise him up; and if he have committed sins, they shall be forgiven him (James 5:15 KJV).

In fact, there's even a gift of healing that's been given for the purpose of ministering healing to fellow believers.

> A spiritual gift is given to each of us so we can help each other. ...The same Spirit gives great faith to another, and to someone else the one Spirit gives the gift of healing (1 Corinthians 12:7,9 NLT).

By contrast, we don't see a gift of "exorcism" that's to be used on the fellow believer. Why? Because exorcism is for the unbeliever. Some might suggest that exorcism would be covered under the "gift of miracles." But clearly, we see that the Bible draws a distinction between an exorcism and a miracle, just like it draws a distinction between a healing and a miracle. Miracles and exorcisms are clearly listed separately here:

> On judgment day many will say to me, "Lord! Lord! We prophesied in your name and cast out demons in your name and performed many miracles in your name" (Matthew 7:22 NLT).

In fact, we don't even see instructions in the Scripture for casting demons out of fellow believers, nor do we see Christians being warned in any New Testament book about the dangers of possession. This is, of course, to be expected, since the Scripture clearly affirms the fact that Christians cannot be possessed (demonized).

Though it may seem obvious, it must be also noted that a sickness is not at all the same thing as a demon. Certainly, demons can use sickness. Still, one is a sentient spiritual being; the other is a disorder in the natural body. So no, saying that Christians can't have demons isn't similar to saying that Christians can't get sick.

What about the daughter of Abraham?

He saw a woman who had been crippled by an evil spirit. She had been bent double for eighteen years and was unable to stand up straight. When Jesus saw her, he called her over and said, "Dear woman, you are healed of your sickness!" Then he touched her, and instantly she could stand straight. How she praised God! (Luke 13:11-13 NLT)

The explanation here would go something like this: "The daughter of Abraham was demon possessed, which demonstrates that God's children can be demon possessed."

Two things to note. First, we don't know if this is an example of full-on demonic possession, as evidenced by the fact that Jesus didn't perform an exorcism. Jesus simply declared the woman to be healed of her sickness. He addressed the disease, not the demon. Still, what we do know is that this demonic spirit was making use of a crippling disease. That disease was the demon's weapon of choice.

Second, the woman being a daughter of Abraham simply meant that she was of Jewish descent. This occurrence took place before Christ's crucifixion, so she could not have been a Spirit-filled, born-again believer in the New Testament sense. New Testament believers are referred to as the "real children of Abraham" (see Galatians 3:7).

Didn't Paul tell the Galatians that they had been bewitched or placed under an evil spell?

Oh, foolish Galatians! Who has cast an evil spell on you? For the meaning of Jesus Christ's death was made as clear to you as if you had seen a picture of his death on the cross (Galatians 3:1 NLT).

Here's the verse again in the KJV.

O foolish Galatians, who hath bewitched you, that ye should not obey the truth, before whose eyes Jesus Christ hath been evidently set forth, crucified among you? (Galatians 3:1 KJV)

Our word *bewitched* comes from the Greek word *baskainó*, which means "to slander" or "to fascinate" as in "deceive."

Here, Paul is simply referring to the fact that the Galatians had believed another gospel—a gospel of legalism. They were being told that circumcision was necessary for salvation. Legalism and witchcraft work hand in hand. So Paul is not saying that the Galatians have demons in them. He's simply correcting them for having been deceived. Notice that he doesn't instruct them to undergo some process of protocols or an exorcism. He doesn't even mention demonic attack. What's the solution that Paul gave to them having been "bewitched"? He simply tells them to believe the truth, to stop believing the false teaching.

I am trusting the Lord to keep you from believing false teachings. God will judge that person, whoever he is, who has been confusing you (Galatians 5:10 NLT).

So this *"evil spell"* Paul is referring to isn't demonic possession, it's deception. And that is consistent with everything we've been going over in this book.

What about sozo?

Doesn't the Greek word *sozo* mean to "save, heal, and deliver"? And doesn't this mean that our salvation comes with deliverance and healing too?

Sozo can, in fact, mean saved, healed, or delivered, depending upon the context in which it is used. But remember, "deliverance" doesn't always mean "exorcism." God delivers Christians from whatever can bind them. Since Christians can't be possessed, possession is never something from which the believer needs to be freed.

Isn't deliverance the children's bread?

The most common response I hear when someone is confronted with the reality that Christians can't be demon possessed is the phrase, "Deliverance is the children's bread." Many fall back on this phrase because they've heard it repeated so often. Of course, Christians can be delivered from demonic deception and attack. Of course, God's power is available to the born-again Christian for freedom from spiritual bondage. However, most would probably be surprised to know that this phrase isn't anywhere to be found in Scripture.

Here's the often misapplied text:

> *Right away a woman who had heard about him came and fell at his feet. Her little girl was possessed by an evil spirit, and she begged him to cast out the demon from her daughter. Since she was a Gentile, born in Syrian Phoenicia, Jesus told*

her, "First I should feed the children—my own family, the Jews. It isn't right to take food from the children and throw it to the dogs" (Mark 7:25-27 NLT).

The explanation goes something like this: "This Gentile woman brought her demon-possessed daughter to Jesus. When she asked Jesus for an exorcism on behalf of her daughter, Jesus told her that He must first feed God's children. So, Jesus must be saying that exorcism is first for God's children. Therefore, if God's children need exorcism then God's children can be demonized. Deliverance is the children's bread."

Aside from the fact that deliverance doesn't always mean exorcism, there are a few things to note here.

First, this story is about much more than just exorcism. It's about Jesus' ministry work as a whole. Jesus is simply explaining to the Canaanite woman that His ministry was first for the Jew, that it wasn't yet His time to minister to the Gentiles.

Second, Jesus Himself is the *"bread"* referred to in this passage.

I am the living bread that came down from heaven. Anyone who eats this bread will live forever; and this bread, which I will offer so the world may live, is my flesh (John 6:51 NLT).

Deliverance isn't the children's bread, Jesus is. Jesus doesn't give deliverance, He is deliverance. When you get Jesus, you receive deliverance in whatever form you need it. And since the believer cannot be demonized, deliverance for us never takes the form of exorcism. Christians only need to be set free from what can actually affect them. Demonic possession cannot affect them.

Still, one might insist, "But this is a story specifically about exorcism!" However, if we're insisting on being specific with how we interpret this portion of Scripture, then we'd have to be specific about what Jesus meant when He referenced children. When Jesus refers to the children, He is specifically speaking of the nation of Israel, not born-again believers.

We can't have it both ways. Either we are specific or general in the interpretation and application of this portion of Scripture. If we are being general with our interpretation, then we must conclude that this is about more than just exorcism—it's about Jesus' broader ministry being available to first Jew then Gentile. If we are being specific with our interpretation, then we must conclude that the term "children" is a specific reference of the nation of Israel, not New Testament believers. In either case, from both angles of interpretation, it's clear that Jesus is not saying that New Testament believers can be demon possessed. Not even close.

The text is not a pretzel; it's not meant to be shaped and twisted to our desired outcome. We have to take it for what it means, not for what we want it to mean. Of all the Bible verses used in an attempt to prove the unbiblical notion of Christian demon possession, I find this the least convincing, so I'm surprised it's used so often in this manner. This was simply about Jesus' ministry assignment to Israel first and the inclusion of the Gentiles. This isn't about "saved or unsaved" but about "Jew and Gentile." This isn't even remotely about Christians and demon possession. Again, I'm surprised it's used in that context, but I had to include it since it is so often referenced in this conversation.

SPOTTING MISUSED SCRIPTURES

Whenever you see a Bible verse that warns Christians of the enemy or you see the enemy attacking or affecting a believer in Scripture, it's never a reference to demon possession. Careful study of the Scriptures will always reveal this fact. There may be misconceptions that I haven't covered in this section, but rest assured, any verse that anyone presents to you as a supposed example of Christian demon possession will never turn out to be an actual example of Christian demon possession. Study the Word.

There are still many examples we could go over: Paul being "bound" to go to Jerusalem; James and John being of a different "spirit" when wanting to call down fire on their enemies; the fowls or the "evil one" snatching up the seeds of the word in the parable of the sower; and on and on. There is no shortage of passages that can be warped in an attempt to make them fit the desired belief. Nevertheless, in every single case, if you will commit yourself to study without clinging to preconceived notions, the clear teachings of Scripture will always prevail.

Thoroughly going over every single misapplied Bible verse on the subject of Christians and demon possession would require a book unto itself. I've already covered the most popular misapplied texts. So at this point, it's best that I just give you two common habits that often cause believers to come to faulty conclusions and inaccurate Bible interpretations on this subject.

#1 - Misunderstanding Key Words and Phrases

We often misunderstand the meaning of key words and phrases. For example, preconceived notions can tempt us to force certain meanings upon phrases like "fill your heart" and "Get thee behind me, satan." Or we might insist the word *deliverance* always means "exorcism." This is why we must study the actual meaning, the context, and the application of these words and phrases and then compare them to the backdrop of Scripture as a whole. No single ambiguous verse should be used to contradict the overall very clear teachings of Scripture. No preconceived idea should be forced on biblical texts.

#2 - Confusing Influence for Possession

Whenever a warning is given to believers about their spiritual enemy, those who believe that Christians can be demon possessed will jump on the opportunity to claim that this validates their belief. But just because Scripture warns of the enemy's ability to attack, deceive, destroy, and tempt doesn't mean that it's always talking about full-on demon possession. It's possible for Christians to be attacked and influenced but never owned or possessed by a demon. Don't confuse influence or attack for possession.

SCRIPTURE OVER STORIES

Realizing that the Bible teaches Christians can't be demonized (possessed) can be very confusing for some. Because of what I had been previously taught, I personally found it to be quite intellectually and emotionally jarring. However, the truth is not to be blamed for the confusion. The cause of confusion is the clinging to the belief that Christians can be demon possessed even though that belief conflicts with the clear teachings of Scripture. Once you let that idea go, and this can be rather difficult to do, the pieces fall into place, and you're left with clear, simple, applicable truths that can be used to experience both progressive and instant freedom. This is where you have to be fully committed to choosing to believe the Bible over man-made teachings.

For many, however, the doctrinal discussion isn't really the issue. No, the real challenge comes for those who have witnessed professing Christians manifest demons. What to do with these stories and experiences? We can't just pretend we didn't hear these testimonies. Every time I teach on this subject, a small handful of believers will sincerely and kindly press me with responses such as these:

+ "I was a born-again Christian for almost ten years when I manifested a demon. What does this mean?"

+ "I saw our worship leader get delivered, and demons spoke through him!"

+ "Demons can enter Christians. I've seen it multiple times. They enter when they gain a legal right."

+ "My pastor's wife, who didn't even believe in modern-day demon possession, manifested a demon and got delivered."

+ "For years, my grandfather had angry, intrusive thoughts every time he heard someone preach. He was definitely a Christian but manifested a demon. Then he went through an exorcism, and now he is free!"

It's inevitable that every time I share the truth about Christians and demon possession that someone passionately shares a story that seems to contradict that truth.

So where do we go from there? How do we explain this? What should we do with our experiences? What about those Christians who manifest as if they're demon possessed? What about the testimonies we hear from Christians who think they had demons expelled from them? The key is not in rejecting these experiences but in biblically understanding these experiences for what they actually are. Is this possible? I'll give you a few biblically consistent explanations. No single one of these explanations applies to every case, but at least one of them is bound to apply to any case.

#1 - The believer might be confusing deliverance for exorcism.

Have you ever been so angry that your body began to shake? Have you ever been so scared that you could hardly stand? Have you ever been so frustrated that you let out a grunt or an annoyed yell? Our emotions can be quite powerful. Our emotions can cause incredibly intense responses. Also, our emotions can coincide with genuine spiritual encounters.

- The prophet Isaiah cried out when he saw the Lord (Isaiah 6:5).

- Peter became excited with wonder at the Lord's transfiguration (Matthew 17:4).

- The guards had a physical reaction and fell to the ground (Matthew 28:4).

- The shepherds were terrified of the angels (Luke 2:9).

In Scripture, there are many examples of human reactions to supernatural encounters. Even in very real, very powerful, very holy encounters with God we are still very human. Every part of us was created to respond to God—this includes the emotions. Encounters with God's power can most certainly cause emotional responses in us. Just because we respond emotionally to God's touch doesn't mean that the encounter was fake. You can have very real emotions in response to a very real encounter with God. Emotions aren't bad. They are part of the human response. When a believer is being set free from a stronghold, in many cases, they are being released from years and years of deception. In a breakthrough moment, one can be overcome with emotion. Again, this emotion doesn't mean that the encounter was fake.

Believers may tremble, sob, and even cry very loudly when being set free or having an encounter in God's glory. Deliverance can be very emotional, and that's to be expected. Deliverance can even induce physical responses. I can recall at least two instances where I sobbed and shook on the floor as God released me from a bondage or a deceptive way of thinking. When people are being touched by God's power, they may shake and cry.

But intense reactions to deliverance mustn't be confused for manifesting demons as in exorcism. It's one thing to be set free from a stronghold during an intense deliverance. It's another thing to be set free from demon possession, which means that the demon inhabited you or attached itself to you so that it was able to speak through you, scream through you, or control your physical movements.

Christians can have liberating, powerfully emotional encounters with God, but we need to make sure that we understand that this is not the same thing as exorcism. When we mistake these reactions for demonic manifestation, that's when confusion sets in. A highly emotional deliverance can very easily be confused for an exorcism from demonic possession.

That believers confuse intense deliverance for exorcism is one explanation as to why some believe that they were simultaneously born again and possessed.

So what about when a demon seems to be speaking through a Christian or controlling their body? Like in the instances where they're growling and so forth? To answer those questions, we look to explanation number two.

#2 – The believer could be responding to the programming they received from erroneous teachings or reacting in a way they think is necessary to be free.

I've heard from many believers who confessed to having been caught up in the emotion of a moment and exhibiting behavior that made it appear as if they were manifesting a demon. Only later do they realize that the programming of erroneous teachings had contributed to their outbursts. That's a difficult thing to admit to one's self, but this does happen.

This doesn't mean they weren't having a spiritual experience or a genuine encounter with God at the time. This just means that their response to that spiritual experience was of the flesh.

Caught up in the hype and emotion of a moment, programmed by inaccurate teachings, some are so desperate to be free from their bondage that they'll go along with whatever they think will work. This doesn't mean they're being intentionally deceptive. But they may watch others thrash around and think to themselves, even if just subconsciously, *Maybe that's what I have to do to be free.* It also doesn't help when ministers use manipulative language like, "Sometimes you have to choose between your dignity or your deliverance." That sort of talk just preys upon the desperate in an attempt to get a reaction and pressures people into certain behaviors.

You can see the difference between authentic demonic manifestation and theatrics. Sometimes, you can see that the individual is just very emotional, desperate for freedom, and attempting their best impression of what they think a demon might do. When being interrogated, you can see them pause to try to think of what a demon might say. This is why real demonic manifestation will raise your hairs, while fake demonic manifestations just look like bad acting in a high school play.

I have spoken to many believers who admitted to me that they acted out a demonic manifestation because they thought that's what was required of them in order to be free. They weren't necessarily being deceptive, but they were going along with what they thought would bring freedom. Furthermore, most of these believers weren't even aware of what they were doing at the time. It's not until they learn the Word, mature in the Spirit, and come to know truth that they're able to look back on those moments and realize what was happening to them. Again, this is not easy to admit. But if someone is truly a born-again believer, this is a legitimate explanation as to why they seemed to manifest a demon. The alternative would contradict the clear teachings of Scripture.

This doesn't apply to every case, but this does happen.

#3 – The believer could have a mental illness that's causing what looks like demonic manifestation.

Yes, there are spiritual aspects of mental illness. But those who struggle mentally are among the most severely abused and negatively affected by unbiblical approaches to deliverance for the believer. This is also why we have to pray fervently for those who suffer with mental illness and are exposed to erroneous teachings about spiritual warfare. Many are left with severely worsened mental health problems.

Personally, I know that my anxiety was so bad at one point that I could begin feeling the symptoms of a heart attack by just thinking about heart failure. I would have physiological responses to thoughts and suggestions. My body would literally begin to feel what I feared.

Think of those with Obsessive-Compulsive Disorder (OCD), anxiety, or other mental illnesses. Sit them in a room filled with people who all believe that Christians can be demonized, tell them exorcism is their only hope at freedom, and then have them listen to inaccurate Bible teachings. Let them hear hours of teachings that tell them things like, "You can have a demon and not know it," "Christians can be possessed," "If you feel uneasy right now, you probably have a demon," or, "If you made a sinful mistake, your demon probably reentered."

Imagine that these vulnerable individuals are sitting in a meeting where an authority figure, with a microphone in hand, comes near to them while saying something like, "Someone around me has a demon. I can feel it!" Think of how all the suggestions made might incite a reaction. "You'll feel the demon in your throat." "You might feel your heart racing." "You'll likely feel like throwing up." Of course, these individuals will feel physiological responses to adamantly repeated suggestions. Especially if they somehow tie these suggestions in with Scripture, the reactions will be almost unavoidable. We often confuse things like Post-Traumatic Stress Disorder (PTSD) in born-again believers for demonic possession.

Take someone with intrusive thoughts and tell them their thoughts are a result of demonic possession. Walk close by someone with OCD while saying, "I can sense a dark spirit around you." Or pack a room filled with people who all insist that most Christians have demons hidden in them, and then put someone who struggles with mental illness in their midst. What do you think will happen? What will these people begin to feel? How might some of them react?

Then these desperate people are paraded in front of others and used as examples of Christians who were supposedly possessed. They feel better for a few days or even weeks; then they go right back to where they started because they never addressed the issues of strongholds or the flesh. Their cycles repeat, and their situations get worse and worse. This would also explain why some have to go through multiple deliverances. Worse still, many ministers unintentionally use pressure tactics and highly suggestive phrases that bring about what looks like demonic manifestation from those who are mentally ill.

I believe in and practice deliverance. I believe in and practice exorcism. Demon possession is real. Spiritual warfare is real. But Christians cannot be possessed, and believers who suffer with mental illness can have their struggles exploited, even if unintentionally, to make it seem as though they are possessed.

#4 – The individual could be acting.

This one is very, very rare. In some instances, people just pretend to be demonized. Anyone who practices deliverance will tell you that, on rare occasion, there is someone who just wants attention and fakes a demonic manifestation. Again, very rare.

#5 – The individual could be a false convert.

Here's what we know from Scripture: Christians cannot be demon possessed.

Either someone is truly born again or truly demon possessed. They can't be both, and they have to discern for themselves which it is. I tend to believe that it's more often an issue of actual Christians thinking they're possessed than actual demoniacs who think they're Christians. Most of the time, it's the case that the individual wasn't actually possessed. But in some instances, it could very well be that the person was a false convert who was actually demonized.

Some might say that it's arrogant of me to question someone's salvation. Honestly, that's not what I'm doing because that's not my place. All I can do is present biblical truths. I'm not saying whether they're saved or not. All I am saying is that the Bible is clear on the fact that someone cannot be both "saved" and "demonized." Which one they actually are is between them and God.

> *Therefore if any man be in Christ, he is a new creature: old things are passed away; behold, all things are become new* (2 Corinthians 5:17 KJV).

That term *"old things"* refers to everything about the former spiritual state.

> *Who hath delivered us from the power of darkness, and hath translated us into the kingdom of his dear Son* (Colossians 1:13 KJV).

We are no longer part of, attached to, inhabited by, possessed by, or related to the kingdom of darkness in any way. "Demon-possessed Christian" is a contradiction in terms, like "square circle" or "married bachelor."

FIVE EXPLANATIONS

We have five possible explanations for what some believe to be accounts of Christians being demonized, and none of these explanations go against biblical orthodoxy. All five of these explanations account for and offer clarification on supposed cases of Christian demon possession. So if we have five explanations that account for these experiences and that adhere to Scripture, why on earth would we reach for the one explanation that contradicts Scripture? Having five biblically consistent ways to see the situation, there's no need to cling to the interpretation that an actual Christian can be demonized. Of all the explanations that are possible, why we would ever reach for the one explanation that contradicts Scripture is troubling to me.

This stubborn clinging to that belief demonstrates either the need to be right, the inability to conform a belief to the Bible, or a lack of reverence for the authority of God's Word. If we're not willing to see the Scripture for what it teaches, and we're not willing to apply its truths to our experiences and to correct our beliefs, then it's not Scripture we believe—it's our own preconceived ideas. We don't need to dismiss our experiences; we simply need to understand them in the light of truth. Let's not elevate our preconceived ideas over the reality of Scripture. Scripture holds more authority than our stories. Christians cannot be demon possessed.

There's a story about a psychologist who was attempting to treat a patient who believed he was dead. The psychologist tried everything he could—counseling, medication, scientific explanation. Nothing worked. Every time the psychologist attempted to persuade the patient that he was alive, the patient would find a way to reject the explanation and cling to his belief. One day, the psychologist asked the patient, "Tell me. Do dead people bleed?" The patient responded, "Of course, not. Everyone knows that dead people don't bleed." "Right. So if we make a small cut on your hand and you bleed, will you finally be convinced that you're alive?" The patient maintained, "When you cut me, I won't bleed. I'm not alive. I'm dead. I've told you this many times."

No longer tolerant of his patient's insistence, the psychologist broke his professionalism, pulled the patient's hand toward himself, and made a small cut on his hand. The patient began to bleed tiny drops. The patient looked down at the tiny cut on his hand, his eyes opened wide, his jaw dropped—he had made a realization. Seeing the surprised look on his patient's face, the psychologist was sure he had made a breakthrough. The patient looked up at the psychologist and gasped, "I was wrong. Dead people do bleed!"

I can only guide someone to truth; I can't believe the truth for them. When Christians say things like, "I used to think Christians couldn't be demon possessed until it happened to me," they're really saying, "I used to believe what the Bible teaches until I had an experience that seemed to contradict it."

So what should Christians think if they believe they were possessed and believe they underwent an actual exorcism? What should we do if a Christian undergoes what they think is an exorcism and it actually seems to bring about positive results? Remember, sometimes Christians confuse deliverance from torment and strongholds for exorcism. But if a Christian is convinced that they were fully possessed by a demon and then set free, I would agree that they were indeed set free. But set free from what? Actual demon possession? No. In the case of true believers, it's not that they were freed from demon possession; they were freed from the lie that they were possessed in the first place. The truth set them free.

However, they could have skipped the ritual that resembled an exorcism and gone right to the believing part. That's what I'm trying to get believers to do—skip the protocols and go right to believing the truth. After their experience with what they thought was an exorcism, they finally came to believe the truth—that satan no longer has them. The problem is that they arrived at that belief because of the religious protocol, not because of what the Bible says. If it was the protocol that convinced them they were free, then only a continuation of protocols will keep them believing in that freedom.

On the other hand, if they come to believe the truth simply because of what God's Word teaches, then no feeling, emotion, thought, or experience will ever again convince them that God gave them over to be possessed by a demonic being. Then they will live in the freedom of that truth, permanently.

Everyone who is faced with truth is confronted with correction. What we do with that correction will either cause us to grow or get stuck where we are. If you believe that Christians can be demonized, then it might be tempting to just dismiss what I've shown you in the Scripture. It's easy to ignore this; it's difficult to truly consider it. But if you are to reject what I'm presenting, dismiss it for the right reasons. Don't dismiss this just because it's different from what you've heard. Don't dismiss this just because you may have a story that seems to contradict it. Don't dismiss this just because another passionate teacher claims to be an expert in this area and says otherwise. Study what I've shown you. See if it isn't true. Don't study to prove a point. Let the Scriptures speak for themselves. And then don't ignore that truth. It's comfortable to just go back to business as usual, but growth can be uncomfortable.

Demons are real. Christians sometimes need deliverance. Believers should practice exorcism. But born-again Christians cannot be demonized.

WHY DOES IT MATTER?

Whenever I say that Christians don't need exorcism, many think I am saying, "Christians don't need deliverance." So what ends up happening is that Christians become defensive because they think I'm speaking against their experience when, in fact, I'm just challenging the way they describe and understand it.

Here, some might quip, "So what? Oppression, depression, regression, possession, deception, attack, or influence—it's all the same. Who cares what words we use as long as people are getting set free?"

Such a suggestion doesn't take into account that the belief that Christians can be demon-possessed is itself a bondage. That's why I'm so adamant about making sure this point is clear. It's been said, "One of satan's greatest lies is that Christians cannot be possessed." I disagree. I think that one of satan's greatest lies is that Christians can be demon possessed. That belief opens the door to perpetual torment, bondage, and confusion. That lie:

- Robs the believer of a life of victory.
- Magnifies demonic power, and minimizes the Holy Spirit's power.
- Creates a subculture of belief whose adherents must subject themselves to an endless stream of protocols, rituals, rites, incantations we call prayers, and a paranoid, hesitant approach to life.
- Forces one to believe that more than just the Holy Spirit's power is needed.
- Places the emphasis on human expertise, instead of the Holy Spirit's authority.
- Distracts from the real problems of deception and disobedience.

I've seen the torment this belief creates, and I've seen the freedom and relief that come when a believer realizes the truth and begins to choose a life of spiritual discipline rather than a constantly demanding yet discouragingly fruitless superstitious seeking. Break the cycle by breaking the power of this lie.

In all its warnings about demons, in all its instructions on spiritual warfare, nowhere, anywhere in the entire New Testament do we see any instructions for casting demons out of believers. That's not to say that we can't be attacked. However, nowhere in the New Testament do we see Christians undergoing exorcism. Nowhere in the New Testament do we see Christians having to undergo special rituals and sessions to find freedom. Now that you know the truth, you're faced with a choice. Embrace the Scripture or cling to religious ideology. The choice is yours, but I highly recommend you side with the truth of Scripture.

So much has been built on this simple but effective lie. This single belief, that demons can inhabit God's children, has led to the complication of the freedom that God has given to those who simply obey and live by faith. In getting us to believe this lie, the enemy succeeds in keeping us distracted from addressing our actual problems. The path to freedom is in the basics of the Christian life—holiness, obedience, discipline, faith, prayer, exercising authority—not in the powerless superstitions created by man or borrowed from other belief systems. Freedom comes by living in the Holy Spirit.

THEN WHO RECEIVES EXORCISM?

Many wonder, "If we don't cast demons out of Christians, then who is exorcism for?" It's for the unbeliever. The primary reason Christians hesitate to cast demons out of the unbeliever is because they misapply this portion of Scripture:

> When an evil spirit leaves a person, it goes into the desert, seeking rest but finding none. Then it says, "I will return to the person I came from." So it returns and finds its former home empty, swept, and in order. Then the spirit finds seven other spirits more evil than itself, and they all enter the person and live there. And so that person is worse off than before. That will be the experience of this evil generation (Matthew 12:43-45 NLT).

We find many useful revelations in that text from Matthew 12. We see that demons wander the earth after leaving an individual. Demons return in an attempt to reenter. Demons have wills of their own. Demons are observant. Demons communicate with one another and even call for backup. Demons can vary in their level of evil. These are all helpful insights.

To the point, this is how that portion of Scripture is misapplied: "If we cast demons out of the unbeliever and they don't get saved, we put them at risk of being seven times worse than before. Therefore, we mustn't cast demons out of the unbeliever."

The concern is well-founded, for the Bible indeed teaches that demons can return with seven others. But there are a few reasons as to why we should set the captives free, even if our theology causes us to hesitate. What does the Bible teach about casting demons out of unbelievers?

Paul expelled a demon from an unbeliever in Acts 16:

> One day as we were going down to the place of prayer, we met a slave girl who had a spirit that enabled her to tell the future. She earned a lot of money for her masters by telling fortunes. She followed Paul and the rest of us, shouting, "These men are servants of the Most High God, and they have come to tell you how to be saved." This went on day after day until Paul got so exasperated that he turned and said to the demon within her, "I command you in the name of Jesus Christ to come out of her." And instantly it left her (Acts 16:16-18 NLT).

There are four other very good reasons why we should cast demons out of unbelievers:

#1 - Deliverance is for today and essential.

If we look at the ministry model of Jesus, we see that He often taught, healed the sick, and drove out demons. Casting out demons isn't negotiable. Deliverance was as much a part of Jesus' ministry as healing and teaching.

> *That evening many demon-possessed people were brought to Jesus. He cast out the evil spirits with a simple command, and he healed all the sick* (Matthew 8:16 NLT). (See also Matthew 4:23-25 and Acts 10:38.)

The following Scripture speaks of the continuation of Jesus' deliverance ministry through those who believe His message.

> *These miraculous signs will accompany those who believe: They will cast out demons in my name, and they will speak in new languages* (Mark 16:17 NLT).

How many of the demoniacs that Jesus freed do we imagine were born-again believers? Of the thousands daily who sought Jesus before He would finish His work on the cross, how many had been born again through their faith in His sacrifice?

To deny deliverance to the unbeliever is to reject a major portion of Jesus' ministry. Since only the unbeliever can be demon possessed, we would be missing a major function of ministry if we were to deny them freedom. This is why I have written to you that one of satan's greatest lies is that Christians can be demon possessed. That lie causes Christians to treat their strongholds like possession and remain bound; that lie also distracts us from practicing exorcism for the benefit of those who truly need it—the unbelievers. What a tricky lie, indeed!

Clearly, Jesus drove demons out of the unbeliever and so should we. Deliverance is too important to leave undone for the sake of a poor application of a single Bible verse. People are in bondage. People are hurting and tormented. We can't allow a religious rule to keep us from ministering to people who need it. What could be more religious than, for the sake of tradition, turning away the captives? Jesus regularly contradicted the traditions of man. He healed on the Sabbath. Likewise, we can and should cast demons out of unbelievers, despite what modern Christian superstitions might dictate.

#2 - Tomorrow isn't promised.

None of us have the guarantee of seeing tomorrow. This goes for those who are demon-possessed too. In turning away the bound, we demonstrate our presumptuous ways.

> *Look here, you who say, "Today or tomorrow we are going to a certain town and will stay there a year. We will do business there and make a profit." How do you know what your life will be like tomorrow? Your life is like the morning fog—it's here a little while, then it's gone. What you ought to say is, "If the Lord wants us to, we will live and do this or that"* (James 4:13-15 NLT).

The Scripture declares, *"... Indeed, the 'right time' is now. Today is the day of salvation"'* (2 Corinthians 6:2 NLT). We don't know who will still remain upon the earth tomorrow, so why risk a soul? Why put off the deliverance? We must cast demons out of the unbeliever now, for now may be all they have.

#3 - Exorcism could lead to salvation.

Think of the demoniac in Mark 5. He was set free and then decided to follow Jesus.

> *As Jesus was getting into the boat, the man who had been demon possessed begged to go with him* (Mark 5:18 NLT).

And Mary Magdalene likewise committed herself to Christ after having been delivered from demon possession. The Bible mentions that she had seven demons cast out of her.

> *After Jesus rose from the dead early on Sunday morning, the first person who saw him was Mary Magdalene, the woman from whom he had cast out seven demons* (Mark 16:9 NLT).

Note that her exorcism didn't take place on that Sunday morning. She had already been delivered for quite some time, since just before she started following Jesus. Mark noted her testimony to help distinguish her from the other Mary. The point is that she followed Jesus as a result of her exorcism.

Exorcism can lead to salvation.

> *Or despisest thou the riches of his goodness and forbearance and longsuffering; not knowing that the goodness of God leadeth thee to repentance?* (Romans 2:4 KJV)

We cry slogans like, "Set the captives free! Deliverance is for today! Jesus still delivers!" Yet we turn away those in desperate need of freedom for the sake of theology. This is the burden of legalism, the powerlessness of religious thinking. Hyper-focused on a strict misapplication of Scripture, too many believers say to the demon-possessed unbeliever, "I have to leave you in bondage, for my doctrine tells me so."

Yes, the unbeliever may end up worse off if they don't repent after exorcism, but the fate of their eternal soul will be far worse if we stand by and do nothing. I wonder how many demon-possessed people would have already been freed and then born again were they not ignored. It's possible that someone's deliverance could draw them to salvation.

This may raise the question, "Then why do we need deliverance ministry at all? Why not just get everyone saved? Then we wouldn't have to cast demons out of anyone."

Such thinking fails to take into account that deliverance ministry is more than just exorcism. Additionally, many may only come to Christ after they've been set free from demonic possession. When someone experiences such liberty after having lived under the hopelessness of demonization, they more often than not commit to following Christ. It's too deep of a spiritual breakthrough to not want the Lord after having experienced it. So we should cast demons out of unbelievers, because it could be what God uses to draw them to salvation.

#4 - We don't say the same about evangelism.

The basic idea behind refusing to cast demons out of unbelievers is that we don't want to potentially make their situation worse. That's understandable. We don't want to put people in positions where their demonization will increase sevenfold. It's wise to consider if the demoniac has at least some willingness to be free. The demoniacs Jesus delivered came to Him or at least allowed themselves to be brought to Him. Still, this doesn't mean that we should never cast demons out of unbelievers, because that's who exorcism is for.

Because the people of Capernaum saw the miracles of Jesus, they were put under stricter judgment for their unbelief.

> *And you people of Capernaum, will you be honored in heaven? No, you will go down to the place of the dead. For if the miracles I did for you had been done in wicked Sodom, it would still be here today. I tell you, even Sodom will be better off on judgment day than you* (Matthew 11:23-24 NLT).

Did this stop Jesus from performing miracles? Imagine saying to the Lord, "Lord, You shouldn't do miracles, because then You could potentially bring a harsher judgment on the people who see the miracles yet still choose to not believe."

Moreover, what about those who know the truth yet reject it? Aren't they in a worse position than if they simply never knew the truth in the first place?

> *And when people escape from the wickedness of the world by knowing our Lord and Savior Jesus Christ and then get tangled up and enslaved by sin again, they are worse off than before. It would be better if they had never known the way to righteousness than to know it and then reject the command they were given to live a holy life* (2 Peter 2:20-21 NLT).

We don't withhold the gospel from unbelievers for fear that they may one day fall away from the truth and end up worse. So why would we withhold deliverance from the bound for fear that they may receive seven more demons?

Aside from the fact that only unbelievers can be demonized, those are four biblical reasons as to why we should cast demons out of unbelievers.

A MAJOR INCONSISTENCY

Even so, there is actually another major inconsistency that needs to be brought to your attention. Those who believe that Christians can be demonized also believe that we shouldn't cast demons out of unbelievers—to prevent seven more demons from entering, of course. But really think about this: If we shouldn't cast demons out of unbelievers because the demon may return with seven others, then why wouldn't the same apply to casting demons out of Christians, since they too can supposedly be demonized?

Of course, some might reply, "Well, Christians can only be re-possessed if they open a door or give the enemy legal right." But the danger would still remain. The believer, in that case, would be one or two mistakes away from being demonized sevenfold.

So it's inconsistent to believe that we should practice exorcism on supposedly demonized Christians, while also saying that we shouldn't practice exorcism on demonized unbelievers. If both can be possessed, then both of them could eventually end up "seven times worse." The same truth would have to apply to both believer and unbeliever.

Here, some might suggest that Christians are protected by the Holy Spirit so that the demon can't re-enter with seven more. But this is what I've been saying all along.

However, I don't believe that the Holy Spirit only protects us from "sevenfold" demonization. I believe He prevents demonization altogether. It's not like the Holy Spirit has a minimum amount of demons He'll allow. Imagine that, "I won't let seven more in, but I'll make an exception for just one." These are the kinds of bizarre contradictions that arise when you just can't let go of this unbiblical notion of Christian demonization.

So either the Holy Spirit protects the believer from demon possession or not. Either exorcism is for the unbeliever, or it isn't for anyone.

Finally, if one is so concerned that a demon may return to an unbeliever after exorcism, they need only to command the demon to never return.

> *When Jesus saw that the crowd of onlookers was growing, he rebuked the evil spirit. "Listen, you spirit that makes this boy unable to hear and speak," he said. "I command you to come out of this child and never enter him again!"* (Mark 9:25 NLT)

Even if the unbeliever were to "open a door" or give a "legal right" to the kingdom of darkness, the demon you expelled would still have to obey the order it was given to never return. Another demon may take its place, but since that demon would only be entering for the first time, it wouldn't be able to bring seven others with it.

A FINAL THOUGHT ON THIS MATTER

If you're confused now about what you believe, just know that things become clearer as you elevate God's Word. The confusion comes from the unbiblical belief and trying to hold on to that unbiblical belief even after having been confronted with the truth. Here's my advice: always side with Scripture. Religious people will be upset with you for not following their protocols and man-made beliefs. Well-meaning Christians may be upset with you for disagreeing with them. Voices of truth always upset the establishment. I don't know about you, but I don't mind shaking things up a bit.

Of course, I don't pursue controversy. I pursue truth. But sometimes on the way to truth, controversy is met. Don't look for controversy. Don't avoid it either. Just pursue truth, and accept whatever comes with it. Be bold for truth. Be different and set apart.

I too have had my share of criticism over this topic. People tell me that this truth I share is keeping people in bondage, which is ironic since Christians who believe they can be possessed are the very same who struggle most. Any believer I know who has embraced the truth has lived in complete authority over demonic beings.

The conversation is so intense because of what's at stake. Once this doctrine of Christian demon possession goes, there's a lot that leaves with it. This single belief opens up the Christian to a complicated world of extra-biblical approaches to the spiritual realm. Allow yourself to be liberated. Come into the truth. Believe in the freedom God has given to you. Don't compromise your authority with spiritually limiting beliefs. Side with Scripture. Trust the Holy Spirit's power.

14

THE STRONGHOLD OF FEAR AND TORMENT

T orment is a vicious assault of the enemy. Nightmares. Voices. The constant sense of a dark presence near you. This isn't just anxiety; it's affliction of the mind. Your sleep is disrupted. It's difficult to enjoy anything at all. Panic attacks, compulsive behavior, and always believing the worst is about to happen. Add to this the barrage of intrusive and sometimes even perverted or blasphemous thoughts. Angry words, curse words, perverse words flash through your mind.

Perhaps you even catch yourself in horrific day dreams—visions of loved ones being harmed, of loss, of pain, of injury, of violence, of disturbing images. Twisted, perverse sexual thoughts may dominate your mind—even sometimes possibly culminating in sexualized dreams.

Demonic manifestations may occur around you, things like objects being moved. In severe cases, you may even see demonic beings, wicked faces, shadowy figures, or hear these beings clamoring around the room—you may even hear their steps.

I've heard of believers who would suddenly begin thinking hateful and blasphemous thoughts during any church meeting or worship service. I've known of Christian leaders who would hear voices.

These are all accounts of one thing: torment. Torment comes in many different forms, but the root is always fear. Torment can be as simple as anxiousness and as intense as hallucinations. But it's all fear.

Torment can last for days, weeks, or even years. I've spoken with and prayed for some believers who even dealt with this stronghold for decades, not knowing how to be free. This stronghold is the one most often confused for demonic possession, because the symptoms are so similar.

Torment of the mind can be debilitating. It can affect everything about you—your work, your relationships, your involvement in ministry, your physical health, and worst of all, your spiritual life. You may have come to the point where you've tried everything. You may be at the point where you find it difficult to enjoy anything at all in life. This, sadly, leads to isolation and that isolation worsens the problem. It's also the tragic reality that torment of the mind can cause such hopelessness in people that they may even consider suicide.

Torment of the mind is perhaps one of the most vicious strongholds, because it comes with an ugly sense of despair and darkness. As difficult as it may be to believe, you must know you can be free.

Dear reader, by the time you've reached this chapter, you already know that Christians can't be demon possessed. What you're dealing with is a spiritual attack from the outside, though it may not feel like it because you are most certainly affected (but not inhabited) on the inside. So how do we overcome the stronghold of torment?

Scripture reveals that Paul the apostle was tormented by a messenger of satan:

> *If I wanted to boast, I would be no fool in doing so, because I would be telling the truth. But I won't do it, because I don't want anyone to give me credit beyond what they can*

see in my life or hear in my message, even though I have received such wonderful revelations from God. So to keep me from becoming proud, I was given a thorn in my flesh, a messenger from Satan to torment me and keep me from becoming proud. Three different times I begged the Lord to take it away. Each time he said, "My grace is all you need. My power works best in weakness." So now I am glad to boast about my weaknesses, so that the power of Christ can work through me. That's why I take pleasure in my weaknesses, and in the insults, hardships, persecutions, and troubles that I suffer for Christ. For when I am weak, then I am strong (2 Corinthians 12:6-10 NLT).

Paul uses the phrase *"a messenger of Satan."* So we know that he was being harassed by a demonic being. The demon was allowed to *"torment"* him. This demonic being could have used human persecutors to harass Paul, or it could have done the harassing itself. In either case, it was limited to "torment." This spirit was referred to as a messenger because of the nature of its attacks—it spoke, it communicated.

This being is described as a *"thorn in the flesh."* In the original language, the word "thorn" is describing a pointed object. The definition is "stake" or "thorn." We know that Paul didn't literally have a stake piercing his physical body. So if someone wants to believe that Paul was speaking of his literal "flesh," then they also have to commit themselves to the belief that he was speaking of a literal wooden stake, which is silly. Simply put, the figurative language of *"thorn in the flesh"* was used to describe the literal reality of a *"messenger of Satan."* The phrase *"thorn in the flesh"* is the analogy, and the *"messenger of Satan"* is the subject of the analogy. Thus, Paul was not saying the messenger was in his physical body. This is further evidenced by the fact that God did not remove this thorn, despite Paul's pleadings.

Based on Paul's written testimony, we know it's possible to be tormented by a demonic attack, even while not being possessed. We also know that it's possible for the enemy to attack with torment, even if you're a believer.

What's the solution given? *"My grace is all you need"* (2 Corinthians 12:9 NLT). This grace is the empowering presence of the Holy Spirit. How then do we cooperate with His work?

REMINDER

Don't forget to apply these basics in your fight against the stronghold of fear and torment:

Dealing with Deception and Open Doors

+ Put on the Armor of God (Chapter 2)
+ Rely on the Spirit of Truth (Chapter 4)
+ Close Open Doors (Chapter 5)
+ Identify Strongholds Through God's Word, the Spirit's Voice, and Sound Teachers (Chapter 6)

Dealing with the Demonic (Chapter 7)

+ Know God's Authority
+ Align with God's Authority
+ Give a Command

- Fast and Pray to Increase Faith

Dealing with the Mental and Emotional (Chapter 8)

- Honor the Basics
- Choose to Believe the Truth
- Fight Reinforcing Lies
- Renew the Mind

#1 - Don't Panic

The stronghold of torment comes with its own unique set of challenges. How can you grab hold of your thoughts when it seems like someone else is doing the thinking for you? Assuming you've already dealt with the potential demonic aspects of this stronghold, you can now move on to this first step: don't panic.

The root lie behind the stronghold of torment is simply the illusion of the enemy's power over you. The attacks are so very intense—the visuals, the sounds, the feelings. But they're all exaggerations of the enemy's power.

There's a story about a great man of faith by the name of Smith Wigglesworth. After several hours of ministering and praying for people at a revival meeting, Mr. Wigglesworth became physically exhausted and went home to sleep for a few hours. Roughly half an hour after he fell asleep, he was awakened by the sudden shaking of his bed. He could feel someone sitting at the foot of his bed. When he rolled over to see what had shaken him from his sleep, he saw a demonic being sitting there and staring at him. He cleared his eyes to make sure that he was actually seeing the demon. He was. Yet after hardly a moment's pause, Mr. Wigglesworth quipped, "Oh, it's only you." Undisturbed, he rolled back into his sleeping position and fell asleep.

> *For God has not given us a spirit of fear and timidity, but of power, love, and self-discipline* (2 Timothy 1:7 NLT).

What would most believers do in that situation? Sadly, I think most would panic. I dare say they would lose sleep in the nights that would follow. Therein lies the problem. Most Christians freak out when they're being attacked. I know demonic attacks can be tormenting, and I don't want to seem indifferent to the suffering of God's people. However, we certainly can add to the torment by the way we respond to it. In fact, many Christians who suffer with this stronghold are simply tormented by the fact that they're being tormented. They can't get over the idea that they're being attacked. They allow it to worry them and consume their thoughts.

I was ministering in Northern California and hosting a seminar on spiritual warfare and deliverance. When it came time for the question and answer segment, a lady told me, "Brother David, sometimes when I pray, I see the image of a snake." I responded, "That's not good. It sounds demonic." She continued, "I know. So what should I do about it?" I explained, "This sounds like a demonic attack of distraction. You need to rebuke it and then continue praying." She stressed, "No, but you don't understand! This happens only when I'm praying. What does it mean? What should I do? Is it a generational curse?"

"Ma'am, whatever it is, it sounds demonic, and if it's demonic, you have authority over it. You need to rebuke it and then continue to pray." She didn't like my answer one bit, so she repeated her question about four more times. She wanted me to delve into her family history, speak on the symbolism of snakes, and give her specialized prayers to be used specifically against "snake demons."

Dear reader, the same power that drives out spirits of infirmity and spirits of witchcraft and spirits of all kinds is the same power that works on "snake demons." It's simply the power of the Holy Spirit. Trying my very best to not offend her, I struck the kindest tone I could find in my voice, "Ma'am, in all honesty, the enemy is trying to distract you when you pray and it's working."

I find this to be a pattern with many of God's people. They want ultra-specific solutions for their ultra-specific problems. They stress about meanings, origins, and demon types. It's like they're getting caught up in their own Christianized version of dungeons and dragons. Some obsess because they find excitement, entertainment, and identity in demonology. Others stress because they've been taught that they need to understand the demonic power from all different angles before God's power can work. Both responses are forms of obsession. We insist on ultra-specific solutions because we don't trust the general truths of God's Word.

When believers become attacked and tormented, they worsen the problem by obsessing over it and asking self-condemning questions: "Is God angry with me? Did I commit the blasphemy of the Holy Spirit? Did Jesus reject me?" In doing this, they ignore the root of the torment and then add a few torments of their own. I've seen it too many times, and it breaks my heart:

"David, I think I'm dealing with a curse. I yawned while I was reading my Bible. Please help!"

"Pastor, please, I had a nightmare. It was so demonic. Help, I don't know what to do."

"David, I feel like everyone around me is against me. Is this a punishment from God or am I being spiritually attacked?"

I could give you literally hundreds of other examples. When I hear such things, I am overcome with righteous indignation. First, I get angry with the enemy for attacking God's people with such deception. Second, I get angry with those whose teachings just add to the confusion and fear.

Believer, when you're being attacked by the enemy, don't be ignorant of his many deceptive devices, but don't lose your peace over the mere fact that he's acting against you either. That's part of the Christian life. You're a target. Of course, the enemy is going to attack. Honestly, I'd be more concerned if he wasn't attacking me. We so often make our struggles worse by adding worry to the already heavy weight. This is partly why some can't get free. They're agitating the problem with things they thought were solutions.

They spend hours online researching spiritual warfare. They obsess over different man-made methods of freedom. Unfortunately, there's a lot of information out there that just makes the problem worse. Moving beyond the Scripture, many just reverse-engineer teaching from the occult and New Age and then slap a Christian label on it. Adding instructions not based on Scripture and placing more burdens on the already afflicted, some will have you believing that there's more criteria you have to fulfill before you can be free. Worsening the problem, some will even teach you that everything is a demon. Then your torment gets even worse, because you keep adding more things to your list of worry.

If you're going to overcome this stronghold, the first step is reacting to the torment with confidence in God. This is actually one of the keys that gave me major breakthrough with panic attacks. A panic attack is, of course, only one example of a torment, but it makes a great illustration for this point.

Here's what I learned to do: The moment I would feel a pain or dizziness or that heavy sense of dread, I would allow myself to feel it. I wouldn't ignore it. I would face it and say, "Is this the worst you can do, devil? Is this all you have?" I would pause and just let myself feel my heart racing, my hands sweat, and my head pound. In the very moment of the panic attack, I would say, "God, thank You that You are my Protector. Thank You that You love me and that You watch over me." In doing this, in not avoiding what I was feeling in the moment, I realized that even though it felt real and felt dangerous, it couldn't really hurt me.

That's the truth about torment—it's scary, but it can't harm you.

My old way of dealing with panic attacks was to try to avoid thinking about the physical sensations and to pretend it wasn't happening. In doing so, I just built up dread. However, in facing what I was feeling and choosing peace despite what I felt, I was able to overcome the power behind the attack—fear.

> *I prayed to the Lord, and he answered me. He freed me from all my fears. Those who look to him for help will be radiant with joy; no shadow of shame will darken their faces* (Psalm 34:4-5 NLT).

The fear is real; the danger is not. I know what it's like to be so convinced of the enemy's power that I can't enjoy a moment in life. I know what it's like to be so crippled by fear that getting out of bed is a battle. From mild torments like social anxiety, doomsday thinking, and uneasiness to intense torments like intrusive thoughts, voices, compulsions, and hallucinations—it's important that you don't respond with panic. By doing so, you just add another layer to the struggle.

I'm not saying we should be in denial about our issues or that we should ignore the fact that we may be struggling. Nor am I advocating for positive thinking alone. I simply mean that panic isn't the appropriate response for the believer when it comes to any kind of attack or stronghold.

At the moment of the attack or thought, that's when you need to call upon the Holy Spirit. In key moments, the Holy Spirit empowers us to face our challenges. When a sorcerer interfered with Paul's preaching of the gospel, the Holy Spirit empowered him to resist the demonic attack.

> *But Elymas, the sorcerer (as his name means in Greek), interfered and urged the governor to pay no attention to what Barnabas and Saul said. He was trying to keep the governor from believing. Saul, also known as Paul, was filled with the Holy Spirit, and he looked the sorcerer in the eye. Then he said, "You son of the devil, full of every sort of deceit and fraud, and enemy of all that is good! Will you never stop perverting the true ways of the Lord? Watch now, for the Lord has laid his hand of punishment upon you, and you will be struck blind. You will not see the sunlight for some time." Instantly mist and darkness came over the man's eyes, and he began groping around begging for someone to take his hand and lead him (Acts 13:8-11 NLT).*

That portion of Scripture reveals one of my favorite truths about the Holy Spirit. He comes through in the moments you need Him most. We know that Paul was already filled with the Holy Spirit when he was born again. So in this story, Paul wasn't receiving power, he was accessing the power he already carried. This "sudden" power is yours too. You already have the Holy Spirit living within you. Whenever you are attacked or challenged, the Holy Spirit will empower you for whatever the moment requires of you.

No matter the torment—whether it be intense or mild—your initial reaction needs to be calling upon the Holy Spirit, not panicking over what you're experiencing. This, like anything worthwhile, may take practice. Prayer, not panic, must be the believer's initial response to any tormenting thought. If you're suffering evil or enduring affliction, cry out for the Holy Spirit to rescue you.

> *Is any among you afflicted? let him pray. Is any merry? let him sing psalms* (James 5:13 KJV).

You may be hearing voices in your head, or you may have intrusive thoughts. You may be filled with anxiety or just generally anguished in the mind. Even in those intense moments, you can choose prayer over panic. By allowing your first response to be prayer instead of panic, by involving the Holy Spirit in the first few split seconds of an episode of mental torment, you take charge of the situation. Like sailing in a storm, you have to stay focused on your destination even when you're being tossed about. These torments are all shadow, no substance. Like projections on a screen, these attacks seem bigger and more tangible than they actually are. They are elaborate shows designed to distract and intimidate you. These theatrics can be persuasive if you give in to the illusion of their power.

This is where we must call upon our Helper the Holy Spirit. In doing so, you create a moment of pause so that you can catch your breath and then choose to believe the truth. This positions you to take step number two, which is to be persuaded of God's love.

#2 - Be Persuaded of His Love

Even in your suffering, you are connected with God. Perhaps one of the most emotionally agitating lies that comes with being mentally afflicted is the idea that the torment is somehow proof that God has abandoned you. Just because you suffer from a mental health issue or from an unhealthy pattern of thinking or emotional pain or demonic attack doesn't mean that you're a fake Christian or that God has tossed you by the wayside. Just because you may be afflicted with tormenting dreams or intrusive thoughts or crippling fears doesn't mean that God no longer loves you.

> And I am convinced that nothing can ever separate us from God's love. Neither death nor life, neither angels nor demons, neither our fears for today nor our worries about tomorrow— not even the powers of hell can separate us from God's love. No power in the sky above or in the earth below—indeed, nothing in all creation will ever be able to separate us from the love of God that is revealed in Christ Jesus our Lord (Romans 8:38-39 NLT).

Nothing can separate you from God's love. Neither fear nor panic attacks, neither OCD nor intrusive thoughts, neither hallucinations nor voices—not even demonic dreams and mental anguish can separate us from God's love.

God's patience has not been worn thin with you just because of your suffering. You haven't been rejected. God isn't on the verge of giving up on you. His mercies are new every morning (Lamentations 3:23). He's patient with our weaknesses and compassionate toward our plights. Grounding yourself in the reality of God's love is a major key to having the torment lifted.

Demons cannot disconnect you from God's love. Torment cannot disconnect you from God's love. To be persuaded of God's love is to be persuaded of victory and identity.

> And as we live in God, our love grows more perfect. So we will not be afraid on the day of judgment, but we can face him with confidence because we live like Jesus here in this world. Such love has no fear, because perfect love expels all fear. If we are afraid, it is for fear of punishment, and this shows

that we have not fully experienced his perfect love (1 John 4:17-18 NLT).

Those who are loved by God have nothing to fear. The God with unlimited power cares for you with an everlasting love. In the end, what have you to fear if everything for you ultimately ends in being with God?

Don't be afraid of those who want to kill your body; they cannot touch your soul. Fear only God, who can destroy both soul and body in hell (Matthew 10:28 NLT).

First of all, Jesus taught that only God could touch the soul. Only God can destroy both body and soul. In other words, only God can decide your eternity. Think of all the horrors and threats the enemy uses to torment your mind. No matter what the enemy threatens or what the natural mind worries about or what the emotions feel, the truth of God's love is liberating because God's love is the ultimate safety net. No matter what happens to you or what doesn't happen for you, you are eternally loved.

The Lord hath appeared of old unto me, saying, Yea, I have loved thee with an everlasting love: therefore with lovingkindness have I drawn thee (Jeremiah 31:3 KJV).

The threats and afflictions are projections, as tormenting as they might be. None of the attacks—thoughts, emotions, demonic voices, hallucinations, and so forth—can separate you from God's love. So even in your torment, you must choose to think about what the Holy Spirit is saying. You haven't been rejected. He didn't leave you. You can be victorious. You are loved by God. The Holy Spirit doesn't just remind us of that truth—He affirms it. He convinces, persuades, and pleads. As all the other voices scream for your attention, the Holy

Spirit's voice pierces through the noise, calling you to believe better things. He is the One who sheds the love of God abroad in your heart.

> And hope maketh not ashamed; because the love of God is shed abroad in our hearts by the Holy Ghost which is given unto us (Romans 5:5 KJV).

In God's love you find firm footing, secure identity, and boldness.

#3 - Don't Identify with the Torment

There is a big difference between acknowledging that you're being tormented and identifying with those torments. To acknowledge you're being tormented is to say, "This is happening to me, and I need help." To identify with your torment is to say, "There's something inherently wrong with me, which is why I will always attract torment." Born-again believers are new creations.

> This means that anyone who belongs to Christ has become a new person. The old life is gone; a new life has begun! (2 Corinthians 5:17 NLT)

You are not your intrusive thoughts. You are not your torments. You are not the voices, the hallucinations, or the night terrors. You are not the fears or the insecurities or the panic attacks. You are not the compulsions, the blasphemous thoughts, or the perverse ideas. You don't belong to the enemy. You are God's child.

Your mind is simply functioning under its old training, and it needs to be renewed. While you're being renewed, remember who you are. The Holy Spirit's presence in you is the affirmation of your identity.

For all who are led by the Spirit of God are children of God (Romans 8:14 NLT).

Learn to separate your identity from your struggles. Instead of saying things like, "I have a blasphemous mind," say instead, "Those are blasphemous thoughts. I can choose to reject them." This doesn't mean that you don't carry any responsibility for your decisions, mistakes, and thoughts. Certainly, God holds us all accountable for our decisions. This just means that you aren't basing your identity on your battle.

When panic sets in, think something like, "This is the anxiety passing through. I feel the panic in my body, but I can choose peace." When intrusive thoughts, whether blasphemous, perverse, or tormenting, race through your head, acknowledge this reality: "These thoughts are troubling, but I choose to reject them. God still loves me, and He will help me to reject these thoughts." When you have night after night of sleep terrors and even demonic visitation (different from possession), remember, "I belong to God. No demon can own or inhabit me. These attacks are only threats, but the enemy is limited to what he can do to me." When your insecurity and hurt cause you to assume that people think the worst of you, ask yourself, "Are they really mistreating me? Do they really dislike me? Or am I reading them through the lens of past hurts and insecurities?"

Your torment doesn't define who you are. Your diagnosis is not your identity. Refer to these attacks as "the anxiety" or "the OCD" or "the intrusive thoughts" or "the torments." This helps you to see the thought patterns from a different perspective. For example, whenever I'm tempted to overthink or imagine the worst-case scenario, I ask, "Is this realistic or is that the anxiety talking?"

I'm not giving you a script, and these aren't special prayers. See the truths and principles behind what I'm explaining to you. The point is that you have to begin to separate your struggles from your identity.

You have to begin to see the attacks, the thoughts, and the torments as intruders, as foreigners passing through—not as a core part of who you are.

See your thoughts from the perspective of the spirit realm. Who is there observing your thoughts? Really, think about this. When you have a thought that troubles you, who is the one being troubled by the thought? It's the true you, your inner spirit self.

> *So I am not the one doing wrong; it is sin living in me that does it* (Romans 7:17 NLT).

How could the thought trouble you if it came from the real you? How could you observe the thought if the thought was you? Your inner self is the true you. The outer torments are not you.

Again, I don't want you to misunderstand this point: I am not saying, nor is Paul saying, that we carry no responsibility for sin or sinful thinking. Paul is simply acknowledging that he doesn't identify with that nature—it's not the true him.

If you battle with torment, then it's likely been a battle for a while, and it's likely based on some pretty heavy realities and painful past experiences. This has probably led you to see yourself as "the tormented one" or "the one who isn't right in the head" or "the damaged and broken one." But if you can begin to see yourself from the perspective of the spirit, you would know you're redeemed. Because you're redeemed and belong to God, there's a separation between your identity and the fallen thought patterns of your former nature.

Here again the Holy Spirit helps you to be free, for the Holy Spirit's presence in your life is the distinction, and He will remind you of that distinction. See your tormenting thoughts apart from you. See them as flaming arrows against which you must guard yourself, not as components of who you are.

#4 - Worship

In moments of emotional turmoil and mental instability, worship calls your attention to look upon the glory of God. To see Jesus is to know peace.

> *You will keep in perfect peace all who trust in you, all whose thoughts are fixed on you!* (Isaiah 26:3 NLT)

Here's how the KJV phrases the same verse:

> *Thou wilt keep him in perfect peace, whose mind is stayed on thee: because he trusteth in thee* (Isaiah 26:3 KJV).

Worship captures the attention of the busied mind. It magnifies the Lord and minimizes the chaos. Worship is the tribute in which you present your awe and adoration. It's difficult to be tormented by anything when you're amazed by God.

Discipline of the thought life calls for you to choose your thoughts, but worship makes it nearly impossible to give your attention to anything else but the goodness of God. Worship is more than just the singing of a song. It's a spiritual celebration in response to revelation given by the Holy Spirit.

> *For God is Spirit, so those who worship him must worship in spirit and in truth* (John 4:24 NLT).

Worship is of both spirit and truth.

It is of truth because it requires revelation. You can sing without a revelation, dance without a revelation, and shout without a revelation. But you can't worship without a revelation. Worship is your being responding to what has been revealed of God to it. Worship is a response to something you see in His person or nature. Worship is giving God glory, as you glimpse His glory.

In this sense, it is of the Spirit. Only the Holy Spirit can reveal God to you. Therefore, only the Holy Spirit can inspire true worship within you.

In moments when you feel tormented, retreat to the inner place where there is peace and stability. Set your mind on God. Think of Him. Then worship. Soon, the noisiness of the torment will be drowned out by the high sound of praise and worship. You can worship your way out of a prison.

> So the jailer put them into the inner dungeon and clamped their feet in the stocks. Around midnight Paul and Silas were praying and singing hymns to God, and the other prisoners were listening. Suddenly, there was a massive earthquake, and the prison was shaken to its foundations. All the doors immediately flew open, and the chains of every prisoner fell off! (Acts 16:24-26 NLT)

Imprisoned for doing the right thing, persecuted for walking in God's will, Paul and Silas didn't sink into a victim mentality. Paying barely any attention at all to the chains that bound them, these servants of the Lord began to worship. They didn't fret over being where they were or panic and assume that God had abandoned them. The cold, dark surroundings of the dungeon couldn't disrupt the heavenly atmospheres within them. They were in prison, but the prison wasn't in them. They worshipped, and their worship shook the foundations of their prison.

#5 - Live Clean

Few things can rob you of peace like sin. Not all torment comes directly from sinful mistakes, but sinful mistakes can worsen your torment. Sin makes you paranoid.

> *The wicked run away when no one is chasing them, but the godly are as bold as lions* (Proverbs 28:1 NLT).

Righteousness is the key to boldness. Boldness is necessary if you wish to confront the torment from the proper posture. Torment is like a bully. It wants you to see it as big and bad and threatening. However, the moment you boldly confront torment, it begins to cower.

The believer who is caught up in sinful living has difficulty confronting torment, because he or she thinks they don't deserve to have authority over the torment or they may think that the torment has a right to remain because of their own mistakes. Sin makes you more likely to accept the torment, because you view yourself as unworthy of God's peace.

Yet again, the Holy Spirit helps us here, for He is the Spirit of holiness. He empowers the mortal body to live free from sin.

> *The Spirit of God, who raised Jesus from the dead, lives in you. And just as God raised Christ Jesus from the dead, he will give life to your mortal bodies by this same Spirit living within you* (Romans 8:11 NLT).

#6 - Fellowship with Believers

Torment isolates, and isolation torments. They make each other worse. When one is living with a tormented mind, they find it difficult to be around others—because of suspicion or self-consciousness. Feeling rejected or misunderstood, some believers dread being around others. Though it might be tempting to avoid others for fear of rejection, ridicule, or betrayal, we must commit ourselves to fellowshipping with other believers. Disconnect can be dangerous.

> *A man who isolates himself seeks his own desire; he rages against all wise judgment* (Proverbs 18:1 NKJV).

When we live disconnected from fellow believers, we lack the benefit of outside perspective. Without close friends, it's difficult to share your thoughts and therefore receive honest feedback about your thoughts. In isolation, overthinking goes unchecked, strange beliefs become solidified, and grounding becomes difficult to find. People help keep us balanced and grounded in reality.

Out of pride, some defend their isolated ways by claiming they can somehow be "contaminated" by those who are not as spiritual as they are. Out of fear of being hurt, some defend their disconnect by claiming that everyone is going to hurt them. While it may be true that others aren't as spiritual or that others may hurt you, the benefits of fellowship outweigh any cons. This isn't to say that we should spend our time being influenced by "carnal Christians" or allow others to abuse us. This does, however, mean that we need to take risks on relationships until we find true friendship. The Bible speaks highly of friendship.

> *A friend loveth at all times, and a brother is born for adversity* (Proverbs 17:17 KJV).

Here, one may run into a dilemma. Friends can help you overcome torment, but torment makes it difficult to find true friends.

At this point, I find it necessary to challenge all believers to be willing to take risks on people we deem as strange. Because of my past struggle with anxiety and depression, I've become more conscious in this area. With God's help, I attempt to be intentional about befriending those who find it difficult to connect with others. And as a result, I've found some amazing people hidden, buried, and trapped under mental struggle. In fact, I've seen people go from nearly losing their minds to grounded and joyful in a matter of months, simply from reconnecting with others. There's a reason why the Bible encourages our togetherness.

> And let us not neglect our meeting together, as some people do, but encourage one another, especially now that the day of his return is drawing near (Hebrews 10:25 NLT).

So you may be in this dilemma of trying to find godly people to call your friends. This is a difficult place to be, indeed. The truth is that in order to connect with others, you'll likely have to experience the pain of rejection and ridicule. There are many who don't understand mental torment. Their responses are not so much reflections of you, as they are of themselves. Some will harmlessly joke or make unintentionally insulting comments, while others are outright cruel. But then you'll find some who understand what you're facing or at least are willing to help you face it. Realize too that even those who love us dearly will hurt us, so have some grace and be willing to forgive mistakes. Don't toss out true friendships because of offense.

Reach out to a community of believers. Be honest about your insecurities, fears, and struggles with torment. Then be willing to suffer rejection until you find relationship. That's the only way forward, as uncomfortable as it may seem. If you're serious about being free, reconnecting with others is necessary. Make sure that these individuals with which you connect aren't feeding into your paranoia, strange doctrines, or torment.

The Holy Spirit will bring you around the right people.

Make every effort to keep yourselves united in the Spirit, binding yourselves together with peace (Ephesians 4:3 NLT).

The Holy Spirit in you will connect with the Holy Spirit in them. There may be conflict and misunderstanding in the outer shells of personality, culture, tone, or appearance. But the innermost part of who you are is united with the Holy Spirit, and that's the part of you that will be drawn to connect with other Spirit-filled people. Don't make judgments upon the exterior.

I know of believers who were polar opposites, people who did not like each other one bit, becoming best of friends because they were willing to work past their exterior differences.

#7 - Rest

Rest is not laziness. Rest is not carnal. Rest can be a demonstration of trust. Believe it or not, rest can be spiritually beneficial. Even the Lord Jesus rested.

Then Jesus said, "Let's go off by ourselves to a quiet place and rest awhile…" (Mark 6:31 NLT).

The condition of your physical being can greatly impact your mental and emotional well-being. Those who live in torment often report inconsistent sleep patterns, poor eating habits, and a lifestyle of very little exercise. Mental torment can be spiritual in nature, but it can also be worsened through a poor physical condition.

Again, you may find yourself in a dilemma. After all, how can a tormented mind rest? How can those sleep when they are frightened? How can they look forward to sleep when they have demonically influenced nightmares? How can they rest when they hear voices or can't control intrusive thoughts?

As difficult as it may seem, you're just going to have to do your best to find moments of rest. In the beginning, this will prove to be difficult. But as you put into practice the biblical keys you're being given, you'll find yourself moving closer and closer to peace. So at the start, just do what you can. Set aside electronics. Schedule a proper bedtime. Don't take on too much or too many projects or responsibilities. Take practical measures to get more rest. Don't feel guilty for resting, and don't worry about what can happen while you're resting. Trust God.

I am referring to sleep, but I am also referring to resting in the Lord's presence through prayer, worship, and reading the Word. For example, play anointed Christian music and just rest.

> And whenever the tormenting spirit from God troubled Saul, David would play the harp. Then Saul would feel better, and the tormenting spirit would go away (1 Samuel 16:23 NLT).

Resting in the Lord soothes the mind. Though Saul was tormented by a demon, he found peace when he stopped to rest and listen to anointed music.

While resting, avoid intrusive thoughts that come in a positive light. I've known of believers who disrupted their own time of rest by convincing themselves that God was sending them random messages. For example, some even have had thoughts that they mistook for the voice of the Holy Spirit saying, "Get up and pray right now, this second! Hurry!" Even seemingly positive distractions like this occur and can disrupt rest. The Holy Spirit doesn't mind you resting. The Holy Spirit doesn't pressure you like your intrusive thoughts or torments pressure you. So be aware of the fact that even positive intrusive thoughts can disrupt rest.

This is the nature of intrusive thoughts. It's not that intrusive thoughts are always negative; it's that we only focus on the negative intrusive thoughts because we are so troubled by them. So we fail to catch the seemingly positive intrusive thoughts that prevent rest.

Just relax. While you rest, stop trying to figure it all out. Stop trying to be deep. When resting, stop obsessing over every thought that rushes through your mind—whether negative or positive. Just embrace the Lord's presence.

Take care of the body, and you'll begin to make progress in the mind.

#8 - Be Selective about What You Hear and See

If you're watching or listening to what is violent, perverted, or troubling, how can you expect to have peace of mind? There will be some movies and songs that leave disturbing imprints on your mind. Turn them off. There will be bizarre spiritual warfare and deliverance teachings from well-intentioned ministers that leave you paranoid, confused, and obsessed with demonic power. Stop listening to those kinds of teachings. There will be conversations that cause ungodly thoughts. Stop having those conversations.

You'd be amazed at how the mind and emotions are impacted by the things it consumes every day. This is why vigilance is key. The intrusive thoughts, nightmares, voices, and even hallucinations gain more power and realism as we feed them with what we allow into our minds. Once you stop feeding the mental torment, it begins to weaken, though it may take time to completely vanish. Starvation is a process. Starve the carnal nature of what it uses to strengthen torment.

> *But put ye on the Lord Jesus Christ, and make not provision*
> *for the flesh, to fulfil the lusts thereof* (Romans 13:14 KJV).

Instead, allow the Holy Spirit to fill your mind with truth. This results in peace, among other things.

> *For the kingdom of God is not a matter of eating and drink-*
> *ing, but of righteousness, peace and joy in the Holy Spirit*
> (Romans 14:17 NLT).

15

THE STRONGHOLD OF ACCUSATION

Have you ever been going about your day with peace in your heart only to be mentally and emotionally deflated by the mere memory of a sin? Maybe you are constantly tormented by your many mistakes, or perhaps there is one sin you committed for which you just can't seem to forgive yourself.

Many believers are unable to enjoy their life in Christ because they are filled with shame over their past or they fear that if they begin to allow themselves to feel the joy of God's forgiveness that suddenly their past sins will return to visit them. Some can't get beyond the idea that their past will return to destroy them or that they just don't deserve to ever be completely free from what they did. Even though they've repented of their sins and asked for God's forgiveness, many still define themselves by their past or never really allow the memory of the mistake to completely fade away. While we can certainly learn from past mistakes, those who are made new in Christ aren't meant to dwell on their past mistakes. If God puts it out of His mind, so should we.

> *I, even I, am he that blotteth out thy transgressions for mine own sake, and will not remember thy sins* (Isaiah 43:25 KJV).
>
> *As far as the east is from the west, so far hath he removed our transgressions from us* (Psalm 103:12 KJV).

The Bible calls the enemy "the accuser."

> *Then I heard a loud voice shouting across the heavens, "It has come at last—salvation and power and the Kingdom of our God, and the authority of his Christ. For the accuser of our brothers and sisters has been thrown down to earth— the one who accuses them before our God day and night"* (Revelation 12:10 NLT).

Satan is the accuser, but Christ is the Advocate.

> *My dear children, I am writing this to you so that you will not sin. But if anyone does sin, we have an advocate who pleads our case before the Father. He is Jesus Christ, the one who is truly righteous* (1 John 2:1 NLT).

God is not the one who reminds you of your past sins; satan is. The fault-finding lies of the enemy are the foundational grounds upon which the stronghold of accusation is built:

+ "Your past is coming back to wreak havoc in your life."
+ "The moment you allow yourself to be at peace and begin enjoying your life in Christ— that's when it will all come down."
+ "You shouldn't enjoy the goodness of God too much, because of your past mistakes."
+ "Yes, you're forgiven, but this mistake will always be at least some part of who you are."
+ "You knew better when you sinned, so God isn't going to forgive this sin like He forgave the others."
+ "You've asked for forgiveness too many times!"

These are all accusatory lies of the enemy. The stronghold of accusation leaves the believer unable or unwilling to let go of their own mistakes. Because of this, they suffer needlessly and carry heavy emotional weights.

REMINDER

Don't forget to apply these basics in your fight against the stronghold of Accusation.

Dealing with Deception and Open Doors

- Put on the Armor of God (Chapter 2)
- Rely on the Spirit of Truth (Chapter 4)
- Close Open Doors (Chapter 5)
- Identify Strongholds Through God's Word, the Spirit's Voice, and Sound Teachers (Chapter 6)

Dealing with the Demonic (Chapter 7)

- Know God's Authority
- Align with God's Authority
- Give a Command
- Fast and Pray to Increase Faith

Dealing with the Mental and Emotional (Chapter 8)

+ Honor the Basics
+ Choose to Believe the Truth
+ Fight Reinforcing Lies
+ Renew the Mind

THE ROLE OF GUILT

Of course, some guilt is good. We should feel shame when we do shameful things, and we should feel guilt when we are guilty.

> For the kind of sorrow God wants us to experience leads us away from sin and results in salvation. There's no regret for that kind of sorrow. But worldly sorrow, which lacks repentance, results in spiritual death (2 Corinthians 7:10 NLT).

We should regret our regrettable actions. The conscience is to the mind what pain is to the body. By the conscience, which is a gift from God, we know when we have violated the standard of holiness. Guilt informs you that something is wrong. Let guilt serve its purpose—that is, allow it to reveal that you've done something truly wrong. Then repent and move on.

CONDEMNATION VERSUS CONVICTION

This is where we have to recognize the difference between condemnation and conviction. Condemnation is *not* of God. Conviction *is* of God. Condemnation tells you that you *are* a mistake. Conviction tells you that you *made* a mistake. *Condemnation pushes you away from God* in shame and fear. *Conviction draws you to God* in repentance and humility.

When we don't meet the standard of righteousness, the Holy Spirit convicts us of this reality:

> *And when he comes, he will convict the world of its sin, and of God's righteousness, and of the coming judgment* (John 16:8 NLT).

But after you've been forgiven and have dealt with the issue, you need to move on.

> *So now there is no condemnation for those who belong to Christ Jesus* (Romans 8:1 NLT).

I imagine that our conversations with God sometimes go something like this: "God, I'm sorry. Please, forgive me. I repent!" The Lord graciously replies, "I forgive you. Go and sin no more." Then we bring it up again, "Lord, really, I'm so sorry. I can't believe I did that. I really, really feel terrible. Please, forgive me!" The Lord, having chosen to forget the sin asks, "Forgive you for what?"

The believer becomes wrapped up in what I call OCC—Obsessive-Compulsive Confession. That's not a clever play on words. I'm serious. Like the germaphobe who washes his hands again and again, even though they are clean, so some Christians confess again and again, even though they're forgiven.

Either we believe the gospel or we don't. If we do believe the gospel, then we know that God's forgiveness applies to us too. And, yes, the forgiveness of God applies to even those who knew better.

SELF-PUNISHMENT

Moving on may be difficult to do because there is a sense of virtue in feeling remorse over sins that have been forgiven. Some Christians believe the lie that they're only forgiven to a certain degree and that they have to carry at least some guilt as a form of payment for their wrongdoing. Like whipping themselves on the back, many strike themselves emotionally and mentally, again and again, with the memory and the pain of their sinful past. They allow themselves to get over their past partially, but cling to the quiet belief that they don't deserve to rejoice in God's goodness.

> *Purify me from my sins, and I will be clean; wash me, and I will be whiter than snow. Oh, give me back my joy again; you have broken me—now let me rejoice* (Psalm 51:7-8 NLT).

Many Christians refuse to embrace that joy because they are still punishing themselves for sins they think they owe a debt on.

For example, many pastors never fully recover from sinful mistakes, not because God or the people haven't forgiven them—but because they haven't forgiven themselves and still see themselves as the one who "fell." They project their own shame and assume that others have a low opinion of them.

Many believers just can't quite let it go. They gain victory for a few weeks or days and then go back to fretting about the mistake. They live paranoid about the past returning. Their sins are ever on their minds. They can't enjoy God's blessing. They don't allow themselves to have it too good. They refuse to achieve, because they believe they are disqualified from achievement. They reject blessing, because they are punishing themselves for the past.

Have mercy on me, O God, because of your unfailing love. Because of your great compassion, blot out the stain of my sins. Wash me clean from my guilt. Purify me from my sin. For I recognize my rebellion; it haunts me day and night (Psalm 51:1-3 NLT).

Dear reader, if that's you, then it's time to confront the lies. God forgives sin. God forgives liars, murderers, adulterers, and the worst kinds of sins. There's no darkness that can hide His light, no distance you can go that He can't reach. No matter how far you've gone, a single moment of true repentance can bring you all the way home.

FREE, ONCE AND FOR ALL

You can begin to live your life in the joy of forgiveness. You can stop looking over your shoulder and wondering if the day of reckoning is coming. You can begin to live in the joy of the Lord, without guilt or the sense of unworthiness.

Don't keep looking at my sins. Remove the stain of my guilt. Create in me a clean heart, O God. Renew a loyal spirit within me (Psalm 51:9-10 NLT).

Oh, what joy for those whose disobedience is forgiven, whose sin is put out of sight! Yes, what joy for those whose record the Lord has cleared of guilt, whose lives are lived in complete honesty! When I refused to confess my sin, my body wasted away, and I groaned all day long. Day and night your hand of discipline was heavy on me. My strength evaporated like water in the summer heat. Finally, I confessed all my sins to you and stopped trying to hide my guilt. I said to myself, "I will confess my rebellion to the Lord." And you forgave me! All my guilt is gone (Psalm 32:1-5 NLT).

He forgives all my sins and heals all my diseases. ...He does not punish us for all our sins; he does not deal harshly with us, as we deserve (Psalm 103:3,10 NLT).

THE HOLY SPIRIT TESTIFIES

That's the joy and the beauty of the cross. Christ absorbed the wrath of God and left you with the benefits of His sinless perfection. The Holy Spirit is the One who testifies of this to you.

For by that one offering he forever made perfect those who are being made holy. And the Holy Spirit also testifies that this is so. For he says, "This is the new covenant I will make with my people on that day, says the Lord: I will put my laws in their hearts, and I will write them on their minds" (Hebrews 10:14-16 NLT).

When the enemy pressures you to look at your past, look far back enough to see the cross. When the enemy reminds you of your sinful mistakes, the Holy Spirit testifies of the one offering that made you perfect in God's sight, on God's record.

Listen to the Advocate, not the accuser. The devil is a liar, and the Holy Spirit always speaks the truth.

16

THE STRONGHOLD
OF DEPRESSION

DECEPTION BRINGS DEPRESSION

Depression can manifest itself in many forms: lingering sadness, physical fatigue, mental anguish or apathy, emotional sensitivity or numbness, cynicism and negativity, hopelessness and emptiness. Some live under the weight of depression for months at a time, years at a time, or even in waves at various points in life. In many cases, depression can leave you feeling empty, uninterested, tired, or just generally disconnected from life.

Ultimately, depression is the result of deception. The lies we believe become the weights we carry in the soul. There are many lies that can be at the heart of depression: "You are unloved and unwanted." "You have no value or purpose." "There's no hope of life getting better." "You'd be better off dead, and your loved ones would be better with you gone." "Nothing will ever work out for you." "You deserve to be mistreated." "You attract chaos and tragedy."

There are thousands of possible lies that can form the root of depression. The lies we believe become the feelings we feel and the thoughts we think. Those thoughts and feelings form mental and emotional patterns, strongholds of depression. Once you embrace the lie, it begins to affect everything about you.

Now, of course, this does not mean that if you're sad that you are deceived. Even Jesus wept.

Then Jesus wept (John 11:35 NLT).

So not everyone who experiences difficulty and heartache will develop depression, but the enemy can certainly use difficulty and heartache in an attempt to persuade you to believe what he says. All of us will experience loss, tragedy, and heartache, but how we respond to these is key. All of us will experience seasons of sadness, but the state of our spiritual lives depends upon whether or not we fall into deception during those seasons of sadness.

The difference between a moment or season of sadness and the stronghold of depression is deception. Only when we choose to believe the enemy's lies can our naturally occurring responses of sadness turn into full-blown strongholds of depression.

Of course, there are mental health aspects to some cases of chronic depression, but even those with mental health issues can live in victory if they embrace truth. Clinically speaking, you may have depression. Spiritually speaking, depression doesn't have to have you.

THE POWER OF ENDORSEMENT

Think of the power of an endorsement. If a major political figure endorses a virtually unknown up-and-comer, the unknown politician can gain enough votes to win an election. If an unknown author is endorsed by a mega-bestselling author, the author can be catapulted into success. If a famous athlete endorses a clothing brand, that clothing brand can bolster sales. An endorsement lends credibility and believability.

In the same way, the enemy will use your emotions and negative circumstances to make his lies more believable. The enemy may also use your upbringing, abuse, betrayal, tragedy, loss, disappointment, and even trauma to endorse his lies.

For example, he might say to you, "You're worthless." If you've experienced trauma, the enemy can use that trauma as evidence for the case he's building against your worth. He might say something like, "If you were really worth anything to God or to anyone, someone would have prevented that trauma from occurring."

That's just one example of how the enemy might use your emotions or negative circumstances to endorse his deceptive talking points.

Consider also that even existing thought patterns can endorse the lies of the enemy. When you face a trial or disappointment, the already existing negative mindset can cause you to think about that trial and disappointment in the worst-case scenario. Preexisting strongholds can cause you to see a bad situation as the worst situation. Strongholds of depression help to form additional strongholds of depression. This is why this stronghold can be so difficult to break.

Demonic beings and the flesh can seize upon our moments of sadness to plant the seeds of deception. They use the power of our emotions and the persuasion of negative circumstances to cause us to think in unbiblical ways. It's easier to believe you're rejected by God when you feel alone. It's easier to believe that nothing ever good happens to you when you're facing a hardship. So the tribulations of life present opportunities for depression to take root, especially if we do not respond to personal tragedy in a spiritual manner.

REMINDER

Don't forget to apply these basics in your fight against the stronghold of Depression.

Dealing with Deception and Open Doors

+ Put on the Armor of God (Chapter 2)
+ Rely on the Spirit of Truth (Chapter 4)
+ Close Open Doors (Chapter 5)
+ Identify Strongholds Through God's Word, the Spirit's Voice, and Sound Teachers (Chapter 6)

Dealing with the Demonic (Chapter 7)

+ Know God's Authority
+ Align with God's Authority
+ Give a Command
+ Fast and Pray to Increase Faith

Dealing with the Mental and Emotional (Chapter 8)

+ Honor the Basics
+ Choose to Believe the Truth
+ Fight Reinforcing Lies
+ Renew the Mind

BREAKING FREE FROM DEPRESSION

#1 - Be Prepared

People will offend and betray you. Life will throw tragedy and trials your way. We will all experience loss and disappointment. Accept the fact that God never promised us perfectly ideal circumstances on this side of eternity. Paul the apostle himself experienced both welcome and unwelcome circumstances.

> *Not that I was ever in need, for I have learned how to be content with whatever I have. I know how to live on almost nothing or with everything. I have learned the secret of living in every situation, whether it is with a full stomach or empty, with plenty or little* (Philippians 4:11-12 NLT).

If you want to prevent the stronghold of depression from being given a place, you need to determine beforehand how you will choose to perceive the negative experiences of life.

> *Dear brothers and sisters, when troubles of any kind come your way, consider it an opportunity for great joy. For you know that when your faith is tested, your endurance has a chance to grow. So let it grow, for when your endurance is fully developed, you will be perfect and complete, needing nothing* (James 1:2-4 NLT).

Before problems ever arise, make a commitment to not be swallowed up in lies such as, "This always happens to me. This will never get better. God has abandoned me."

Know the Word before the tragedy strikes, so that your foundation is in place before the storm. Before you face loss, betrayal, or any negative circumstances, prepare spiritually. Determine within yourself that you will not allow yourself to embrace the lies of the enemy about you or about God's love for you just because of life's negative occurrences. This doesn't mean you won't experience the emotions of sadness, but it does mean that you won't allow the flesh or the devil to use your trials as an opportunity to build the foundations of the stronghold of depression.

#2 - Take Care of the Body

This may not sound spiritual, but you need to take care of your body if you want to win your battle against depression. Your sleep patterns, diet, exercise routines, and overall physical health can affect how you feel. This doesn't mean that those who battle with other chronic illnesses can't overcome depression. This just means that we must do what we can to take care of the temple of the Holy Spirit.

I know that it can be frustrating when people lend you their simple-sounding, dismissive cures for depression. Overcoming depression isn't just a matter of "getting more sun" or "getting some exercise" or "getting out more" as some casually suggest. Still, we also must acknowledge that care for the physical body is a key component to winning in the war against depression.

Think of the prophet Elijah. After winning a supernatural stand-off against Jezebel's false prophets, Elijah fled away in fear for his life. Elijah was likely tired and worn out, emotionally drained from the work he was doing for the Lord. It was at this point that Jezebel threatened to kill him. What did this mighty prophet do? How did the man who called fire from Heaven respond to the threats of a wicked woman? He panicked.

Elijah was afraid and fled for his life. He went to Beersheba, a town in Judah, and he left his servant there. Then he went on alone into the wilderness, traveling all day. He sat down under a solitary broom tree and prayed that he might die. "I have had enough, Lord," he said. "Take my life, for I am no better than my ancestors who have already died." Then he lay down and slept under the broom tree. But as he was sleeping, an angel touched him and told him, "Get up and eat!" He looked around and there beside his head was some bread baked on hot stones and a jar of water! So he ate and drank and lay down again. Then the angel of the Lord came again and touched him and said, "Get up and eat some more, or the journey ahead will be too much for you." So he got up and ate and drank, and the food gave him enough strength to travel forty days and forty nights to Mount Sinai, the mountain of God (1 Kings 19:3-8 NLT).

Elijah was depressed to the point of wanting to die. He believed the lie that he was no better than his ancestors. He pitied himself. In response, God didn't suggest the prophet was demon possessed. God didn't tell Elijah to undergo an exorcism. In this specific instance, what did the prophet need? The truth, a nap, and some food. He needed rest, to take care of his own body.

#3 - Believe the Truth

I've already covered this key in Chapter 8, but I think it's necessary to show you how believing the truth looks, specifically in the fight against depression.

When the psalmist was discouraged, when his heart was filled with sadness, he decided to make a shift in his thinking.

Why am I discouraged? Why is my heart so sad? I will put my hope in God! I will praise him again—my Savior and my God! (Psalm 43:5 NLT)

Even though depression can sometimes seem only like a feeling that we can't explain or like a heaviness for which we cannot identify a source, it must be remembered that deception is, in fact, the source of depression. You may not be able to immediately identify the lie or you may not be able to point out the source, but deception is the root, even if it is hidden. Trials may cause the emotion of sadness, but only deception can form the stronghold of depression.

There may actually be several lies that you believe that might be contributing to the stronghold of depression in your life.

I showed you how to identify these lies in Chapter 6. I also wrote to you about what it means to choose to believe the truth and then renew the mind in Chapter 8. Here's the dynamic I want to revisit: resisting the reinforcing lies.

Perhaps no stronghold has more effective reinforcing lies than depression. Depression often breeds cynicism, and cynicism rejects hope. Cynicism says:

+ **"You already tried that; it won't work."**
+ **"This is too simple; your problems are more complex."**
+ **"Even if it does work, you're just going to end up depressed again."**

If you're going to effectively resist the primary lies of depression, then you need to also resist the secondary lies that distract you and discourage you from even trying. Consistently believing and walking in the truth really is the key to freedom. Don't allow any setbacks or delays to deter you from attacking the stronghold at its weak points. The only way the enemy can keep you from tearing down the stronghold is getting you to believe it can't be done.

THE JOY OF THE HOLY SPIRIT

I watched a man stand behind the podium at his own daughter's funeral and say, "Father, we celebrate Your will concerning us." The eulogy he gave was beautiful and thoughtful, but what struck me was the joy he carried while giving it. He sang. He danced. He praised God. All while standing in front of his daughter's casket. I wasn't a father at the time, but looking back to that moment now as a father, I am even more amazed by what I witnessed.

What was it that gave that man the strength to sing at his daughter's funeral? What was it that made Paul the apostle celebrate his own persecution? What did the early Church have that made them rejoice when being martyred for their faith in Christ? It was the supernatural joy of the Holy Spirit. Lest you think I'm giving you the "others have it worse" speech, let me put it to you clearly: I'm not saying that you can't be sad because others have it worse; I'm saying you can be joyful even in the very worst of times, because you have what they had.

And ye became followers of us, and of the Lord, having received the word in much affliction, with joy of the Holy Ghost (1 Thessalonians 1:6 KJV).

And the believers were filled with joy and with the Holy Spirit (Acts 13:52 NLT).

The joy of the Holy Spirit is supernatural. You've heard it said, "The world gives happiness, but the Holy Spirit gives joy." In reality, the words *happiness* and *joy* are synonymous. The difference is that the believer gets their joy from the Holy Spirit, and the unbeliever gets their joy from the things of this world. Nothing can outlast its source. The difference between worldly happiness and godly happiness is that one fades, the other does not. The source of the world's joy is temporary. The source of our joy is eternal.

We are supernatural beings, citizens of Heaven, and God's children. There may be chaos on the outside, but you have access to the joy of the Spirit on the inside. You access that joy by believing the truth, living in the truth, focusing on the truth, and insisting on the truth even when you have reason to doubt.

We are heavenly beings. We are of the light. We are of another realm. It's purely supernatural. It's the joy of the Holy Spirit. Remember who you truly are in the Holy Spirit.

17

OTHER STRONGHOLDS

All of the basic keys to freedom can apply to all of the strongholds mentioned here in this book. You might also find it helpful to apply some of the keys I gave you to overcome specific strongholds to other strongholds. All spiritual truths and biblical tactics can potentially have some impact on all strongholds.

Because you've now been equipped with the essentials of freedom, I use this chapter to briefly cover additional strongholds. I show you their symptoms, their sources, and then the solutions or truths that can be used to combat them. These are the strongholds I cover in this chapter:

- The Stronghold of Distraction
- The Stronghold of Offense
- The Stronghold of Confusion

THE STRONGHOLD OF DISTRACTION

If the enemy can't destroy you with disobedience, he'll try to delay you with distraction. The stronghold of distraction is based on the lie that the sacred or the spiritual is not as valuable or as interesting as the immediate or the secular. That's the source lie—that the things of this world will be more satisfying than the things of the heavenly realm. Believing this lie results in apathy toward things like church attendance, prayer, devotion to the Word, and worship. It causes the believer to prioritize things like money, career, and entertainment over the things of God.

What makes this stronghold especially deceptive is the fact that it doesn't remove spiritual practices from your life completely. It only minimizes them. So then the believer who prays for ten minutes a day might settle for their half-hearted commitment to prayer while using the excuse, "At least I'm doing something."

The believer who is caught up in this stronghold usually spends far too much time on their phone, browsing social media, or seeking the entertaining over the eternal. They aren't in sin, but they also aren't going deeper with the Lord.

> *Think about the things of heaven, not the things of earth* (Colossians 3:2 NLT).

When you begin to believe the lie that the immediate deserves your attention more than the eternal, or that the things of this earth are more interesting than the things of Heaven, you begin to live your life content in complacency.

The Holy Spirit counters this deception by revealing to us the deep things of God.

> *But it was to us that God revealed these things by his Spirit. For his Spirit searches out everything and shows us God's deep secrets. No one can know a person's thoughts except that person's own spirit, and no one can know God's thoughts except God's own Spirit. And we have received God's Spirit*

*(not the world's spirit), so we can know the wonderful things
God has freely given us* (1 Corinthians 2:10-12 NLT).

The Holy Spirit shows us the deeper realities of God. Knowing God
is not like studying a textbook; knowing God is like traveling through
the cosmos at light speed, like jumping into a depth from a great height,
like uncovering a rare treasure.

*Unto me, who am less than the least of all saints, is this grace
given, that I should preach among the Gentiles the unsearchable riches of Christ* (Ephesians 3:8 KJV).

I love that—*the unsearchable riches of Christ!* The Holy Spirit calls
our attention to the glorious adventure that is the pursuit of God. Time
and eternity rest in His hand. Mysteries upon mysteries are waiting to
be discovered in His nature and mind. The Source of life itself can be
known by the Holy Spirit. And we trade this for binge-watching TV
shows? We ignore this in exchange for likes and shares?

Allow the Holy Spirit to break the stronghold of distraction by
capturing your mind and heart, by illuminating the imagination, by
drawing you in to the depths of God Almighty—the colorful, vibrant,
and glorious One.

THE STRONGHOLD OF OFFENSE

The stronghold of offense leaves the Christian with a dry prayer life, a
passionless worship posture, and a mind unable to fully receive what
God speaks through His Word. You know you're under this stronghold
if you live in the memory of an offense. And that memory of the offense
makes it easier to offend you. Christians who are already offended are

the easiest to offend again. Offense gives you a sharp tongue, a moody demeanor, and a cynical outlook. It can manifest in sarcasm, passive-aggressive comments, jokes with subtle insults, and even a hyper-critical mind. When people are near someone who carries offense, they feel like they're walking on eggshells. The offended often create a tense, uncertain atmosphere around them.

When writing about a man who had caused quite a bit of confusion and pain to the Church, Paul wrote of forgiveness. He made it clear that forgiveness of the offender was necessary in order to avoid the schemes of the enemy.

I am not overstating it when I say that the man who caused all the trouble hurt all of you more than he hurt me. Most of you opposed him, and that was punishment enough. Now, however, it is time to forgive and comfort him. Otherwise he may be overcome by discouragement. So I urge you now to reaffirm your love for him. I wrote to you as I did to test you and see if you would fully comply with my instructions. When you forgive this man, I forgive him, too. And when I forgive whatever needs to be forgiven, I do so with Christ's authority for your benefit, so that Satan will not outsmart us. For we are familiar with his evil schemes (2 Corinthians 2:5-11 NLT).

As believers, we have died to ourselves. You can't offend a dead man. You can't upset a dead woman. You and I no longer live. Christ lives in us.

My old self has been crucified with Christ. It is no longer I who live, but Christ lives in me... (Galatians 2:20 NLT).

The stronghold of offense is founded upon the lie that we have the right to carry unforgiveness. The truth is that we are to forgive just as God has forgiven us.

Instead, be kind to each other, tenderhearted, forgiving one another, just as God through Christ has forgiven you (Ephesians 4:32 NLT).

We are beings of God's light and love. Our ability to forgive should astound the world and melt the heart of the most egregious offenders.

Of course, this doesn't mean that we accept abuse of any kind. This just means that we practice forgiving others the way God has forgiven us. Does God punish us according to our sins? Does God hold the memory of our sins against us? Does God constantly accuse us of our past wrongdoing? No.

One might ask, "But how? How do I forgive? I've tried and I still feel anger and hurt." Forgiveness is not a feeling; it's a choice to release the individual. You release the individual by choosing to put their wrongdoing out of your mind. This isn't to deny that they hurt you; this is to deny yourself the right to hold it against them.

Make every effort to keep yourselves united in the Spirit, binding yourselves together with peace (Ephesians 4:3 NLT).

Forgiveness begins when you reject the lie that it's right for you to hold offense in your heart. I know this isn't popular to say, and to some degree, even church culture is beginning to soften its stance on this. Still, biblically speaking, we have no right to hold offense, ever.

Then Peter came to him and asked, "Lord, how often should I forgive someone who sins against me? Seven times?"

"No, not seven times," Jesus replied, "but seventy times seven!

"Therefore, the Kingdom of Heaven can be compared to a king who decided to bring his accounts up to date with

servants who had borrowed money from him. In the process, one of his debtors was brought in who owed him millions of dollars. He couldn't pay, so his master ordered that he be sold—along with his wife, his children, and everything he owned—to pay the debt.

"But the man fell down before his master and begged him, 'Please, be patient with me, and I will pay it all.' Then his master was filled with pity for him, and he released him and forgave his debt.

"But when the man left the king, he went to a fellow servant who owed him a few thousand dollars. He grabbed him by the throat and demanded instant payment.

"His fellow servant fell down before him and begged for a little more time. 'Be patient with me, and I will pay it,' he pleaded. But his creditor wouldn't wait. He had the man arrested and put in prison until the debt could be paid in full.

"When some of the other servants saw this, they were very upset. They went to the king and told him everything that had happened. Then the king called in the man he had forgiven and said, 'You evil servant! I forgave you that tremendous debt because you pleaded with me. Shouldn't you have mercy on your fellow servant, just as I had mercy on you?' Then the angry king sent the man to prison to be tortured until he had paid his entire debt. That's what my heavenly Father will do to you if you refuse to forgive your brothers and sisters from your heart" (Matthew 18:21-35 NLT).

Forgiveness isn't a one-time occurrence. Sometimes, it's not just the offense we need to forgive but the remembrance of the offense. We must forgive every time we recall how we've been hurt. This becomes easier each time you choose to relinquish wrath, each time you choose to stop imagining revenge, each time you choose to stop building the case against your offender. You may be in the right. They may be in the wrong. You may feel bothered that they seem to be getting away with offending you. But you need to embrace this truth—we have no right to be offended.

You may not be able to forgive, but God can. Forgiveness is a supernatural work of the Spirit. Only He could so transform you that you can forgive like God forgives. Ask Him, and then choose to commit your mind to the truths that are consistent with God's forgiving nature. To forgive like God forgives, you need His Spirit.

Pray for your offender. Verbally bless your offender. Reject the anger. You may have to do this repeatedly, but you have to be committed to forgiveness if you want to go free. Reject the lie that you have a right to hold a grudge, persist in blessing the one who hurt you, and then release them to the Lord through prayer. Remember how God forgave your debt, and then go and do likewise.

THE STRONGHOLD OF CONFUSION

Many believers feel stuck in confusion about their calling, their lives, and their beliefs. Hearing so many messages from so many sources, they begin to wonder where they can find certainty and solid ground. It's in this place of not knowing where to go or what to do, this spiritual season of "in-between," that causes far too many Christians to be paralyzed in perplexity.

What is the source of confusion?

Confusion is the conflict that results when you can't deny the truth yet won't deny the lies you've embraced. Confusion comes when you cling to both lies and truth at the same time. If you want to be rid of confusion, you must resolve this conflict. If you want to resolve this conflict, you must stop clinging to the lies. Even though it may not be immediately identifiable, deception hides behind all confusion. Deception is the root of all confusion.

For example, let's say there's a man looking for a wife. In his desperation, he begins to date a nonbeliever. The lie he believes is that Christians can date nonbelievers. But he buries that lie deep, somewhere in the back of his mind where it can't inconvenience him or conflict with his passions. After weeks of dating this woman, major conflicts begin to arise. So he finally begins to pray about his relationship. Suppressed in his subconscious is the truth he buried—the truth that he shouldn't be in this relationship.

Then, as he prays, his passions begin to fight him. Now he's going back and forth. "I should be in this relationship. I shouldn't be in this relationship." He may even begin to pray for God to bless his mess. Now he's confused. Part of him thinks he should "work it out." Another part of him feels "I need to end this." But until he admits the lie he told himself, he will remain confused.

As another example, let's say a woman is praying about what she should do for God. She believes the fear-based lie that if she does anything God didn't instruct her to do that she will be harshly judged. So instead of using her talents and abilities for the advancement of God's Kingdom, she's stuck waiting for some ultra-clear, ultra-specific instruction on what she should do for God. She's unaware of the fact that the Bible already gives general commands: to live holy, evangelize, serve in a local church, study the Word, worship, pray, and so forth.

She's waiting for the heavens to split open and an audible voice to instruct her. She also doesn't realize that God progressively reveals His will; He guides as we go. So what does she do? Nothing. She's stuck waiting for God to give her a step-by-step manual for her every day. When that doesn't happen, she's confused. "What should I do for God?

I don't know my calling! I'm waiting for Him to reveal it." She feels discouraged, overlooked, frustrated, and, yes, very confused about what to do. All of this would be solved if she stopped believing the lie that she has to wait for ultra-clear instructions. Once she realizes the truth, that she should just live by the Word and do something with what God gave her, she's free from the confusion. And as she begins to do something, God clearly reveals her next steps.

We can be confused about relationships, callings, doctrine, and many other aspects of life. If you're in confusion, God didn't put you there.

> *For God is not the author of confusion, but of peace, as in all churches of the saints* (1 Corinthians 14:33 NKJV).

When you can't see a clear path forward or are unsure about what to believe, who to trust, or where to go, that's confusion. This is why we so need the precious Holy Spirit. The Holy Spirit speaks clearly through the Scriptures. The Scriptures are "God-breathed," they are of His Spirit.

> *All scripture is given by inspiration of God, and is profitable for doctrine, for reproof, for correction, for instruction in righteousness: That the man of God may be perfect, thoroughly furnished unto all good works* (2 Timothy 3:16-17 KJV).

When you're caught in confusion, search the Scriptures. There, you will find the instructions from the Holy Spirit. Do what the Word clearly says, and the Holy Spirit will reveal His specific instructions for your life. Your obedience to what is written in the Word will make it easier for you to hear the whispers of the Holy Spirit to your heart.

STAYING FREE

You were created to live in victory. To seize this victory, to win in the battle for truth, you need to apply God's armor and then lean upon the strength of the precious Holy Spirit. He will help you to shore up spiritual weak points (close doors), identify strongholds, and then begin to tear them down.

First, you must deal with the demonic aspects of the stronghold by knowing God's authority, aligning yourself with God's authority, and then exercising a divine command. If this does not cause the demon to shut its mouth, you need to fast and pray. Prayer and fasting will help rid you of compromise and doubt, thus aligning you with God's authority. If even this doesn't seem to work, you are now likely dealing with self, not satan. For after you have exercised divine authority, demons cannot keep influence, so the influence that remains must be of the carnal nature.

All the while, you should be practicing the basics of Christian discipline—daily prayer, devotion to the Word, holiness, and obedience toward God. Such living will give you the proper footing you need to choose to believe the truth, fight reinforcing lies, and renew your mind.

Whatever God does not deal with instantly, He will help you to deal with progressively. This is when you have to commit to applying the truths I have shown you from Scripture. This is when you will be tempted to look for quick fixes and embrace religious doctrines that will put you back in a cycle of bondage.

> *So let's not get tired of doing what is good. At just the right time we will reap a harvest of blessing if we don't give up* (Galatians 6:9 NLT).

You have to persist in doing what you know leads to freedom. If for no other reason, this is why most believers just can't be free. They simply choose to avoid commitment to God's process. Yes, God can do anything instantaneously. But at some point, you need to be committed to dealing with the problems of self.

When the problems of the flesh arise again—and they most certainly will—apply the biblical methods of deliverance and freedom. Many Christians panic when they face a hardship or have to deal with problems they have dealt with before. So don't confuse the battle with self for the bondage of satan. Just because you battle doesn't mean you're bound. You can only be bound again if you stop believing the truth. And the truth is that you have been given everything you need to continue in victory.

Many believers become trapped in decades of bondage, simply because they are impatient with God's process. They give up before any progress can be made. Giving up is evidence that you don't believe God's way will work. If you believed, beyond all doubt, that God's path to freedom would work, no matter how long it took, you would stay in the process. Make up your mind now—you're going to be free, and you're not quitting.

The Holy Spirit gives you patience for the process. Use the patience He gives to you.

> *But the Holy Spirit produces this kind of fruit in our lives: love, joy, peace, patience, kindness, goodness, faithfulness, gentleness, and self-control...* (Galatians 5:22-23 NLT).

You stay free by living according to the Word and staying faithful to the Holy Spirit's process—no matter the delay or the setback. Keep going. You'll notice some progress over a few days, then weeks, then months. Then before you know it, you'll look back at where you started and say, "I'm free. I am truly, truly free!"

The Holy Spirit exposes the lies and reminds you of the truth. He instantaneously breaks demonic power and progressively works His power in you to help you overcome self. He calls you to be free, sets you free, and then keeps you free. Truly, the Holy Spirit is the Bondage Breaker, and He lives in you.

ABOUT THE AUTHOR

David Diga Hernandez is an evangelist, bestselling author, YouTuber, healing minister, and friend of the Holy Spirit. His evangelistic healing ministry holds Miracle Services all around the world and reaches millions of people through media. David carries a grace to evangelize the lost and to lead believers into closeness with the Holy Spirit.

From

David Diga Hernandez

Discover Your Identity as a Carrier of God's Presence, Power, and Glory!

Do you sometimes wonder how God can consider you a friend in light of failures and defeats? Does your own insufficiency cause you to wonder whether the Holy Spirit truly dwells within you? Do you wonder why your own faith experience is so different from that of the heroes in the Bible?

Scripture makes it clear that *communion with the Holy Spirit* is the key to living the kind of empowered and authentic Christian life we see modeled in Scripture. The Holy Spirit works within us to form hearts that truly worship, minds that understand the depths of God's Word, and hands that accomplish the miraculous. This book will acquaint you with the mysterious third Person of the Trinity, helping you to draw closer to Him so that you may become a carrier of God's Spirit—a chosen friend of God.

If you desire to know God in a deeper and more intimate way, if you want your soul to be set ablaze with a passionate love for Him, if you want to walk in the fullness of all that He has created for you, then this book is for you!

Purchase your copy wherever books are sold

From
David Diga Hernandez

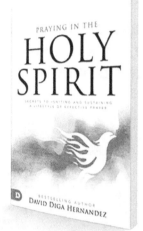

If you've ever been frustrated in your prayer life, this book is for you

Do you ever feel like your prayers are not effective? Does your prayer life lack vitality and consistency?

The secret to a thriving prayer life is not a formula—it is the supernatural power of the Holy Spirit. As you learn to engage with the Spirit of God, your prayer life will soar to levels you never dreamed were possible!

In *Praying in the Holy Spirit*, internationally recognized evangelist, teacher, and healing minister, David Hernandez presents bold answers to tough questions about prayer and offers revelatory insights to help you commune with the Holy Spirit in powerful ways.

Move beyond striving and struggling in prayer. It's time to pray in perfect faith from unhindered union with the Holy Spirit.

Purchase your copy wherever books are sold